Henri de Lubac
Christian Resistance to Anti-Semitism

Henri de Lubac

Christian Resistance
to
Anti-Semitism

Memories from 1940–1944

Translated by
Sister Elizabeth Englund, O.C.D.

IGNATIUS PRESS   SAN FRANCISCO

Title of French original:
Résistance chrétienne à l'antisémitisime
© 1988 Librairie Arthème Fayard

Cover design by Roxanne Mei Lum
Cover calligraphy by Joan McGrady-Beach

To the memory of Fathers
Pierre Chaillet
(1900–1972)
Gaston Fessard
(1897–1978)
Yves de Montcheuil
(1900–1944)

Members of the Society of Jesus,
sons of the Church,
courageous and charitable,
men of God,
very beloved brothers.

and

To Adrien Nemoz,
who was the first
to come to the holy hill
seeking the light but explosive bag
with which he would run
through a thousand dangers—
and who still today retains in his heart
the purity of an enterprise
wholly inspired by our Faith.

Contents

7

8 CONTENTS

14 Yves de Montcheuil   215
       Appendix 1   236
       Appendix 2   241

Epilogue   243

Abbreviations   249

Index   251

Preface

We all know of Fr. de Lubac's participation in the spiritual resistance to anti-Semitism during the tragic years when France was occupied by the nazis. In particular, he is known to have been one of the principal theologians of the clandestine *Cahiers du Témoignage chrétien* [Notebooks of Christian witness], which, from November 1941 until May 1944, allowed the voice of the Church and of the persecuted to be heard. Many today have difficulty forming any idea of the nature of this witness or, above all, of the historical context in which it was given. On the other hand, as one can easily understand, the written sources of a clandestine activity are rare and, from a distance of more than forty years, difficult to interpret. So it happens that some historians, even those who are genuinely well informed, do not appreciate the full value of certain facts, particularly if they themselves did not participate in the events. This holds even more true when the questions under consideration are delicate ones in which the historians do not necessarily have any particular competence, such as matters relating to the internal life of the churches.

A theologian and historian by profession, Cardinal de Lubac is one of the last great actors from whom we may gather testimony about some of the major fundamental facts in the history of the Church in France during the years 1940–1945. We therefore asked him to put down in writing certain recollections, which had often been recalled only by chance during a conversation and which were in danger of being lost forever or, what would have been worse, passed on after his death in an imprecise or biased way. He decided to comply with our request and wrote the memoir you are about to read, the

9

final draft of which was completed early in 1984. These pages, entrusted at that time to several friends, were in no way intended for a forthcoming publication. Their interest and timeliness, the authority of their author and the light which reading them threw on such an obscure period of our history made us then consider publishing part of them as an appendix to a study on the Jewish character of the apostolic Church. But then we thought that this memoir really should be published in its entirety. Although he found it impossible to revise and complete it, after having reread it, Cardinal de Lubac did not object to our publishing it as it is.

Cardinal de Lubac does not merely give us here unpublished recollections, which he alone could relate, about the clandestine *Cahiers du Témoignage chrétien*, the Chaine Declaration, his activities with the Catholic faculties in Lyons, to the Ecole des cadres d'Uriage and to the Chantiers de jeunesse [work camps], or even his mission of August 1942 to Cardinal Saliège at the request of Cardinal Gerlier. That would all be enough to justify its publication. But the author of these recollections goes even farther. Examining controversial documents with his twofold competence as historian and theologian, he contributes decisive clarifications on more than one point. Such is the case, to cite only one example, with Ambassador Léon Bérard's famous report to Marshal Pétain. An experienced theologian and a lucid observer involved in the life of the Church, Cardinal de Lubac excels at defining the nature, limits and stakes of the relations of the Church with the temporal order and the state in critical circumstances. Finally, these recollections cannot fail to be above all a personal witness: a witness which the Christian conscience cannot, without denying itself, be excused from bearing over the past twenty centuries, even if, under certain circumstances, it was at the cost of one's life. It was this witness which, from the first days after Hitler's rise to power, Cardinal Saliège bore to the public, when he declared on April 12, 1933:

Not only do I myself feel struck by the blows that are falling on the persecuted, but I shudder with all the more distress when I find that it is not some confused ideal, some cold, abstract idea that is misunderstood and ridiculed . . . but that living, personal being whose breath has run through and borne the entire history of Israel: Yahweh, he whom I call "the good God", the Just One par excellence. . . . I cannot forget that it was in Israel that the tree of Jesse flowered and that there it brought forth its fruit. The Virgin, Christ, the first disciples were of the Jewish race. How could I not feel bound to Israel like a branch to the trunk that bore it! . . . Catholicism cannot agree that belonging to a particular race places men in a position that entitles them to fewer rights. It proclaims the essential equality of all races and all individuals.

Michel Sales
October 6, 1987

Foreword

To the extent allowed by my often-failing memory, supported by various notes written already well after the events themselves and also by conversations with Mme. Renée Bédarida and Abbé Charles Molette, marvelously penetrating in the interpretation of documents and their dates, I offer here, to satisfy as well as possible a few younger friends, an oversimplified account of several incidents concerning anti-Semitism in which I found myself involved forty years ago, during the Occupation. I am placing them in a more general context, whose outline I am simply borrowing from some of the most readily accessible works. I do not claim to contribute any sensational revelation. This will be for me simply an opportunity to complete the account of several facts in order to make them better understood and occasionally, in the process, to correct, or at least to qualify, certain assertions or judgments. I am liable to have made a few mistakes myself. In any case, my point of view, which I hope is never partial in the sense of being unfair, can only be extremely partial in the sense of being incomplete.

Henri de Lubac

Chapter 1

Anti-Semitism Prior to 1940

Much information will be found in the first parts of Pierre Pierrard's work *Juifs et catholiques français, de Drumont à Jules Isaac (1886–1945)* [French Catholics and Jews, from Drumont to Jules Isaac (1886–1945)] (Fayard, 1970) on anti-Semitism in France during the period between the two world wars, on the favorable reception that nazi propaganda found there and on the twofold penetration of anti-Semitic doctrines in those that were already commonly known and those that came to certain Catholic circles from Germany. One will also find there numerous examples of the courageous and multifaceted resistance with which the Catholic conscience resisted this scourge. I will cite only one minor but characteristic example. In 1935, Oscar de Férenzy, who was of Swiss origin, published (through Flammarion) *Les Juifs et les Chrétiens* [Jews and Christians], a work whose preface was written by Fr. Devaux, superior of the Sion Fathers; over a long period of time, he increased the number of lectures he gave on this subject, heedless of the abuse that poured in on him. In substance, his response to all was: "I defend Israel because Jesus was the descendant of David. I defend Israel because I am a Christian; as a Christian, I have the duty to come to its aid." The journal he founded in 1936 (whose patrons included Mauriac, Maritain and Frs. Dieux, Bonsirven and Devaux) lasted until May 20, 1940 (P. Pierrard, 282).

My attention had at that time been drawn more particularly to the subject for several years by two men: one was Fr. Victor Fontoynont, S.J., a professor of theology at the scholasticate at Lyons-Fourvière, my good, long-standing adviser, formerly a professor of philosophy at the colleges of Bollengo (Piedmont) and Mongré (Villefranche-sur-Saône), then prefect of studies at Fourvière, a duty that he had just handed over to Fr. Henri Rondet. While working to complete his old project of translating the Greek and Eastern Fathers, inspired by thoughts of ecumenism, he was at the same time, in his rare free moments, lovingly working on a monograph that he was not able to finish, that of a "Hebrew vocabulary" similar to his famous Vocabulaire grec [Greek vocabulary], which has recently been republished.

My second instructor was Abbé Jules Monchanin. Before leaving Lyons in obedience to a vow he had made to devote himself entirely to India, he had organized meetings there between Christians and Jews. In collaboration with Mme. Belensson, he also participated in the Parisian Jewish-Catholic Foyer on rue Froidevaux, a "little oasis of peace in the midst of hatred". In 1937, in a series of lectures held on the premises of the University Parish (rue d'Assas) in order to fight against the rise of anti-Semitism, he had examined "the spirit of Judaism, the common task of Jews and Christians, the fullness of Christ realized in the culmination of the Judeo-Christian lineage", and it was following in his footsteps that I had described a little later "the dream of Israel and the universality of the Church". Monchanin never ceased to explain on every occasion that "it was not possible to tear out half of the Bible", that "one perverts the New Testament by removing its historical roots",[1] and he did his best to rouse sleeping consciences

---

[1] Archbishop Lustiger of Paris later emphasized this in an important interview published in Hebrew in one of the main journals from Jerusalem and taken up again in French in the review Le Débat (Gallimard, no. 20 [May 1982], 163–91) under the title "Puisqu'il le faut . . ." The author draws attention to the latent danger of Marcionism, which, by rejecting (or ignoring) the Old Testament, cuts Christ off from his Jewish roots and thereby, in "dehistoricizing" him, tends to make him a new pagan god. "Oser Croire" (Centurion, 1985), 51–79: "Puisqu'il le faut . . ."

by showing them that "the anti-Semitism of the nazis extends even to God himself".[2]

But sleeping consciences did not let themselves be roused easily. And in the final years between the wars, especially after Hitler's rise to power, various causes led to a new and more serious wave of anti-Semitism. The flood of Jewish émigrés (they were seldom called "refugees") posed social problems that were difficult to resolve. The French Jews who were already assimilated did not always view this influx favorably. As these new arrivals were often socialists or communists, they aroused suspicion, which redoubled after Léon Blum's rise to power; at the same time, their growing number provoked mass xenophobia. Sixty-five percent of the party founded by Doriot (Parti Populaire Française), which won over a number of intellectuals, belonged to the working class.[3] Suspicion of too many foreigners, of Jewish foreigners, then of all Jews became for some of the French more lively than their suspicion of Hitler—all the more so since the phenomenon of

---

[2] Before leaving for India, he and a Jewish friend had composed in Hebrew a "Prayer of Israel to the Virgin", to be engraved under a statue of the Virgin in the Jewish quarter of Paris:

> Virgin of Israel who gave birth to the Messiah,
> Remember your people who are suffering,
> Waiting for their Redeemer
> And fighting for the Kingdom to come.

> Daughter of Abraham, Virgin, Mother and servant,
> You, chosen from among us,
> Whom all generations proclaim blessed,
> On whom the Spirit rests,

> Spread the wings of the Shekinah
> Over our people and all peoples.

> L'abbé Jules Monchanin (Tournai, Casterman), 176

[3] Marcel Bourdot, in La France et la Question juive (F.Q.J.), 1940–1944 (Center for Contemporary Jewish Documentation, Sylvie Messinger, 1981), 266–72.

Hitler was poorly perceived and at times even totally misunderstood by a number of intellectuals and politicians,[4] despite many warnings, and since some circles of believers were obsessed by their pacifist idealism. Pastor Boegner went so far as to say, "I wonder if we were not all struck blind"[5] at the moment

---

[4] Gabriel Marcel and Gaston Fessard, *Correspondance annotée* (Beauchesne, 1985), 142–44, 185–87. The *Revue des deux mondes*, on the other hand, welcomed the very clear-sighted articles by Robert d'Harcourt. On d'Harcourt, see *Cahiers Robert d'Harcourt*, 1 (December 1981, a special number of the *Nouvelles de l'Institut catholique de Paris*). Cf. below, Chap. 3, n. 17. In Lyons, the *Salut public*, an evening paper with a "growing audience among . . . the Lyons bourgeoisie", was "perspicacious": Jacques Prévotat, in *Revue d'histoire de la Seconde Guerre mondiale*, 128 (October 1982), 96 (according to Latreille from Lyons), etc. *La Semaine Sociale* from Clermont-Ferrand, whose theme in 1937 was "the human person in peril", provided strong leadership and led a vigorous indictment against totalitarianism (A. Latreille, Lyons Symposium, 73). It is more than an exaggeration to claim that up until 1945, "the battle against racism and anti-Semitism . . . was carried on by leftist organizations with only weak Christian participation", only pointing out, moreover, that "weak participation" contributed by Anglo-Saxons (cf. François Delpech, *Sur les Juifs, études d'histoire contemporaine* [P.U.L., 1983], 358). More than one author has misused the words "right" and "left", which in such subjects are often misleading. It was not any tendency toward the right or the left which determined the action of men like Chaillet, Fessard or de Montcheuil; cf. below, Chap. 11, n. 11. There is a fundamental truth expressed in this reflection by F. Lovsky, *Antisémitisme et Mystère d'Israël* (Albin Michel, 1955), 496: "We do not think it necessary to say we are changing the political opinions of Christians in order to guard against anti-Semitism: it is enough quite simply to stress the Christianity of Christians."

[5] Marc Boegner, *L'Exigence oecuménique* (Albin Michel, 1968), 119. It is true that Boegner is speaking of the "strange meeting" in Holland in January 1940 between Protestant bishops from Nordic countries, whose lack of realism defies belief. One Scandinavian bishop admired Hitler as the "greatest man the world has ever seen"; the archbishop of Finland wanted the West to conclude an immediate peace, reconciling with Germany in order to save the Christian faith from Bolshevism, etc. "I had", he concludes, "to spell it out" (*L'Exigence oecuménique*, 121). But similar, less spectacular cases occurred in France before this, and *"la drôle de guerre* ('the phony war', 1939–40) was lulling the French conscience to sleep": Stanislas Fumet, *Histoire de Dieu dans ma vie* (Fayard, 1978), 414.

of the war. So blind that, while the war of 1914 had given
rise to that "sacred union" that made Barrès write his beautiful
chapter "The Israelites" in *Les Diverses Familles spirituelles de
la France* [The various spiritual families of France], the 1940
disaster immediately provoked a kind of war of revenge
against Israel.[6] The prisons of the "French state" continued
to receive—in greater number—the Jews whom the prisons
of Daladier received.[7] The overcrowded mass of refugees—or
rather, of those "diverted"—from Germany and central
Europe by Hitler after his victory, Jews for the most part,
continued to rot away, piled up in miserable camps that were
already full before their arrival—and the country as a whole
knew nothing about it.[8] Without needing any pressure from
the conqueror,[9] the council of ministers who had gathered at
Vichy on October 1, 1940, would propose the first foundations
of a special statute for Jews, and it was the head of state who
would at first prove to be the most severe.[10] Undoubtedly,

[6] A contrast noted by J. B. Duroselle, in *F.Q.J.*, 14.

[7] During the war, thousands of Germans, Jews in great number, had already
been arrested as "suspects of collusion with the enemy" and interned in Paris
(May 14, 1940, at the Buffalo stadium and at Vel d'Hiv) and in the camps
in the south of France. Cf. Philippe Bourdrel, *Histoire des Juifs en France* (Albin
Michel, 1974), 387–88.

[8] Cf. Marc Boegner, *L'Exigence oecuménique*, 124: "We had already been
criticized vehemently from abroad. Had not one journalist from the United
States published an article entitled 'From Hitler's Concentration Camps to
the French Concentration Camps'?" The situation was worse after the defeat:
"From one day to the next, France had to shelter thousands of non-Aryans
from Germany, Austria, Czechoslovakia 'entrusted' by the occupying power
to the care of the French authorities" (ibid., 147). On the Gurs camp visited
by Boegner: ibid., 149–50. Boegner had preached during Lent in 1938 on
"the Gospel and racism" (published in 1939).

[9] The fate of Jews in Algeria became worse than that in metropolitan
France, even though there was no Germany there to exert pressure. Cf. P.
Bourdrel, 390–93.

[10] Pétain supposedly insisted in particular "that Justice and Education con-
tain no Jews": Pascal Ory, in *F.Q.J.*, apparently quoting Paul Baudouin. The
latter reportedly said: "If we continue to abstain, the Germans are going to

CHRISTIAN RESISTANCE TO ANTI-SEMITISM
he was encouraged in this by his two close advisers, Alibert and Ménétrel, both of whom were steeped in the doctrines of Maurras,[11] but he was not of their school.[12] A victory over the Jewish peril must have seemed to him, as it did to other politicians of various origins, a first, very appreciable compensation for our defeat. For, like so many others, Pétain seems not to have read *Mein Kampf*, even in the expurgated translation that was the only one Hitler had authorized for use by the French. Pétain seems to have been totally unaware of the totalitarian spirit and its implacable harshness—and he was preparing to finesse Hitler a little like Stresemann had formerly finessed Briand, to look him in the face at Montoire as he had looked mutinous soldiers in the face in 1917, with the hope of similar success. No one among those responsible, either before or after the downfall and change of government, seems to have noticed or taken seriously the threat uttered by Hitler in his speech of January 30, 1939: "If the international Jewish community succeeded, in Europe or elsewhere, in pushing the people into a world war, the end result would not at all be a Bolshevization of Europe and a victory for Judaism but

---

make some brutal decisions" (September 10, 1940), in Jacques Duquesne, *Les Catholiques français sous l'Occupation* (Grasset, 1966), 178. Cf. Robert Aron, *Histoire de Vichy* (Fayard, 1954), 254; *F.Q.J.*, 118 (Claude Lévy) and 129–30 (Jacques Madaule).

[11] Pierre Laval, in 1935, when he was received by Pius XI, had tried to plead the cause of l'Action française; the Pope had replied: "The lifting of sanctions and censures against these gentlemen does not depend on us but on themselves, that is to say, on their retraction." After that, Maurras had written to the Pope, who had answered him; a formula for submission had been presented but dismissed as unsatisfactory; the Carmel of Lisieux had intervened; Pius XI had accepted a new formula of retraction, a little before his death, and it was Pius XII who confirmed his decision. Cf. François Charles-Roux, *Huit ans au Vatican* (Flammarion, 1947), 53.

[12] The fact that Pétain was at that time surrounded by men from *l'Action française* was not, however, a coincidence. For if he admired the Church, it was in the same way that Maurras did, as an agent of order and national cohesion. Cf. J. Duquesne, 22–23.

the extermination of the Jewish race in Europe." No one, however, could imagine (nor would they be able to for a long time yet) the methodical savagery determined to persevere in the execution of this threat to the very end.[13] Pétain and his ministers, like most of the men of the Third Republic, seem to have been completely unaware of the formidable spiritual drama that was relentlessly pursuing its course and of the diabolical hurricane with whose violence any attempt to compromise could only intensify.[14]

But outside official circles, outside political and diplomatic milieux, outside the dominant literary movements, several men, and more particularly several Christians, had become aware of this drama. "They knew perfectly well", as one of them wrote,

> what the totalitarian enterprise and the ends it was pursuing
> meant not only with respect to the expansion of the temporal
> power of the German Reich but also, and I would say above

[13] Many French people were long deluded by the external correctness of the occupying forces. Hitler's plans concerning the Jews were entrusted to the superior officers of the SS; now the latter, "following the example of their master Heydrich, were not vulgar roughnecks but intelligent, often cultivated and superiorly organized fanatics"; in François Delpech, *Sur les Juifs, études d'histoire contemporaine* (P.U.L., 1983), 182. The celebrated ambassador Otto Abetz, such a friend of France, so passionately interested in French culture, so appreciated by so many Parisian intellectuals, was not, in this regard, unworthy of Heydrich's agents.

[14] René Schwob had written in *Esprit*, 8 (May 1, 1933), "Protestation d'un chrétien", 167, after Hitler came to power: "As always, diplomats and politicians were unable to foresee anything." This was very much the case in the years that followed; but the "as always" goes too far: in this instance the reference is to something quite apart from ordinary politics and diplomacy. In exceedingly moderate language, J. B. Duroselle regretted that our "technocrats" at that time took hardly any interest in "the romantic doctrine of nazism" (*Mélanges offerts à André Latreille* [Lyons: Audin, 1972], 362). On the birth of the new "French state": Robert Aron, *La France de Vichy* (Fayard, 1954), chap. 2, "Vichy, 1–10 juillet 1940" (95–159). In the years before the war, internal politics and social conflicts monopolized the attention of many.

all, with respect to intellectual and moral perversion, a veritable enterprise of negation, the eradication of the values by which we have lived ever since the three great currents coming from Jerusalem, Athens and Rome first met.[15]

[15] Jean-Marie Soutou, in a statement made on June 25, 1979, at the annual conference of the *Alliance israélite universelle*. The *Annales* of the A.C.J.F. and the *Chantiers* of the J.E.C. (Jeunesse étudiante catholique [Students' Catholic Association]) gave increased information and warnings about nazism during the 1930s. Cf. A. Michel, "Les mouvements de jeunesse catholique et le nazisme dans l'entre-deux-guerres", *Colloque de Biviers* (1984). Albert Gortais, secretary general of the A.C.J.F. from 1936 to 1938 (and again in 1940 in Lyons), had been able to observe nazism up close in 1937 during a stay in a *Hitlerjugend* camp; he would be one of the earliest workers in the Resistance.

Chapter 2

Lyons 1940–1941:
"Confidential Memorandum" —Pius XI

In June 1940 came the collapse, the consequences of which are well known. Using different methods in each of the two "zones", the way was soon open to anti-Jewish politics and propaganda, stifling censorship of any free voice, a police force hostile to any effort toward mercy for the persecuted.

In Lyons, we received several Belgian Jesuits who had shifted their large scholasticate from Louvain (where I had stayed ten years earlier). Among them was Fr. Pierre Charles (1883–1954), a close friend of Frs. Auguste Valensin and Pierre Teilhard de Chardin, former fellow students at the theology scholasticate at Ore Place (Hastings)—reinstalled at Lyons in 1926 after a long exile. Fr. Charles was soon to continue his exodus as far as Latin America, where he would continue to teach theology for five years, escaping Hitler's thunderbolts, which he had drawn down on himself by unmasking the fraudulent "Protocols of the Elders of Zion" (cf. P. Pierrard, 232–35 and 264–66).[1] During his brief stay in Lyons, I showed him around the city, and his vigorous words confirmed in me the effect of my past conversations with Abbé Monchanin and of the daily presence of Fr. Fontoynont.

Finally, in the months that followed, two other friends arrived. First came my old friend Fr. Gaston Fessard,

[1] Pierre Charles, *Nouvelle Revue théologique* (Louvain), January and November 1938. Cf. F. Lovsky, *Antisémitisme et Mystère d'Israël* (Albin Michel, 1955), 338. See *Cahiers sioniens*, 1 (1954), 35.

demobilized and kept at Lyons by our Provincials with several
other members of our two Paris houses of *Etudes* and *L'Action
populaire*. Then, at the end of December, arrived Fr. Pierre
Chaillet, a friend of six or seven years, having returned from
Hungary for a long interlude at Fourvière, where he was a
professor for a few years. Both men were a great consolation
to me.

A "chair of the missions" had been established by the *Propaganda Fides* at the Catholic faculties of Lyons, and I was asked
to give two lectures there. These took place in January 1941.
The first was a general talk inspired by my book *Catholicisme*
as well as by an unpublished work by Fr. de Montcheuil
on the "raison d'être of the missions", by some unpublished
notes of Abbé Monchanin and by numerous missiological
writings by Fr. Charles. The second was entirely a "reply
to objections": it gave me an opportunity to attack racism.
After an introduction that refuted the myth of the "curse of
Ham", I finally came to the subject close to my heart, using
as a foundation the Christmas Message of Pius XII, part of
which *La Croix* had just published in a French translation:
"At a time when earthly authorities are making their power
felt, Christians are giving way by a timid flight" and are
thus becoming, through their silence, "the intermediaries
of theories and prejudices coming from circles that are
foreign and hostile to Christianity".[2] Then followed an
account of racism according to Hitler, Chamberlain and
Rosenberg, refuted with the help of Charles and his friend
Teilhard; then a reminder of the fate of the Polish, "which
will perhaps be tomorrow the fate of the 'denordicized' French

[2] *La Croix*, January 16, 1941, and *Semaine religieuse de Lyon*. Through the
media as a whole, I would say, "most Catholics in France could have known
only a misleading summary of this message." Cf. *Le Fondement théologique
des missions:* La sphère et la croix (Ed. du Seuil, 1946), 77. During this same
month of January 1941, Alfred Michelin, coeditor of *La Croix*, complained,
with respect to Pétain—but in vain—about censorship that mutilates the
teaching of the Pope.

as well"; and finally the recalling of Pius XI's battle against this "neopaganism" and of the hymn addressed long ago by St. Augustine to the Church as mother: "By a bond not only of common life but of true brotherhood, you unite citizens to citizens, races to races, in a word, all men to each other, by reminding them of their common origin."[3]

In my naïveté, I still believed at that time that I was expressing the common sentiment of a very large part, if not all, of French Catholicism. I will also admit that if I had been able to foresee in concrete terms what was going to take place in the course of the following four years, I too would have undoubtedly been afraid and "given way by a timid flight". While the first of my lectures was reproduced in the journal *L'Union missionnaire du clergé* of January–April 1941, the second of course remained unpublished until 1946. With my anguish increasing daily over a situation that grew worse by degrading consciences, and feeling incapable of undertaking any action whatever, I decided to address a confidential memorandum "to my Superiors" on April 15, 1941, in order to make known to them the fruit of my reflections.[4] The following lines, which treat the question of anti-Semitism more specifically, are extracted from this:

> Anti-Semitism is rampant in its most contemptible form, through a campaign destined to rally public opinion to its side: the press, pictures, cinema (a repugnant film imported from Germany has just appeared in Lyons), and it is beginning to be

[3] Op. cit., 77–101. St. Augustine, *De moribus Ecclesiae catholicae*. Cf. Charles Journet, in *Nova et Vetera* (Freiburg, July–September 1941), 225–31: "It is not only in the form of anti-Semitism, it is in itself that racism has been condemned by the Church. But it is in the form of anti-Semitism that it shows its true nature and reveals its secret to us."

[4] The text of this memorandum has recently been published, with the willing agreement of my Provincial, Fr. Henri Madelin, in the work by Jean Chelini, *L'Eglise sous Pie XII, la Tourmente, 1939–1945* (Fayard, 1983), 295–310.

rampant as well in an unjust form in arbitrary laws. Let us recall the decree of the Holy Office of March 21, 1928: "The Apostolic See condemns in the clearest possible way (*maxime damnat*) hatred directed against the people who were once the chosen people of God, that hatred which is today referred to under the general name of anti-Semitism."[5] But should a Catholic need an express condemnation in order to disapprove of a campaign that arouses the basest passions or to be concerned about legislation that strikes indiscriminately, with retroactive effect, one whole category of Frenchmen, without any regard to their merit or lack of merit, solely because of what is called their "race"? The measures are already much more severe in the "occupied zone", and there is no attempt to hide the fact that the other zone will follow suit and that the result will be one single legislation for the whole of Europe. . . . The anti-Semitism of today was unknown to our fathers; besides its degrading effect on those who abandon themselves to it, it is anti-Christian. It is against the Bible, against the Gospel as well as the Old Testament, against the universalism of the Church, against what is called the "Roman International"; it is against all that Pius XI, following St. Paul, claimed as ours the day he cried out: "Spiritually we are Semites!"[6] It is all the more

---

[5] In *F.Q.J.* (1981), 203, François Delpech wrote: "In 1928, anti-Semitism was condemned by the Holy Office, but the latter condemned at the same time a small group of Christians who rightly wanted to fight against anti-Semitism." Cf. *Sur les Juifs* (P.U.L., 1983), 269. Such an antithesis gives the reader a false impression. There is no relationship between these two facts here linked together. Many other "small groups" and bodies fought against anti-Semitism with the explicit or implicit approval of ecclesiastical authorities. Pius XI himself and Cardinal Van Rossum had at first supported the association of *Amis d'Israël*, founded by Franceska Van Leer and two Dutch priests; but it had then "deviated from its original goals" (Charles Journet, "Antisémitisme", in *Nova et Vetera* [Freiburg, July–September 1941], 225). On the "rather rash mystical inflation of the founders", who "began to have an exaggerated sense of themselves as prophets", see Stanislas Fumet, *Histoire de Dieu dans ma vie*, 300–302. Their reference to Léon Bloy, says Fumet with some indulgence, "was not a reference for theologians without genius".

[6] Cf. Pius XI, September 6, 1938, to a group of Belgian pilgrims: "Through Christ and in Christ, we are spiritual descendants of Abraham. No! It is not

important to be on guard, for this anti-Semitism is already gaining ground among the Catholic elite, even in our religious houses.[7]

The cry of Pius XI: "Spiritually we are Semites!" immediately and justifiably became famous.[8] But this was not an isolated cry. Two months earlier, in three other speeches, on July 15, 21 and 28, given before three different audiences, the elderly Pope had opened his soul, and each time the doctrinal fullness of what he said was wholly vibrant with moving tones: "The children of all these races are men, not any animal or being whatever, and human dignity consists in the fact that all make up one single family, the human race. This is how the Church teaches us to think, feel and treat these matters. It is her response to the discussions that are at present shaking

possible for Christians to participate in anti-Semitism. We recognize the right of anyone to defend himself, to take the necessary means to protect himself against whatever threatens his legitimate interests. But anti-Semitism is inadmissible. We are spiritually Semites." On the essential importance of these last words: Yves Congar, *L'Eglise catholique devant la question raciale* (Cerf, 1953), 16-17.

[7] This memorandum (and what followed it) was welcomed by Fr. Joseph du Bouchet, who was then my Provincial (cf. below). This was also true of my Rector, Fr. Auguste Decisier. I never knew what the Fr. Assistant, Norbert de Boynes, thought of it. He was at that time staying in Fourvière, but he was soon to leave again (for Rome) before I had a chance to meet him.

[8] F. Lovsky, 12, brought out the essential importance of these words, their close connection with the text from the Holy Office and the continuity one can find between it and the position formerly stated by Bernard Lazare, who had "the great merit of linking anti-Semitism to the unique existence . . . of a particular people: anti-Semitism does not relate to any minority whatsoever, national or religious, but to Israel. There is a connection between the mission of Israel in the world . . . and the opinion of the world with respect to the people who embody this precise mission. So we see the Holy See . . . stress with the greatest clarity that anti-Semitism is not only *one* undifferentiated form of animosity between peoples, since the Apostolic See, . . . just as it reproves all hatred and animosities between peoples, reproves it to the highest degree." Cf. Bernard Lazare, *L'Antisémitisme, son histoire et ses causes* (defin. ed., 1934), 1:39-42.

the world. . . . For her part, all men are the object of the same motherly affection; all are called to the same light."[9] And all these speeches were echoes of the encyclical *Mit brennender Sorge*, promulgated the preceding year (March 14, 1937), which denounced "the vain attempt to imprison God, the creator of the universe, . . . within the narrowness of the blood relationship of a single race".[10] From February 24, 1934, on, that is, even before the death of Marshal Hindenburg removed the last curb on Hitler's absolute dictatorship, Pius XI had declared: "We are living in historically tragic times. . . . We are living in times when racial pride has been exalted to the point of being a pride of thoughts, doctrines and practices, which is neither Christian nor human."[11] That someone like Céline, in his deranged anti-Semitism, breathed out his fury against the Pope, whom he affected to call "Isaac Ratisch" (the Pope's surname being Ratti), is not at all

[9] To the students of the Roman College of the Propaganda, July 28.

[10] Cardinal Pacelli, the future Pius XII and at that time Secretary of State, in complete agreement of thought with Pius XI, was, with the assistance of Msgr. von Preysing, Bishop of Berlin, and of Cardinal Faulhaber, Archbishop of Munich, the principal author (and probably translator into German) of this encyclical. Von Preysing, a Bavarian who was the former secretary to Faulhaber and the friend of Pacelli, whom he had first known in Munich, was the most energetic and perceptive of the German bishops; Pius XII always trusted him, consulted him in the nominations of bishops and encouraged his "frank and courageous" attitude, like that of von Galen in Münster (details in Victor Conzemius, *Eglises chrétiennes et Totalitarisme national-socialiste* [Louvain, 1969], 44–45 and 113–14). Von Preysing had very quickly seen the anti-Christian and demonic character of Hitlerism; from 1936 on, he considered further negotiations with the nazis to be senseless.

[11] On the activity of Pius XI in this field: Romano Guardini, *Le Chrétien devant la racisme* (French trans., Alsace, 1938, under the pseudonym of Lucien Valdor). In his speech of January 12, 1953 (receiving the announcement of his elevation to the cardinalate), Cardinal Ottaviani recalled both "the years of nazi violence" and "the red-hot anti-Christian ferocity": *L'Eglise et la Cité* (Imprimerie Vaticane, 1963), 4. R. Fontenelle, *Pius XI* (Ed. Spes), 423–28, gives the list of Pius XI's texts on nazism which would follow one after the other from June 1933 until Christmas 1938.

surprising.[12] But that in the whole of our country, and even
in a part of our clergy, there was scarcely any perception of
the epic grandeur of this battle led by the head of the Church,
whose only weapons were words, against the new *credo* of
racism, that, right after the disaster of June 1940, there was
even more receptiveness to the monstrous propaganda of the
victor, this is what surprised me, staggered me.

Since that time, several historians, even Catholic historians,[13] have attempted to minimize the significance of *Mit
brennender Sorge*. They have tried to persuade us that it was
"not as clear-cut as the encyclical *Divini Redemptoris* against
atheistic communism, which dates from the same period".[14]
This makes one wonder how they could have read it. Let it
be judged by its very title, or by passages such as the following:

> Whoever takes race or state or the form of state or the possessors
> of power or any other fundamental value of the human commu-
> nity . . . and divinizes them through an idolatrous cult, that
> one overturns and falsifies the order of things created and or-
> dained by God. The culminating point of Revelation reached
> in the Gospel of Jesus Christ is definitive; it is forever binding.
> This Revelation knows no extension added by the hand of man;
> it does not allow itself to be supplanted and replaced by arbitrary

---

[12] Any more than are the stupid insults by Lucien Rebattet in *Les Décombres*,
533: "Ratti, the antiracist, would prefer to give proofs of the rights of man
to atheists and to the Sanhedrin by promoting negro or yellow bishops. The
most ardent wish of this honorary rabbi has certainly been to cardinalize five
or six Jews" (quoted by René Rémond, *L'Anticléricalisme en France de 1815 à
nos jours* [Fayard, 1976], 281). And again: "the old wretch Ratti", "that evil
old fossil". The work appeared in Paris in 1942. Rebattet was the editor of
Je suis partout.

[13] Thus F. Delpech, *Sur les Juifs*, 213; cf. 254: "It is good that M. Margiotta-
Broglie has shown that there was also a problem with Pius XI." An amazing
feat!

[14] March 19, 1937. It should not be forgotten that these two encyclicals
were completed by a third, promulgated several days later, on March 28,
"in which the moral principles of a just political overthrow are defined"
(Charles Molette).

"revelations" which certain spokesmen of the present time claim
to derive from what they call the myth of blood and race.

Whoever, in sacrilegious ignorance of the essential differences
between God and creature, between the God-man and the children of men, dares to raise a mortal being, even if he be the
greatest of all time, to the level of Christ, and much more,
above him or against him, that person deserves to hear himself
called a prophet of nothingness, to whom the frightening words
of Scripture apply: "He who sits in the heavens laughs at them."

And this terrible accusation:

The experiences of recent years bring the responsibilities completely to light: they reveal the intrigues which from the beginning were aimed solely at a war of extermination.[15]

It is distressing to find coming from the pen of someone
like the aging Loisy anathemas against "the catastrophic pro-
gram of Pius XI" and against his role "beside Hitler and Mussolini in the conspiracy against freedom of spirit under the
guise of a fight against communism"; to hear it said that "Pius
XI is the most harmful Pope we have had in many generations".[16] These texts slightly precede *Mit brennender Sorge*,
but, as we have seen above, Pius XI had already declared his
verdict against Hitler a long time before this, and he had
repeated it many a time.[17] He had not waited until his last

[15] These texts will be quoted by G. Fessard, *France, prends garde . . .*, 34.

[16] Texts quoted by Emile Poulat, *Critique et Mystique* (Le Centurion, 1984),
157–59; "No [Pope] other than Pius XI has been the object of his indignation
to this extent" (158, n. 24). Others besides Loisy have reproached Pius XI
for the Lateran Treaty (in February 1929) because of the Concordat that
accompanied it; Fr. Fessard, on the other hand, has analyzed it very well in
his book *"Pax Nostra"*; see particularly p. 324: "The creative boldness of
Christian politics, such as Pius XI practiced by carrying through the Lateran
Treaty to a successful conclusion, consisted in trusting that, in surrendering
to the other the maximum possible amount of what is temporal and earthly,
he would make all the more transparent the spiritual quality of the Word
which he was to represent in the world."

[17] See the texts in Georges Jarlot, S.J., *Pie XI, doctrine et action sociale,
1922–1939* (Rome: Gregorian University Pub., 1973), 380–86. There is a

days to denounce that "paganism of state" that Loisy thought he saw him support.[18]

The thesis of a belated reversal by Pius XI has nevertheless been supported by the Italian Carlo Falconi, who also found fault with *Mit brennender Sorge* itself. His bill of indictment, written in the face of more than one known fact, should be quoted as a model of systematic distortion of reality:

It has been fashionable to contrast the ambiguities and hesitations of Pope Pacelli to the resolution and firmness of Pope Ratti's language. Now it is indisputable that in the final period of his pontificate, Pius XI worked a certain reversal in his politics of sympathy for totalitarian regimes and even went so far as to speak some moving words with respect to the Jews. But it is nonetheless true that these extreme *retractationes* were more verbal than real and sometimes more confidential than public and imperative. The famous speech on Catholics as the spiritual heirs of the Jews, for example, was given behind closed doors and was not even recorded by *l'Osservatore Romano* [Pius XI addressed it to Belgian pilgrims, who had offered him a missal as a gift, on September 6, 1938, before the general audience].
. . . [As for] his unjustly famous encyclical *Mit brennender Sorge*, it has been defined as an encyclical against nazism. This is so little true of the encyclical that it does not even dare to attribute to nazism as such, but only to some of its trends, the widespread dogmatic and moral errors in Germany. The sole reproach that Pope Ratti permitted himself to address against the leaders of the Third Reich, with all due respect to their rank, and the sole reason that made him decide to write, was that they violated the Concordat. Pius XI was not concerned about anything else.[19]

---

good historical account in R. Fontenelle, *Pie XI* (Spes, 1939), chap. 19, "La croix gammée", 415–47. From 1930 until his death, Pius XI never relented in his battle against nazism.

[18] Cf. his address of December 24, 1934 (G. Jarlot, 382).

[19] Carlo Falconi, *Le Silence de Pie XII* (Monaco: Ed. du Rocher, 1965), 75 and 76, etc.

How is it, then, that everyone was so mistaken about it? "In its substance, a crushing blow, in its release, a clap of thunder: such was the encyclical *Mit brennender Sorge*", wrote François Charles-Roux, our ambassador to the Vatican at that time,[20] expressing the general impression. Spread abroad and distributed secretly in thousands of copies between March 17 and 21, it was read in all the churches of the Reich. "Perhaps never", wrote Robert d'Harcourt, who heard it read, "did we feel more acutely, almost physically, the power of the Catholic communion, the strength of our attachment to Rome. . . . None of that whole packed crowd of people who were listening to the reading of the pontifical document in an attitude of prayer could maintain any illusion about the gravity of its significance and of its consequences."[21] A German friend who heard it in another church told me of a similar impression.[22]

How is it that the Grand Rabbi of Paris, Julien Weil himself, could have been mistaken, then, and persisted in his error, when, on February 11, 1939, the day after the death of Pius XI, he addressed this public homage to him:

> The death of His Holiness Pius XI moves me deeply and pain-fully. Judaism wholeheartedly joins the universal veneration that surrounded the august Pontiff, admiring and honoring him as a great servant of God, a true apostle of social justice, peace and the human fraternity. On numerous occasions, Pius XI denounced with luminous firmness and clarity the pernicious errors of racist paganism, and he condemned anti-Semitism as

[20] Op. cit., 99. It was Cardinal Pacelli who had organized, in coordination with the nuncio in Berlin, its unannounced "release".

[21] "En Allemagne après l'encyclique", in *Etudes*, 231:293ff.

[22] The attention of the congregation had been subtly caught by seeing the priest, after the reading of the day's Gospel, open the tabernacle, withdraw a paper from it and make his way to the pulpit. In August 1942, Grand Rabbi Kaplan, aware of the Judeo-Christian solidarity, would recall Pius XI's assertion "Spiritually we are Semites" in asking Cardinal Gerlier to intervene; and again, in 1947, he would invoke this "testimony of the great Pope" (*N'oublie pas* [Stock, 1984], 57 and 142).

irreconcilable with the Christian faith and as an instigator of iniquities and odious violence. I am sure that I express the feelings of all my fellow Jews in saluting with respect the great figure of Pius XI and in giving in our prayers a religious expression to our homage of regret and gratitude toward this great servant of the God of justice and love.[23]

Following Pius XI, and nearly on the eve of the war, just after the bloody outburst organized by the official forces of nazi anti-Semitism on November 9 and 10, 1938 (the *Kristalnacht*), Cardinal Verdier, Archbishop of Paris, had raised a protest in conjunction with Cardinals Van Roey (Malines) and Schuster (Milan): "Very close to us, in the name of racial rights, thousands and thousands of people were tracked down like wild beasts, stripped of their possessions, veritable pariahs who are seeking in vain in the heart of civilization for shelter

[23] Quoted in Philippe Bourdrel, *Histoire des Juifs en France*, 568 (app. 11). In the conclusion of *Epreuve de force*, which appeared in June 1939 (Bloud et Gay), G. Fessard exalted "the splendid figure of Pius XI", who set the faith of the Church in the incarnate Transcendent One against the nazi and communist myths (133). Similarly, at the end of his reply to the inquiry of the journal *Volontés* (same date): "When, in 1937, Pius XI published his two encyclicals in rapid succession . . ., when on every occasion this old man, threatened with imminent death, still continued to face all dangers . . ., it was then apparent that the Bishop of Rome could be and was in fact not only the defender of a particular city, like the bishop of the High Middle Ages, but the defender of the entire human city against the return of barbarism." On these two encyclicals, cf. Roger Aubert, in *Nouvelle Histoire de l'Eglise* (Seuil, 1975), 603–5.

Here is an example of the long-term effect of the words of Pius XI. In 1942, the regional head of censorship in Pau would send to Vichy the following note, dated July 25, 1942: "On February 12, 1942[?], *La Revue des jeunes* (Fr. Carré, O.P., editor) presented the main board of censors in Pau with a treatise entitled 'Several Clarifications on the Jewish Question'. The censor then explained that this text, which he banned, risked distressing the consciences of certain fearful Catholics by invoking the witness of Pope Pius XI and by uniting them to the Semitic family at the very moment when the government was trying to effect an ethnic dissociation" (Archives of the C.D.J.C., 368, quoted by Renée Bédarida at the symposium of March 1979, mimeographed text).

and a piece of bread. There you have the result of the racial theory."[24] In 1939, when we were at war, all the bishops of France insisted on the entire moral legitimacy of our side, sometimes going so far as to speak of a crusade for the assistance of Christian civilization. This was something new: in 1914, they had simply recognized that the right was on our side. Pius XI having died in the meantime, on February 10, 1939, Cardinal Pacelli, who succeeded him under the name of Pius XII, promulgated his first encyclical, *Summi Pontificatus*, on October 27. In it, he declared his position "against exacerbated nationalism, the idolatry of the state, totalitarianism, racism, the cult of brutal force, contempt of international agreements, against all the characteristics of Hitler's political system; he laid the responsibility for the scourge of the war on these aberrations."[25] Once our own disaster occurred in 1940, crowning Hitler's successive aggressions, Pius XII again let the voice of the Church be heard, without any ambiguity or softening. It was on December 24, 1940:

> We find ourselves faced with actions as irreconcilable with the prescriptions of positive international law as they are with natural law and even with the most elementary sentiments of humanity, actions which show us into what a polluted, chaotic circle the juridical sense, led astray by purely utilitarian considerations, can sink. It is in this category that we place: premeditated aggression against a small, hardworking and peaceful people under the pretext of a nonexistent danger that they neither intended nor were capable of; atrocities . . . ; illegal use of destructive force even against noncombatants, fugitives, the elderly and children; a contempt for human dignity, freedom

[24] Quoted by Michel Riquet, S.J., *Chrétiens de France dans l'Europe enchaînée* (S.O.S., 1972), 31–32.

[25] François Charles-Roux, 351–52. On October 1, Cardinal Cerejeira, patriarch of Lisbon, had published a pastoral letter on "the neopagan doctrines", leveled almost entirely against Hitlerism, and it had been reproduced by *l'Osservatore Romano* (348–49).

and life that gives rise to actions that cry out for vengeance before God; anti-Christian and even atheistic propaganda. . . . The memory of the short-lived duration of negotiations and agreements in the end paralyzes any efforts capable of leading to a peaceful solution.[26]

The numerous declarations of our bishops belonged to the past. For the most part, following the stunning collapse, they seemed to have disappeared with a world that had been engulfed. Even the voice of the sovereign Pontiff no longer reached us. On the contrary, what dominated was the "masochism of self-accusation . . . fostered by some of the media at that time and in more than one official speech". It was a "penitential" vocabulary, orchestrating the addresses given by the head of state, a vocabulary with political intentions in view but which a certain naïvely supernatural spirit on the part of many priests and their flocks was only too tempted to accommodate. The apostolic nuncio, Bishop Valerio Valeri, had to recommend that *La Croix* not speak of "divine vengeance", and Msgr. Guerry, recently named archbishop coadjutor of Cambrai, reacted against this torrent of masochism being exploited by the victor in his Grenoble journal, *L'Action catholique*. He dared to recall there soberly, in moderate language that was still for a short time tolerated by state censorship, which was itself closely controlled: "Let us not have the souls of defeated men. . . . We took up arms to remain faithful to promises made and to affirm respect for treaties."[27]

---

[26] Quoted, ibid., 362–63.

[27] Cf. M. Riquet, loc. cit., and J. Duquesne, 26–34. Guerry's article "brought a lively reaction from the German press, which judged that the French had understood precisely nothing". Gabriel Marcel's reaction, in *Esprit*, was in harmony with that of the nuncio and of Archbishop Guerry.

Chapter 3

Fessard and Chaillet:
"France, Take Care"

The memorandum addressed to my superiors was accompanied by a certain number of documents serving as supporting material. I had submitted my idea for this to Fr. Fontoynont, my personal adviser, who had greatly encouraged me and later approved what I had written. I spoke of it to my two friends Gaston Fessard and Pierre Chaillet, with whom I had rather numerous conversations during this period. As I recall, I had them read my text—not to convince or arouse them, for they certainly had no need of this, as I well knew. Both were most capable of understanding the situation and better than I at acting accordingly. They were two exceptional personalities. And their former work—scholarly research and apostolic activities—had prepared them for the task that now lay before them.

Fr. Chaillet, professor of theology at the Fourvière scholasticate since 1935 (he would remain there until 1942),[1] had made a careful study of the nazi movement from its origins, in its doctrine and in its actions, during prolonged stays in central Europe; he had organized assistance for German and Austrian emigrés and exiles, particularly of the Jewish race.

---

[1] For the curriculum vitae of Fr. Chaillet from 1930–1931 (Innsbruck, Vienna and Lyons) until 1939, see Renée Bédarida, "Le Père Pierre Chaillet, De la théologie de Moehler à la Résistance", Biviers Symposium, September 1984, on spirituality, theology and the Resistance (published by the University Presses of Grenoble).

In *La Vie intellectuelle* of June 1938, he had published the premonitory article "The Freedom of the Church", in which we read: "The visible Church is the principle of total commitment of Christian fidelity . . . , she cannot fail in the fidelity of her witness."[2] Ever since his stay in Rome (1936–1937), where he prepared for his teaching career with a thesis on the ecclesiology of the Catholic School of Tübingen, which he was not able to finish (for he saw things on a grand scale and wanted first to translate the works of Drey, the founder of the school), he had encouraged the new translation of the important work *L'Unité de l'Eglise* by Johann-Adam Moehler, for which he provided an introduction.[3] Thanks to a Franche-Conté tenacity placed at the service of his Faith, he had surmounted all the obstacles that, during this troubled period, seemed to make a project, which was very close to his heart, appear fanciful: the publication of a great collective work, which, in the form of a "homage to Moehler", would affirm through the close collaboration of German and French theologians, in the face of religious nationalism and threats of an "Aryan Christianity", that *the Church is one*. The work had appeared simultaneously in Munich in German and in Paris in French in 1939, on the eve of the war. In his own contribution, "The Mystical Principle of Unity", we can already see what a profound theologian he would have been if a higher vocation had not diverted him forever from a life of study.[4] Speaking from experience, he had also published in 1939 the little book *L'Autriche souffrante* [Suffering Austria], in which he said:

[2] *Vie int.* (June 1938), 173.
[3] This was the second volume of the series "Unam Sanctam", which Fr. Yves Congar had just started for Editions du Cerf.
[4] *L'Eglise est une, hommage à Moehler*, French ed. (Bloud et Gay, 1939), 194–220; cf. Introduction, 3–16. See the account quoted by R. Bédarida. We should also point out that he had published (Vrin, 1934) a translation adapted from the German Jesuit Bernard Jansen, *La Philosophie religieuse de Kant*.

The triumph of Hitlerism in Germany was to mark an outburst of racist terror. . . . The Third Reich intends to resolve the problem of racial purity by the relentless extermination of those whom the Nuremberg laws leave defenseless in the face of the outburst of the basest instincts. . . . We know the disgust and indignation aroused in the civilized world by this shameful hunting down of people treated like unclean beasts. One need only have been a witness in Vienna to find it impossible to resign oneself to a complacent silence and complicity."[5]

He was thereby striving to awaken the consciences of so many heedless French faced with the "growing shadow of the swastika over Europe", and he was already making an appeal for "spiritual resistance".[6] Little read by our politicians, the book did not escape the vigilance of the nazi censors, and from 1940 on, it would be inscribed on the famous Otto list of forbidden publications.

As for Fr. Fessard, he too had long been preparing himself to understand and judge.[7] Accompanied by Fr. de Montcheuil, he had attended in 1934 one of the first nazi congresses in Nuremberg, and both had been seized by a grieved horror. The first work he published, in 1936, was *"Pax Nostra", examen de conscience international* ["Pax Nostra", an international examination of conscience], a work that from the very first line of its introduction referred to Hitler. In it he had written:

[5] This passage is quoted by R. Bédarida in the collection *La France et la Question Juive*, 214–15. On Austria at that time and Anschluss (annexation): François Charles-Roux, *Huit ans au Vatican, 1932–1940* (Flammarion, 1947), 110–29.

[6] *L'Autriche souffrante*, 117 and 124.

[7] On the first works of Fr. Fessard, striving during the 1930s to define a Christian attitude as far as international relations are concerned and determining the response of a conscience that has remained Christian in the face of nazi anti-Semitism, see the account of Jacques Prévotat: "Quatre jésuites devant le totalitarisme nazi", Biviers Symposium, September 1984, on Spiritualité, théologie et Résistance.

Christian Revelation has come to create the world a second time. . . . It has expanded to its widest limits the horizons of the human community where every "I" finds its birth, and at the same time it has consolidated to the maximum degree the existence of this "I", this tiny element of that community. The revelation of universal brotherhood in Christ, the revelation of the absolute value of each man, such are the two poles between which we must orient our two loves, that of peace and that of country. It has been rightly said that the message of Christ has revealed us to ourselves as *persons*. And, in fact, this term is perfectly suited to designate the twofold, paradoxical quality that we receive from our supernatural destiny: on the one hand, it serves to indicate so well to us that each one of us acquires, by reason of this destiny, a value immeasurably beyond that of the rest of nature, that it becomes for all the object of sovereign respect, and on the other hand, in this absolute value communicated by Christ, our freedom finds the sole end worthy of it: the realization of a perfect community among all.[8]

The books and articles that Fr. Fessard had published after this on the subject of communism and nazism, each time proceeding through a more concrete analysis and a closer study of the circumstances, were at the same time all founded on this doctrinal basis. *Epreuve de force*,[9] written soon after the Munich Treaty and appearing in June 1939, was not long in joining Fr. Chaillet's work as a victim of the Otto list. So the two friends would share the honor paid to Hitler himself, whose Mein Kampf would also appear on the list.[10] The interest that Fessard had long shown in the religion of Israel and in the numerous present-day Jewish problems, an interest

---

[8] *"Pax Nostra", examen de conscience international* (Grasset, 1936), 39–40. I quoted these pages in a conference given to the Ecole des cadres d'Uriage in 1941: *Explication chrétienne de notre temps* (Ed. de l'Orante, 1942), 27. (On Uriage: Raymond Josse, "L'Ecole des cadres d'Uriage, 1940–1942", in *Revue d'histoire de la Seconde Guerre mondiale*, 61 [January 1966], 49–74.)

[9] *Epreuve de force, réflexions sur la crise internationale* (Bloud et Gay, 1939).

[10] Cf. Henri Amouroux, *La Vie des Français sous l'Occupation* (Fayard, 1961).

mixed with a courage that was as prudent as it was intrepid, would quite naturally continue in new forms imposed by the temporary triumph of nazism.

As early as December 15, 1940, invited at the suggestion of our confrere Victor Dillard to preach the sermon one Sunday in Advent at the church of Saint-Louis de Vichy, Fr. Fessard had warned his listeners to be on guard against racism, and the text of this sermon (somewhat blue-penciled by the inevitable censorship) had appeared in February 1941 in *Cité nouvelle*,[11] a journal newly founded by the Jesuits, destined to replace in the "southern zone" both *Etudes* and the *Revue de l'Action populaire*. There had been at first a question of making him the editor, but the choice fell to Fr. Desbuquois, whose more flexible temperament gave more hope of survival to the journal. Fr. Fessard had also published in one of the first two issues of *Temps nouveau* (the weekly version of *Temps présent*, which Stanislas Fumet, who had also become a resident of Lyons, had just by some miracle revived), on December 27, 1940, a warning article: "*Custos, quid de nocte?*"[12] Born, or rather reborn, on December 20, this journal, after having been "suspended" twice, specifically for having protested against the ignoble film *Le Juif Süss*, was to be definitively banned on August 15, 1941, by a telegram from Admiral Darlan.[13]

In his cramped quarters on rue Sainte-Hélène, Fessard lost

[11] The entire text of the sermon would be reinstated in the work by Fr. Fessard, *De l'actualité historique* (D.D.B., 1960), 1:77–93.

[12] "Christians, could we remain oblivious to the insidious solicitations of despair, egoism and obsequious servility!"

[13] The rebirth and survival, however brief, of Fumet's weekly was a kind of miracle, due, according to J. Duquesne, 141, to "the intervention of a rather anarchistic member of the Laval cabinet". The reality was a bit different: see below, Chap. 12, nn. 11, 12 and 13. In response to Darlan, Fumet would write to him that he had committed a great blunder by suppressing *Temps nouveau*: for all French patriots in the free zone, it was an invitation to join resistance movements (*Histoire de Dieu dans ma vie*, 462).

no time. From the spring of 1941, having noted that it was from then on pointless to seek to enlighten minds by writing for publication, he had begun a work in which he would set forth the truth without pointless precautions, but without yet knowing what precise use he could make of it. This was what would become, at the end of several months, the first *Cahier* of the *Témoignage chrétien*: "France, Take Care Not to Lose Your Soul!"[14] Along with the many other things he read, he used—very freely—my memorandum to my superiors and several appended documents; but the organization of thought, the simple, strong plan that he adopted and the overall writing were his alone. The strictness of his logic, his passion for truth, his habitual independence of spirit can be recognized in it from beginning to end. When, in the autumn, he had to return to Paris to the *Etudes* house, to which he had belonged since 1934,[15] he left the finished manuscript for this in Lyons, in the hands of his friend Chaillet. Did he already know that this would be the first number of a whole series of

---

[14] If it is true, as Marcel Ruby recalls, in *La Résistance à Lyon* (Lyons: L'Hermès, 1979), 10, that "the popular democrats and even more the Jeune République (Young Republic) were very active from the beginning", they were nevertheless not "at the origin of the creation of *Témoignage chrétien*". "In Lyons, in November 1940, France-Liberté appeared, a group with progressive Christian leanings that was closely connected with the Jeune République and that leftists with other leanings rapidly joined; it devoted its energies to the distribution of stickers opposing the Vichy government", etc.; see Marcel Baudot, in *F.Q.J.*, 278–79. Toward the end of 1941, from this group and from several others, would come, at the instigation of Jean-Pierre Lévy and Avinin, the clandestine journal *Le Franc-Tireur*, which claimed to be "without any alterations due to class, race or ideology", but in which the members of the Jeune République would soon be swamped in a rather anticlerical socialist milieu: "Christians have a relatively small part [in it], and atheists, Freemasons and free thinkers are [there] in great numbers." (There were some connections, especially in 1942, with l'Amitié chrétienne and *T.C.*)

[15] It has been written that he had to leave Lyons because his superiors did not trust him; another has said that, on the contrary, his superiors had wanted to protect him, for the Lyons police had begun to suspect him. Unverifiable hypotheses, and perhaps each as false as the other.

Cahiers? I think that he did not. My memories about this are a bit confused. When did this idea come to take shape in some precise fashion in the mind of Chaillet himself? Probably rather late, and perhaps even as a result of the manuscript that Fessard had just handed over to him. What is certain is that Chaillet's will to initiate, with precise information and upon doctrinal bases in the very name of his Catholic fidelity, a resistance that was properly spiritual, independent of political or even simply national trends, had been quickly and firmly decided. This was precisely the concept of his friend Fessard. It imposed on him a rigorous distinction of roles. During the first semester of 1941, put in contact with Captain Henri Frenay through Stanislas Fumet, Chaillet had given Frenay several religious chronicles, signed Testis, for his clandestine journal, *Les Petites Ailes*, which soon became *Vérités*. But that was only a provisional activity. In order to carry out his plan, Chaillet needed complete autonomy. He came to an agreement about this with Frenay, who, as a Catholic, understood it without difficulty: in the necessary secrecy, his work would be, unalloyed, a "Catholic witness". A meeting with a certain number of Protestants who had a similar intention in mind, and more particularly with the intrepid Pastor Roland de Pury, made him choose, at the very last moment, the title *Témoignage chrétien* [Christian witness].[16]

For information about the atmosphere in Lyons, "capital of misery and of hope", during the years 1940–1941; about the first disappointments, indeed, the indignation of Chaillet in the face of a kind of apathy and, at times, even a kind of widespread euphoria in the population that reached to certain

[16] It will be noted that, through the influence of Moehler, Fr. Chaillet had long been interested in ecumenism. This interest must have been deepened through his relations with Fr. Congar and even more with Abbé Couturier, whom he knew during his years in Lyons and who had him give a conference on Moehler in January 1938; he would participate very actively in 1939 in the "Dombes reunion", which had been Abbé Couturier's initiative.

parts of the clergy; about his conflict (which remained friendly)
with those who, like Mounier, thought that a loyal effort at
putting things right could be attempted in accord with the
new regime because they did not have a realistic enough view
either of its fatal subservience to the victor or of the relentless
nazi ideology; about his numerous contacts with present and
future workers in the Resistance through semiclandestine conversations that did not always seem very effective to him or
which he judged dangerous; about the various steps by which
he sought less a way in which to commit himself, for that
was already clearly conceived, than the practical means of
implementation; about the first members with whom he
formed an association, in the first ranks of which was Louis
Cruvillier, whom he met through Alexandre Marc; in short,
about everything to do with the essential origin and preparation of the *Cahiers* (as well as about all the rest of their history),
the fundamental work is and will remain that of Renée Bédarida,[17] who, after having participated herself in the dangerous
enterprise, later became its historian at the cost of long and
minute research carried out with great care.

In her determination to collect all valuable information,
Renée Bédarida included an episode that was not very clear,
without contesting its authenticity but also without covering
up the implausibility of certain details and the contradictions
between the various accounts given of it. With new research
and the evidence of other witnesses, it seems possible today

[17] *Les Armes de l'Esprit: Témoignage chrétien (1914–1944)*, with the collaboration of François Bédarida (Les Editions ouvrières, 1977), 378 pp. To be
completed through various papers given later by the author at the symposia
held on this period of our history. R. B. repeatedly and with reason insists
on the perfect understanding between Chaillet and Robert d'Harcourt, whose
clear-sightedness, Catholic spirit, decisiveness and heroic courage were, from
the beginning of nazism, consistently exemplary; d'Harcourt would be the
principal author of *Cahier 24–25, Puissance des ténèbres* (March 1944). On
d'Harcourt, see the paper given by Jacques Prévotat at the Biviers Symposium,
September 1984.

to see with more certainty that the episode was authentic but of negligible interest.

In June 1941, Frs. Daniélou and Varillon, accompanied by a Catholic student, Jean Neyra (a future Jesuit), came one day from Mongré (Villefranche-sur-Saône) to see their confrere Fr. Fessard. According to the first version of the story, itself subject to variants, they asked him to write "within the week" a pamphlet destined for a group of young students in Lyons of whom Neyra was a part: the pamphlet would be duplicated and distributed clandestinely in Lyons on July 14. Fessard acceded to the request and within that one week met with one of the visitors. Surprise, perhaps a slight disappointment, but above all, great admiration! The author actually showed him a thick memorandum of fifty pages, scholarly, well structured, solidly documented, in which "the whole mechanism of Hitler's ideology was taken apart" and all the shrewdness of the nazi methods of propaganda was systematically analyzed. It was not what they were expecting, but what joy to hold in one's hands such a work, written in so few days! Having heard of it, Neyra returned to Fessard: he in his turn was also struck by the "rigorous logic" of the writing as well as by the "clarity", indeed the "violence", of the author's remarks, which were nevertheless marked "with a tranquil assurance". The manuscript was handed over to Neyra, to do as he wished with it! At once changing his plan, giving up the idea of the pamphlet he had wanted to distribute to his Lyons comrades, he jumped onto the train for Marseilles with his precious booty in hand, intending to confide it to an unknown friend who would distribute it in the Midi La Voix du Vatican. According to some, the printing was carried out; but despite a later search, no indication has been found that would help to verify this. According to others, the Marseille plan fell through. Returning then to Lyons, Neyra got in touch with a manufacturer who was himself associated with a printer—but without any more success. Finally, the manuscript, or rather one of the copies (the last!) that had been made of it in the meantime, fell into the hands of Fr. Chaillet: according to some, through an unknown intermediary; according to others, sent by Fessard himself, suspecting that his confrere would know how to make use of it.[18] At the time when he left Lyons, toward the end of August or the beginning of September, he left his work to Chaillet. The latter, who until then did not suspect a thing, soon saw the good use he could make of it: it would be the first *Cahier du Témoignage chrétien*!

This account, reconstructed from various testimonies given separately, orally and a long time after the events (sometimes twenty-five or thirty-five years later), then revised by a chronicler who judged herself to be better informed (we do not know by whom) about the Marseille incidents, seems so incoherent (in addition to the contradictions indicated in the passage) that another, more sober version has circulated about it: Fessard was asked by his visitors to write something and he did so; that is, he simply drew from his work, which was already well advanced, to say the least, material for a pamphlet for the use of the students, making the necessary adaptations— unless this pamphlet, written in its entirety in response to the request, then suggested to him the idea of enlarging it, so that it ended up as the famous booklet. . . . Supposing that this version is the right one, there is no doubt in any case that the pamphlet delivered to the student was larger and more solid than anticipated.

Renée Bédarida saw very well, without raising any doubt

---

[18] Fessard had no need, as one chronicler imagined, of being put in touch with Chaillet late in the day through a third party outside the Society. One other historian remains in the dark; J. Duquesne, 154, after a list of those who encouraged Chaillet in his enterprise: "Several days later, Fr. Chaillet received the manuscript from Fr. Fessard. It was decided. He was going to publish it"; on p. 151, he was more precise about the intervention of Fessard but seemed to believe that the latter knew nothing directly from Chaillet: "Before leaving, [Fessard] confided his text to Fr. Chaillet, who, he had learned, wanted to launch something."

about the visit or the request made of Fessard, that these were of only minor interest and that, on the other hand, Fessard and Chaillet, these two Jesuit friends, did not have to hide from each other for a long time or have a third party put them in touch with each other—especially since they were both in close association with a third friend, less enterprising than they but staying at the same time in the same town and sharing, as they all well knew, their common sentiments. Besides, if Fr. Fessard had had to leave Lyons during the summer, it is difficult to see how all the incidents recounted above in one or the other of their versions could have taken place. If, on the contrary, he left toward the middle of October, as we now know to be certain,[19] it is just as difficult to see how he could have, in the midst of his growing obligations in Lyons, succeeded in finishing between July and then the whole booklet inspired by the request for the pamphlet; nor can we see how for his part Chaillet, receiving the mysterious manuscript,[20] could also have found time (in addition to his pressing activity in what would be "l'Amitié chrétienne") to reflect on it sufficiently to come up with the idea of a collection of *Cahiers*, and to take all the necessary steps to finish everything required for the preparation, printing and distribution—even with the effective assistance of Frenay and Cruvillier—since the Fessard *Cahier*, which was supposedly handed over at the time of his departure, after October 15, began to be distributed on November 16. That would have been perhaps a little tight! But nothing obliges us to think

[19] Letter from G. Fessard to Gabriel Marcel, October 11, 1941: "My departure [from Lyons] is fixed for next Wednesday. My trunks are ready, my good-bye visits almost finished." His first card from Paris to G. Marcel would be on November 11: he has seen the friends about whom Marcel was waiting for news: Jean Wahl, Mme. Ergaz, Daniel Halévy, Marcel Moré. "I have found my home once again and hope to be able to work a little more than last year."

[20] "By chance", as one author has written!

that Fessard waited until the last day to confide his text to Chaillet. Let us conclude in any case that, even if there is no reason to question the fact itself, which has given rise to such varied and debatable interpretations, that fact remains of little interest. Fr. Daniélou, who had visited Chaillet in June, does not seem to have seen in that event anything worth particular mention and did not, if I am not mistaken, relate anything about it.[21]

If one of Fessard's visitors or one of those who wrote about this visit thought he could attribute the significance to it that we have just seen, that proves at least one thing: even in front of visiting friends, Fessard knew how to be discreet.[22]

There would be no reason to dwell so long on this "diverse fact" if the myth springing from it, with all its different variants, were not continuing to grow. In 1984 we found a new version of it in the essay *Les Jésuites, histoire de pouvoirs* by journalist Alain Woodrow (with the collaboration of Albert Longchamp). The author, who has not given way to sheer fantasy, tells us that "François Varillon was at the origin of the proposal made to Fr. Gaston Fessard to write a pamphlet", that "the pamphlet became a manuscript of fifty pages", that,

---

[21] We know, however, that he would become an ardent distributor of the *Cahiers*.

[22] As he would always be. A silent worker, although always concerned to reflect on the most current questions, he would for a long time be seldom cited among "the living forces and inquiring minds of French Christianity" of his time (the expression comes from Fr. Joseph Robert, O.P., at the Biviers Symposium, with respect to the union established among notable Catholics by the weekly *Sept* during the 1930s). In the note given by Delpech, who was not, moreover, sparing with proper names, on the first *Cahier* of the T.C., Fessard's name was omitted (*Sur les Juifs*, 240). If in the period after the war this name would appear more frequently, it would be rather as an untimely foil. Fessard nevertheless remains, for the clear-sighted historian of our time, one of its great figures. *France, prends garde de perdre ta liberté!* [France, take care that you don't lose your liberty!], by G. Fessard, would appear in 1945 and 1946 in the Editions du Témoignage Chrétien, founded at that time by Chaillet.

"printed in two versions, one in Lyons and the other in Salon-de-Provence, the booklet was the first of the *Cahiers*", and ends with this admirable phrase: "The continuation of the operation was entrusted to Fr. Pierre Chaillet"![23]

France, Take Care Not to Lose Your Soul!, printed in mid-November 1941, began to be distributed on the afternoon of November 16.[24] The adventure of the *Cahiers* began. Fr. Chaillet, who conducted the enterprise with the assistance of Fr. Fessard, would manage it until its end, on the eve of the liberation of Paris, abandoning forever his plan for an in-depth study of Moehler and of the renewal of theology in the Church, but in view of higher duties,[25] achieving in action what he had learned from his heroes:

> Just as each Christian must every day, through a permanent victory over the world, renew the interior treasure that has been communicated to him by grace, so the Church must ceaselessly renew herself in a holy battle for the fidelity of her witness. It is this battle which gives the Church her martyrs; it is then that she upholds all that, in the course of history, has given witness to her divine origin.[26]

[23] J. C. Lattès (1984), 182–83, followed by clichés about "cowardice and fears", the "return of conscience", "unarmed but effective power", the restoration of "lost honor". . . , which in their facile abstraction at least do not introduce any other concrete error. The three Jesuits in question having died before the publication and amplification of such myths, I thought it opportune to make this clarification.

[24] Through a slight error, Marcel Baudot, in *F.Q.J.*, 282, dates the first *Cahier* of the *T.C.* as January 1942.

[25] See below, Chap. 10.

[26] Johann-Adam Moehler, *Lettre à la comtesse de Stolberg*, June 24, 1834. Quoted by Pierre Chaillet, at the conclusion of the collection *L'Eglise est une, hommage à Moehler*, 349. Two or three copies of the first *Cahier* of the *T.C.* passed very quickly into the occupied zone, thanks to a wine merchant from Beaune (a city located on the demarcation line, north side), who, during a business trip to Lyons, had taken part in the secret meeting of a small group of Resistance workers that perhaps included Fr. Chaillet. Fr. Fessard, however, seems not to have been aware of this before the end of the summer of

N.B.: Jacques Maritain's booklet *A travers le désastre* might be considered a preview *Cahier du T.C.* This was the text of a conference given in New York, a copy of which, coming by way of the United States embassy in Berne, reached France through secret channels. The booklet was printed in Gap, under the care of Fernand Belot (who would be one of Fr. Chaillet's principal assistants) and Marcel Arnaud, and widely disseminated in the Southeast before passing into the occupied zone and being republished in 1943 by Editions de Minuit. Chaillet became its distributor in 1941. (Cf. Renée Bédarida, 66–68.)

"The series of *Cahiers du Témoignage chrétien*, carrying on in secret the tradition of those like Charles Péguy and blocking the way of the racist contagion, under the title 'France, Take Care Not to Lose Your Soul', certainly belongs to the finest pages of the French Resistance" (Léon Poliakov, *Bréviaire de la haine* [Paris: Calmann-Lévy, 1951], 340).

1942. He wrote to me on May 11: "Have not yet seen the homework of my child from Sainte-Hélène." A young student at a teachers' college, it seems, brought it back from his vacation, spent with his family in the free zone, and showed it to several comrades. It was undoubtedly in this way that it reached its author as well as Fr. de Montcheuil. The London journal *Volunteer for the Christian City* announced the *Cahier* several months later (cf. J. Duquesne, 115). Even in May 1943, rather few Parisians seem to have known of the *Cahiers*. At that time, a student found by the police in possession of *Défi* [Challenge] (January-February 1943) in the presbytery of Saint-Etienne-du-Mont was imprisoned at Fresnes, where he remained for fifteen months (R. Bédarida, 156).

Chapter 4

Statute of the Jews (June 3, 1941) and the Chaine Declaration

"From October 18, 1940, until September 16, 1941, twenty-six laws, twenty-four decrees, six orders and one ruling concerning the Jews appeared in the *Journal officiel* [Official journal]."[1]

The first law, promulgated on October 18, 1940, issued from that very first Vichy regime, a "mixture of boy scouts, Maurrassism, moral order and old conservatism", as Jean-Baptiste Duroselle describes it.[2] A set of restrictive measures throughout, it was already clearly anti-Semitic. Its "foreman" was Alibert, lord chancellor in the Laval government.[3] From the twentieth on, at the B.B.C. (British Broadcasting Corporation), Maurice Schumann would criticize this "racist legislation, contrary to all national traditions and condemned by the Church".

This law, however, caused scarcely any stir in the country. It passed nearly unnoticed by many, and even a great number of Jews were at first unaware of it. In fact, as the Jewish historian Georges Wellers explains:

---

[1] *Cahiers du T.C.*, 6–7, *Antisémites*. On the anti-Jewish legislation in France from June 1940 to April 1942, see in *F.Q.J.*: Guy Pedroncini, 27–30, Fred Jupperman, 31–41, and, for administrative and police administration, 57–65. Henri Amouroux, *La Vie des Français sous l'Occupation*, 389–400.

[2] *F.Q.J.*, 19.

[3] Claude Lévy, 118.

During the first months after the Armistice, all of France was struck by a whirlwind of preoccupations that could be neither avoided nor postponed: the colossal exodus had dispersed families, who were looking for each other through little announcements in journals, a search that was particularly difficult and hopeless because of the disorganization of the postal system and railroads after the line of demarcation cut France into pieces; fifteen hundred young soldiers were in Germany, imprisoned in the "Stalags" and "Offlags", and their fate worried and distressed innumerable families; others—military and civilian—had disappeared . . . and their relatives lived in anguish; a considerable number of persons were deprived of resources far from their home or usual place of business.[4]

On the other hand, the Vichy camps held almost no one but Jewish foreigners, just dumped by Hitler into France and "toward whom almost no one felt any responsibility",[5] and many Frenchmen were even unaware of the foreign Jews' presence in our land. As for those who had emigrated a long time before, a large number were both Jewish and communist, and at the time when the German-Soviet pact had created such a disturbance, one could scarcely hope for "much hostile reaction to discriminatory legislation", even if it affected French citizens, "very gradually set up by the government of a marshal who enjoyed rather general confidence". Besides, the French Jews affected by the law scarcely wanted to make their lot worse by protesting. For the communists themselves, the Jewish problem had been reduced to merely one aspect of the class struggle, anti-Semitism being only a diversion invented by the capitalist powers: there was no "Jewish entity", but

[4] L'Etoile jaune à l'heure de Vichy: De Drancy à Auschwitz (Fayard, 1973), 270–71. Cf. J. M. Soutou: the average Frenchman did not react at first in 1940 to the first anti-Jewish measures; he was "absorbed in the difficulties of everyday life", and "everything that had been done on the administrative and regulatory level" by the preceding governments had prepared minds "for acceptance or at least for passivity", F.Q.J., 250.

[5] H. Amouroux, 401.

only "Jewish problems to screen out and Jewish capitalists to bring under control".[6] It was only in November 1941 that the clandestine booklet "L'antisémitisme, le racisme, le problème juif" [Anti-Semitism, racism, the Jewish problem] by Georges Politzer appeared; and his point of view really penetrated communist circles only one year later. Let us add that in the beginning there was dissension between the different Jewish organizations, that "native" Jews were themselves quite often more or less "xenophobic"[7] and that from August 15, 1940, two journalists in Vichy itself, at the Parc Hotel, were preparing anti-Jewish broadcasts.[8] As for the *Journal officiel* of October 18, which announced the new statute for the Jews, it explained sanctimoniously that it was not a question of "facile vengeance but of indispensable security".[9]

These facts all help to explain why the first anti-Jewish legislation of October 1940, which was still rather moderate, really aroused little public opinion.[10]

The Catholic hierarchy, however, was not without concern about the law. The two assemblies of cardinals and archbishops discussed it (this duality, imposed by the occupying forces, did not facilitate the understanding needed for a common, energetic action), but they did not decide to produce a public document. Not that the French episcopate was still more or less under the influence of Maurras. As Jean-Marie Mayeur has observed, it had been profoundly renewed since 1926, and neither Liénart (the "bête noire of the integrists") nor Gerlier (former President of the A.C.J.F.) nor Suhard

---

[6] Marcel Baudot, "Les mouvements de résistance devant la persécution des Juifs", in *F.Q.J.*, 273 and 290.

[7] Alexandre Glasberg, *Colloque de Grenoble*, 203.

[8] Alain Loubreaux and Lucien Rebattet, edited by J. L. Tixier-Vignancour.

[9] Cf. J. Duquesne, 250–52.

[10] It does not follow, however, that the distinctions "between Christians and non-Christians, between the French and foreigners" were all purely "theoretical and arbitrary". What is "shocking" in the texts of this first phase is the way in which they are treated. Cf. F. Delpech, 293.

("preoccupied with the indispensable transformations of a missionary Church"), its three heads, had any connections with l'Action française. But their trustworthy support of the Vichy government, rather like that of the immense majority of the French people, went "beyond traditional loyalty", and undoubtedly they too were afraid to break with a "politics of presence" that "had begun in the last years of the Third Republic" and marked "a return of Catholics into civil society".[11] Surely, too, they did not foresee that, through this first statute of exception, which could seem rather moderate, they were getting caught in fatal gears. It was (as it is easy for us to say, after the fact) a serious error.

The first official and public Christian protest came from Pastor Marc Boegner, in a letter addressed to the Grand Rabbi of France, March 26, 1941, in the name of the "Christian conscience" and of the "Reformed Church". In the meantime, Admiral Darlan, who had replaced Laval in power, had just created the general High Commission for Jewish questions, the direction of which he entrusted to Xavier Vallat (March 9, 1941). Some might have thought that Darlan, whose mentality had nothing particularly anti-Semitic in it, sought by this new institution rather to reject any excess in the future by ensuring a regular application of the law. On March 26, the same day as he addressed his public letter to the Grand Rabbi, Pastor Boegner wrote one to Darlan, the trusting conclusion of which would soon be disappointed: "We know, Admiral, that you have the firm desire, through the very institution of a High Commission for Jewish questions, to do everything in your power to avoid any greater trials for French Israelites. . . . The Christian confessions will unhesitatingly support your effort, knowing how difficult this will be."[12]

---

[11] "Les Eglises devant la persécution des Juifs en France", 150–51.

[12] This last sentence, it seems to me, gives us a rather clear indication that Boegner, before writing, made contact with the Catholic "confession", that is, with Cardinal Gerlier, which would have been consistent with his constant

This was a failure to recognize both the opportunism of the new Prime Minister and the convictions of the auxiliary whom he had just appointed. Everyone knows what happened. Darlan was not a man to submit to or to be moved by high principles. Soon the law of June 3, 1941, far from softening that of October 18, 1940, or even from specifying its limits, made it considerably worse.[13]

Xavier Vallat was one of those Catholics in l'Action française who, following Maurras, extolled what they freely called, by watering down the deep feeling of their master, a "reasonable anti-Semitism". At the time of his trial, Vallat would candidly explain: "It was time to put an end to the mortal danger that the Jewish abscess constituted. . . . The Jew was perfectly tolerable in a homeopathic dose. . . . [But] France had been struck by a Jewish stroke of which she almost died. It was very necessary for us to take the scalpel in hand." Several at Vichy had nearly the same opinion, seeming besides to imagine themselves free to direct their policies as they wished without knowing anything of the conqueror's ideology. Vallat would say in his defense: "The French leaders cannot reasonably be reproached for not having known of abominations that even those who would be the victims did not suspect and accused for having knowingly directed the Jews toward the gas chambers and crematorium furnaces." This, at that time, must be recognized. However serious the Vichy government's lack of foresight may have proved to be, a lack of foresight made worse by an anti-Semitic fascination,

---

desire, in any serious circumstance, to proceed in union with him. So, in this event, the Church of France did not entirely commit suicide. If we dare to advance this hypothesis, Gerlier would thus have taken his revenge on the wait-and-see decision adopted by the Assembly; moreover, this way of addressing the authorities by expressing his confidence in being heard, on the other hand, would have seemed good to him, as it did to Boegner.

[13] In the occupied zone, La France continue, a clandestine journal by a group of intellectuals, would rise up on June 20, 1941, against the second statute of the Jews (Baudet, 281).

and however unjust some of its legislative dispositions had
already been, Daniel Mayer is unjust when, carried away by
an excusable indignation, he protested in December 1957, in
Evidences: "There is only a difference in degree, not in kind,
between the acceptance of a *numerus clausus* and the crematorium furnaces, the former leading infallibly to the latter."[14]
Quite different would be the attitude of Vallat's successor,
certainly not designated by him but in opposition to him,
whom Laval—having returned to power—would allow the
all-powerful nazi head Dannecker to impose upon France: the
sinister Darquier de Pellepoix, who had launched as early as
1938 an "anti-Jewish gathering" and who was in the ranks of
the nazis.

One element of the law of June 1941 was particularly
dangerous, all the more so because its immediate effects at-
tracted little attention: it was the order given for a census of
all Jews. The file established by this means would be enor-
mously helpful to the occupying forces later on. Only a few
perspicacious men "were too familiar with what had happened
in Germany, Austria, Poland and Czechoslovakia to fail to
assess immediately the more or less long-term implications
of this measure. From 1933 on, they had heard the story from
varied accounts of those who, fleeing nazism, had come to
seek their help."[15]

Having made these general remarks, I will now pick up once
again the thread of my own recollections.

In a tiny, modest room on the outskirts of Lyons lived a
German, Paulus Lenz-Médoc,[16] and his wife. Lenz-Médoc
had been a declared enemy of nazism from his youthful student

---

[14] Quoted by Pierre Pierrard, 301–7.

[15] J. M. Soutou, speech to the annual conference of the Alliance israélite
universelle, June 25, 1979.

[16] On Paulus Lenz-Médoc, who died on September 7, 1987, cf. J. Prévotat
in "France catholique", November 27, 1987.

days and had led a fight against it even before Hitler's rise to power. He had been the spokesman for the German episcopate in many meetings, had argued for a Christian reconciliation of his country with Poland, had organized protests against anti-Jewish pamphlets and cruelty; so he was consequently imprisoned in 1933. But all this Catholic activity had earned him, thanks to Cardinal Faulhaber, if I am not mistaken, the protection of a Vatican passport; he could be taken out of prison and could legally leave his country without appearing on the list of emigrants. He was living in Paris when the invasion of the summer of 1940 made him seek a precarious refuge in Lyons, armed with a safe-conduct pass obtained from Bishop Bertoli, then adviser to the nunciature. There he was given charge of a course in German literature at the university and gave German lessons to our university seminary students. Bonds of friendship were quickly formed between him and the directors of the seminary and several professors in the faculty. Lenz-Médoc lived not far from the parish church of Saint-Alban, whose curé, Abbé Laurent Remillieux, apostle for liturgical renewal, was also, in the period between the wars, an ardent partisan of French-German meetings to promote the reconciliation of the two peoples. But this cause, which might have led him into a questionable pacifism, was on the contrary to make him rise up, informed by experience, against the horrors of the nazi persecution. As soon as the law of June 3, 1941, appeared, Paulus Lenz-Médoc rushed to the presbytery of Saint-Alban to discuss it with Remillieux. He felt this law must not pass nearly unnoticed like that of 1940. It was necessary to bring it to public attention, to refute the sophisms that had inspired this new statute for the Jews, and this would have to be done by a highly recognized authority. They quickly agreed that it should be a member of the theology faculty and that this member should be Abbé Joseph Chaine, whom they both already knew and who had all the qualifications needed to inspire their confidence. Remillieux therefore contacted Chaine without delay.

Abbé Joseph Chaine (1888–1948) was both a professor in the theology faculty (rue du Plat) and chaplain for the university parish. He was behind the idea proposed to him even before he heard it: a collective declaration, based on solid evidence, made by our faculty must oppose this unjust law with its fearful consequences.

Chaine occupied the Old Testament chair, formerly held for many years by Abbé Augustin Lémann, a Jew converted to Catholicism in 1854 along with his twin brother, Joseph, at the age of eighteen, through reading the Gospels. Both spent their entire existence in an avid study of the Bible and in the love of their people, who had given the Messiah to the world. Both had written copiously. They nearly worshipped the memory of Louis XVI, true initiator of the emancipation of the Jews in France, whose spirit would be betrayed by the Revolution and whose plan would be distorted by its irreligiousness: this accounted for certain abuses in the power acquired by the Jewish society in the nineteenth century. Their exegesis and their views on the history of the Jewish people in the midst of the nations were far from modern methods of criticism, but they did not lack a certain depth. Both had the soul of a prophet. Joseph was the more lyrical: "We will never forget that it was in France that the poor, wandering Jew first received permission to stop his vagabond course. . . . So we thank you, O noble country of France! We thank you, children of France, who were the first among all peoples to extend your hand to us, who looked on us as men and who invited us to sit down and make our home with you. . . . O France, . . . the blessing of the pilgrim of centuries is on you!" Meditating on biblical images, he composed a vast Marian summa. Augustin, in his teaching, showed prophecies being fulfilled in Christ. In a large work that ran to three editions, Joseph celebrated "The Entrance of the Israelites into French Society and the Christian States", all the while regretting that their emancipation had inclined them to modern irreligion. In *L'Avenir de Jérusalem*, addressing Zionists,

Augustin asked them to renounce their "illusions" in order to be open to the hope for "fraternal union of the two peoples of Christ in the spiritual Jerusalem".

If the Lémann brothers had ever been "thought of as oracles in the midst of the clergy", that time was then well over. It has nevertheless been suggested that, having apparently faded after the 1914 war, their influence again rebounded in 1937, thanks to an enthusiastic biography published at that time by a venerable Capuchin, Théotime de Saint-Just.[17] I must admit to being ignorant of this work. But I can say that, having read the *Chronique sociale* from 1912 on, and having known many Lyons priests of all ages and many inhabitants of the "peninsula", I never heard the name of the Lémann brothers uttered until much later by a few priest friends: and they had a benevolent smile for those characters (who were, for all that, quite likable), whose portraits presided over our meals in the Vaise orphanage, where Abbé Jules Monchanin and my dean, Bishop Georges Jouassard, succeeded each other.[18]

In any case, if some old Lyonese influence played a part in Abbé Chaine's decision, it was not that of his distant predecessor at the faculty but that of his uncle, Léon Chaine, an admitted Lyonese, who had in 1901 taken up the defense of Dreyfus in his "Letter of a Catholic Citizen of Lyons to a Bishop".

---

[17] *Le Retour d'Israël et des nations au Christ-Roi: les frères Lémann, Juifs convertis.* Cf. F. Delpech, *Sur les Juifs,* 157–58 and 228–30.

[18] Even that great cemetery, the *Dictionnaire de théologie catholique,* has not retained their names. The young Aimé Pallière, the future author of the *Sanctuaire inconnu,* had for some time taken courses from Fr. Augustin Lémann. In *Etudes* of March 20, 1927, Fr. Léonce de Grandmaison published a fine article about him: "L'Odyssée spirituelle d'un moderniste, du christianisme au judaïsme". See also Jacob Kaplan, *Justice pour la foi juive* (Centurion, 1977), 43–45. One can like Pallière's personality without finding him a "great prophet" (P. Pierrard, 43). After the Second World War, Pallière would receive the long-desired authorization to participate once again "in the sacraments of the Holy Church" (private letter).

Refused at first by all editors, this letter, after new incidents, had finally been inserted by Abbé Naudet in his journal *La Justice sociale* on March 29, 1902.[19] A former student at the French Ecole biblique in Jerusalem and still filially devoted to his master, Fr. Lagrange, Abbé Chaine, at the same time as he willingly argued in favor of a greater openness in the Church to biblical criticism,[20] had also become an apostle for a better understanding of the people of Israel, bringing about a more just appreciation in their regard with respect to both their present and their past. A guileless friend with a gentle and ingenuous charity, to whom we had given the nickname *Catena aurea*, he was to die shortly after the war of an illness made worse by the privations he had imposed on himself in order to provide for those who were poorer than he. He was characterized by perfect honesty and a wise but exacting liberalism.[21]

[19] Léon Chaine would then publish, through A. Stock in 1903, *Les Catholiques français et leurs difficultés actuelles*, in which chap. 4 treated "anti-Semitism" (P. Pierrard, 201–12).

[20] In 1937, when Cardinal Pacelli came to Paris, he succeeded in keeping the biblical question alive for a long time, and this was part of the preparation culminating in the encyclical *Divino afflante Spiritu* of Pius XII.

[21] See in the *Mémorial J. Chaine* (Bibliothèque de la Faculté catholique de théologie de Lyon, 1950) the two notes devoted to him by Georges Villepelet, P.S.S., Superior of the university seminary, and André Latreille, President of the university parish. He had "agreed, in an apostolic spirit, to hand over his whole life, in daily food, to whoever had recourse to him. . . . He held that no armistice could, on pain of bringing about the loss of the French soul, impose a compromise with satanic nazism or even silence and complacence with regard to its temporary victory. How he became the liaison between the universities thrown into the "Resistance", the "Jesuitry" of Fourvière, the university seminary and the driving forces behind the "Témoignage chrétien", . . . his neighbor and accomplice Marrou could say better than I. . . . He himself spoke little about it later, for he had a gift for being silent about his generous actions. . . . He made it a special point to help the Jews. He did this in practical ways, as always, helping his archbishop hide those whom the various police forces were tracking down. But he did it even more courageously with his pen: with his confreres . . . he wrote a little book,

Having immediately made the project of Lenz-Médoc and Remillieux his own, Abbé Chaine informed Louis Richard, P.S.S., about it. Richard was a professor of dogma in our faculty who was at the same time director of the university seminary, ecclesiastical consultant to the *Chronique sociale*, connected with the archdiocese and of great authority in the diocese of Lyons and in all the Southeast.[22] He also confided it to me as well as to Fr. Joseph Bonsirven, S.J. (1880–1958), who was not a tenured professor in our faculty (he taught and lived in the Fourvière scholasticate, which welcomed him when the German offensive of May 1940 forced him to leave that of Enghien in Belgium), but he was a friend of our house and the best able to help us. A priest from the diocese of Albi, having done his biblical studies first in Jerusalem and then at the Biblical Institute in Rome, he entered the Society of Jesus in 1919 and specialized in ancient Judaism and the rabbinate. His two most recent technical works were at the time *Le Judaïsme palestinien au temps de Jésus-Christ* [Palestinian Judaism at the time of Jesus Christ] (1935) and *Exégèse rabbinique et exégèse paulinienne* [Rabbinic exegesis and Pauline exegesis] (1939).[23] But he did not let himself be absorbed by his scientific work: he took an active part in the spiritual combat of the times. From 1927 on, he opened in *Etudes* a "Jewish chronicle", which made the anti-Semites indignant. In 1936, in his work *Sur les ruines du Temple* [On the ruins of the Temple], he sought to show the "inestimable riches of Judaism", "now

---

Israël et la Foi chrétienne, which could be published only in Switzerland but which circulated in France" (A. Latreille, 21).

[22] Very fine and well-documented information on Fr. Richard was given at the Biviers Symposium (September 1984) by Msgr. Pierre Bockel, archpriest of the cathedral of Strasbourg, who was then a student in our faculty and who was in 1943 the main organizer of the threefold *Cahier* of the *T.C.*, Alsace and Lorraine, French lands.

[23] For Bonsirven's biography and bibliography, see the note by Fr. Stanislas Lyonnet in *Biblica* (1958) 2:262–68.

enshrined in a diverted messianism and in a narrow particularism", which he noted "with sadness but also with respect and sympathy for the souls who held them". In 1937, he collaborated in the collective work *Sur les Juifs*, which contained the testimonies of André Spire, Daniel-Rops and Paul Claudel. He also collaborated in the *Bulletin catholique de la question d'Israël*, published by the Sisters of Notre-Dame de Sion, and he vigorously defended the courageous Oscar de Firenzy against the deranged attacks of Hermann de Vries.[24] Finally, each week in 1938, from February to May, he gave a series of lectures on Judaism at the Catholic Institute of Paris.

So we four gathered together and, under the direction of Abbé Chaine—who had already drafted a first outline with the help of Richard—we worked out a text from which he would make an official protest on behalf of our faculty.[25] He would be careful to show the contents of it to two or three of our colleagues in order to get their advice . . . and their signature. The task was quickly accomplished. But in his enthusiasm, he did not adequately assess the obstacles. The colleagues consulted did not disapprove of either the idea or the terms of the declaration—quite the contrary—but they judged the idea of making an official protest to be fanciful. It would find no media willing to spread it or even to make an allusion to it; so it would soon be suppressed and would remain totally unknown by the public. On the other hand, since it would be known by the government through the official censors, our colleagues thought that it would have another effect: that of closing the theology faculty, perhaps even all of the Catholic faculties in Lyons; and the public would be given only some communiqué fabricated in some office of the high police as a reason for the closure. When our

[24] Cf. P. Pierrard, 266–67.
[25] I am not absolutely certain that Bonsirven took part in this first meeting. But he was consulted and then kept informed, and the text would have been communicated to him.

authorities were informed about it, they were of the same opinion. Only anonymous, clandestine writings, not bearing the mark of any identifiable organism, would have a chance—a very weak chance—of enlightening consciences without a catastrophe. We were forced to recognize it.[26] Consequently, the first paragraph of the planned declaration was modified. We will see a little later on what its fate would be.

[26] As Charles Molette has well observed, an official declaration of this kind "would have been not only a gesture outside all administrative norms but even—given the context of that time—a suicidal provocation. . . . From a historical point of view, the importance of this declaration, however, could not be underestimated, not only because of its content and repercussions, but also because of what followed it": Impacts, Revue de l'Université catholique de l'Ouest (1978), 4:8.

Chapter 5

The Text and Fate of the Chaine Declaration

This text has sometimes been called, rather incorrectly, as we shall see, the "text of the Catholic Institute of Lyons". Archbishop Guerry of Cambrai quoted in large part the declaration that issued from Abbé Chaine's initiative (37–38) in his work on *L'Eglise catholique en France sous l'Occupation* [The Catholic Church in France under the Occupation] (Flammarion, 1947), which was published in an attempt to reestablish the truth in the face of often unjust and at times excessive criticism regarding the French episcopate, owing to the passionate atmosphere of the times that followed the Liberation. He preceded the excerpt with these words: "In a widely distributed declaration of June 17, 1941, the Catholic theology faculty of Lyons had denounced the injustices of the law of June 2, 1941" (37). Perhaps he had in hand the original text, which at first professed this. This error has occasionally been reproduced, notably in the work by André Deroo, *L'Episcopat français dans la mêlée de son temps, 1930–1954* ([Bonne Presse, 1955],89).[1]

---

[1] So too Georges Wellers, *L'Etoile jaune à l'heure de Vichy: De Drancy à Auschwitz* (Fayard, 1973), 266: "The Catholic theology faculty in Lyons protested against the statute of the Jews in a declaration dated June 17, 1941, which was widely disseminated." Henri Amouroux, *La Vie des Français sous l'Occupation*, 389: "In a declaration of June 17, 1941, the Catholic theology faculty in Lyons would protest . . ." In *"Le Vicaire" et l'Histoire*, 207, Jacques Nobécourt also speaks of "the Catholic theology faculty in Lyons".

The assertion has been criticized with good reason. A discussion was once again raised about this in a symposium held in Grenoble in 1976, *Eglise et chrétiens dans la Seconde Guerre mondiale, la région Rhône-Alpes*, the *Actes* of which were published in 1978 (P.U.L.) under the direction of Xavier de Montclos, Monique Luirard, François Delpech and Pierre Bolle. Vladimir Rabi contributed a piece to it on "the intervention of the Hierarchy in favor of the Jews: an observation and a question".[2] Not content with reestablishing the truth about the question that we have just seen and that was already recognized—as it emerges from the documents that he himself was quoting[3]—and with establishing a (not always very precise) list of historians who would allow themselves to be deceived,[4] Rabi, on the basis of this, instituted a formal legal action against the episcopate. Picking up every available straw, he brought up a remark made about Cardinal Saliège by Xavier Vallat in the course of his trial,[5] and he tried to prove that the Catholic hierarchy had no choice but to recognize the new

[2] 195–99. A clarifying outline by F. Delpech, 201–3.

[3] Thus the letter addressed to him by Joseph Folliet, after consultation with Bishop Duquaire, the former secretary of Cardinal Gerlier: "Father de Lubac, whose memory is quite faithful, assures that there was no official declaration by the theology faculty. There was a plan for one, due particularly to Abbé Chaine and Canon Richard, both deceased, but this was not retained by the archdiocese nor apparently has it been preserved." Rabi also quotes the letter from a third party, to whom I had replied that "it had absolutely no official value". I believe I also recall having responded to a letter received directly from Rabi in almost exactly the same way.

[4] J. Duquesne has not spoken of an official protest by the faculty but of a protest by "professors", which is also rather imprecise, and he added (something that is not very accurate): "There was no public protest coming directly from the episcopate": *Les Catholiques français sous l'Occupation* (Grasset, 1966), 255.

[5] F. Delpech replied on this point to Rabi, *Colloque de Lyon*, 203: "As for the testimony of the man named Gazagne, testimony instigated by Xavier Vallat or by his lawyers at the time of his trial, it seems to me to be highly suspect." Cf. below, Chap. 7, n. 8.

statute for the Jews as just since, on the left as well as on the right, from Toussenel (1844) to Vallat, a consistently anti-Semitic tradition had called for the revision of the 1791 act of emancipation, which had made the Jews French citizens. He insinuated that in this respect the bishops were even directing, rather than following, public opinion. Going still further, asserting that for two years in succession there had been on their part "nothing, nothing, not the least official protest" (we will soon see how things actually stood), he added: "And then suddenly. . . . " Suddenly, it was not essentially the horrors of the summer of 1942 (which will be referred to later on); it was, according to Rabi, the feeling, which would increase in November with the American landing in northern Africa, that victory was about to change sides. And, in conclusion, he quotes these lines from Bernanos as a condemnation of the Church in France: "If one could trace precisely, from 1940 to 1945, month by month, the curve of probability for an Allied victory, one would see that it coincides perfectly with that of growing membership in the presumed side of victory, which was in turns a German victory and then an Allied victory."[6]

What had been made as an "observation" and a "question" had turned into a terrible prosecution. But the grounds for this abusive accusation were fragile; certain facts were misunderstood; the episcopal texts from the summer of 1942 were presented as a reversal and as a politically opportunistic maneuver. Blind in his fixed prejudice, the author committed a gross error that made him turn the chronology upside down; finally, to apply the vengeful words of Bernanos to the so-called blameworthy hierarchy was inexcusable.

[6]*Français, si vous saviez*, G. Bernanos (Gallimard, 1961), 173. Rabi was able to invoke this text with only apparent grounds because he began by submitting that "popular opinion in France" has modeled itself on "the image of the Hierarchy".

The Lyons text that gave rise to this lawsuit has since been quoted in its entirety by François Delpech.[7] I think it might be useful to reproduce it here:[8]

Draft of a Declaration
of the Catholic Theology Faculty of Lyons

Lyons, June 17, 1941

Faced with the anti-Semitic propaganda that has been released today in our country and with the legislative measures that have just been promulgated with respect to the Jews, we cannot remain silent. The Church has intervened more than once in recent years to condemn anti-Semitism, and the theology faculties have received from the Holy See the order to fight with all available means against the doctrinal errors and perversions that are threatening the purity of Christian moral doctrine. It is for this reason that we make the following declaration, to which we wish to give all possible publicity.

1. We must recognize the state's right and duty to safeguard the life and the unity of the nation, to promulgate laws and to take necessary measures, conforming to the principles of justice and of respect for the human person. In particular, the state has

---

[7] *Eglises et Chrétiens dans la Seconde Guerre mondiale, la France, Colloque de Lyon, 1978* (P.U.L., 1982), 288–89. The author observes that in this text "the reference is particularly to French Jews", "which clearly shows the damaging effects of xenophobia even in the most lucid of minds": *Sur les Juifs*, 290.

[8] The two asterisks (*) indicate the beginning and end of the quotation made by Archbishop Guerry. It can thus be seen that, even if the quotation of the document is incomplete, it nonetheless does not deserve the epithet "truncated version" (*Sur les Juifs*). It reproduces very exactly the four central paragraphs, that is, those in which the principal intolerable points of the new legislation are criticized in a direct and specific way. We can read in *Le Monde* of October 27, 1976: "Even in the truncated form reported by Archbishop Guerry and endlessly reproduced by Christian and Jewish writers, the famous declaration against anti-Semitism by the theology faculty of Lyons, in June 1941, never existed, at least not in the form claimed!" Such an allegation, made in such an abrupt form, is at the very least ambiguous. For it was not a matter of Archbishop Guerry having quoted some fake document, as the vengeful tone of this text would seem to imply. (Cf. C. Molette, 7.)

the right to revise naturalization that has been hastily granted in recent years to foreigners, whoever they may be.

2. We do not contest the fact that there is a Jewish question; but, in France, it does not arise in the same way it does in other countries. It should be resolved in France "à la française" [in a French way]. Now we cannot fail to notice that the recent statute for the Jews has been strongly influenced by foreign principles. The present situation in France might be an explanation [for this], but it could not be for us a justification.

*3. The law of June 1941 on the statute for the Jews is offensive to a whole category of Frenchmen: the Israelites, whom it tends to single out for public opinion as being particularly responsible for the nation's misfortunes, by making suspects of them.

4. It is unjust with regard to French Israelites in that, through its retroactive effects, it repudiates France's commitments in their regard; for it was trusting in French law that they have entered into administration, the army, university, etc., thereby committing their lives and those of their families.

5. It is offensive with regard to Israelites who have recently adhered to a Christian confession, as well as with regard to ecclesiastical authorities, in the distinction it makes between baptisms received before and baptisms received after June 25, 1940, the latter finding themselves under suspicion of disloyalty, which tends to create a category of suspect Christians within the Christian community.

6. Determining Jews by religious criteria establishes a discrimination between Frenchmen based on membership in a religion recognized by the French state before the law of separation. Such a discrimination, which is contrary to the French tradition established over one and one-half centuries ago, is also a discrimination against the principle that "no one can be harassed because of his religious opinions". Catholics have a right to invoke this principle for themselves, if the occasion calls for it, only if they protect that right for others as well.*

The Church cannot forget that the Israelites are the descendants of the people who were the object of the divine election of which she is the culmination, of those people from whom Christ, our Savior, the Virgin Mary and the apostles sprang; that they have in common with us the books of the Old Testament, the inspired pages of which we read in our liturgy, the psalms from which we sing to praise God and to express our hope for his Kingdom; that, according to the words of Pius XI, we, like they, are sons of Abraham, the father of believers, and that the blessing promised to his descendants is still upon them, to call them to recognize in Jesus the Christ who was promised to them.

Consequently, we do not at all wish to seem to approve, be it only through our silence, propaganda harmful to the Israelites, particularly to French Israelites, and one that is not without danger for Christianity itself; or even certain legal dispositions that go well beyond what is required for the defense of our nation and that equity condemns, particularly at the present moment when France needs harmony between all her children if she is to be rebuilt and when the government wishes to promote a national revolution inspired by French tradition and Christian civilization.

Let me insert a parenthetical remark here. People were at that time very poorly informed about what was happening in France from one city to another, from one region to another and, a fortiori, from one "zone" to another. In cards sent between "zones", correspondents had to be extremely prudent or even, on sensitive issues, totally silent. It was only after the Liberation that I learned of a coincidence worthy of note. While we were in Lyons with Abbé Chaine, seeking another way to use our attempted declaration, my confrere Fr. Michel Riquet was taking similar steps in Paris.[9] It had become clear

[9] Michel Riquet, S.J., *Chrétiens de France dans l'Europe déchirée* (S.O.S., 1972), 89–91. In 1979, Fr. Riquet would explain that, having been chaplain for students in Paris (Laënnec Conference) and, on the other hand, having collaborated with Cardinal Verdier, "within these two contexts, from 1933 on, we began to react in Catholic circles against the national-socialist mystique. . . . There was the overall danger which national socialism imposed on the Christian civilization of which we were a part. . . . First and foremost in our motivations was the battle against racism, but in that fight against racism, anti-Semitism was necessarily included. . . . At the Pax Romana congress in Klagenfurt, Austria, I read a message from my mentor and friend Jacques Maritain on 'impossible anti-Semitism'. But the theme of the congress

to him that the "collaboration" inaugurated at Montoire on October 24, 1940, was leading France into the paths of racism and that resistance was required by the Christian conscience. It was the promulgation of the law of June 2 that determined him to intervene. He drafted a note that he had delivered, through Bishop Courbe, on July 11, to the Assembly of cardinals and archbishops (A.C.A.). Here is the tenor of it:

1. As written, the law of June 2, 1941, bearing the statute of the Jews (*Journal officiel* of June 14, 1941, p. 2475, no. 3332), seems to us to be a scandal for the Christian conscience as well as an insult to French intelligence.

It will, in fact, in the final analysis, be interpreted as a sectarian law of exception and oppression against a religious confession. According to the terms of this law, one is of the Jewish race insofar as one belongs to the Israelite confession. Even more, whoever cannot prove his adhesion to one of the other confessions recognized by the Concordat state can be presumed Jewish. The French state, like the German Reich before it, is assessing social purity on the basis of baptismal certificates. This law is therefore very much a law of religious persecution, and the Christian Churches are being used in order to apply it. Duress is thus being exercised over souls in a twofold manner: to tear them away from Judaism on the one hand, and to make them adhere to Christianity on the other.

What should astonish Christians and scandalize non-Christians is that such an abuse is not meeting with any protest from the episcopate, which, for years, has not ceased to claim religious freedom as a common right. The tacit approval of (which is not to say consent to) this unjust oppression of consciences today distresses a great number of young Christians. It discredits the Church in the eyes of those who, in such great

---

included the whole fight against racism in all its forms": *F.Q.J.*, 381–82. The letter of Fr. Riquet of July 11 was pointed out by François Delpech, *Sur les Juifs*, 176–77. The first chapter, "De l'Action française à l'Amitié judéo-chrétienne", in Fr. Riquet's book *Un chrétien face à Israël* (Robert Laffont, 1975), 9–23, is of interest.

numbers during recent years, have become accustomed to think of her as the supreme champion of the human person's dignity and freedom of spirit. It might seem to them that the Church in France, having obtained a little more justice for herself, is now not interested in the injustices committed against others.

2. Intolerable in its present form, the law of June 2 is, moreover, being applied with an odious brutality. After five thousand Jewish foreigners were interned without warning, their families, deprived of any support, are being denied the allocation that should be awarded in virtue of a decree of October 1940 to any family of a person interned for administrative reasons, which is very much the case. The police stations have in fact, and on orders, refused to deliver the certificates of internment that are required for the collection of this allocation.

It would seem that the best way to give witness to truth and to charity would be for the episcopate to make an appeal to the generosity of the faithful, that they might come to the aid of the families and children who are the victims of these laws for which, one might say, the Church is refusing to bear the responsibility, for they are inspired far less by the Gospel than by the exigencies of a nationalism whose excesses the popes have long denounced and condemned. This appeal to charity is within the role of the Church and would be understood by most. This would also be an encouragement to others (St. Vincent de Paul conferences, social secretariats, League aid) who might act effectively in favor of these unfortunate persecuted people.— July 11, 1941.

Two totally independent texts, whose authors were unaware of each other but who would not be long in meeting.

Chapter 6

The Bérard Report: Its Origin

Let us close the Parisian paragraph and return to Lyons for a few days.

During the week in June 1941 when what I have recounted above was happening at the theology faculty, Cardinal Gerlier, Archbishop of Lyons and chancellor of our faculties, was in Spain. He returned to Lyons on the sixteenth. We showed him our text immediately. Although he too judged that making an official declaration out of it could not be considered, he warmly approved of its tenor and, after the beginning part of the text had been slightly altered to hide its origin, he authorized its anonymous distribution—which took place beginning on the seventeenth. Despite what has at times been said about this text, I do not believe that in the final analysis it was widely distributed. We had at our disposal neither the experience, time, material nor any sort of secret organization for that purpose. And it was undoubtedly too serious a writing, in language that was both juridical and theological, to capture the attention of the "man on the street" who found it in his mailbox.

Abbé Chaine's initiative, however, was, insofar as it is possible to judge, soon to bear fruit.

In July, the Assembly of cardinals and archbishops of the occupied zone met in Paris. By exception, Cardinal Gerlier came from Lyons to participate in it. The Assembly worked out a rather long declaration in two parts. It is in the first part that we find the famous formula on patriotism without subservience toward the established authority, about which I will

71

speak later on; this soon came to be the part that stuck in everyone's mind, "widely disseminated, profusely commented on", discussed, turned into a variety of different meanings.[1] But there was a second part, in which "the sense of respect for the human person, for his dignity, his essential freedoms" was recalled as an urgent objective, the Assembly "condemning all injustice and all excess toward anyone whomsoever".

All the archbishops of the southern zone signed this text in the days following the July 24 vote.

Now, if we consider that the Lyons declaration by Chaine was read and approved by Cardinal Gerlier on June 16 and that the Riquet memorandum was sent to the Paris office of the archbishops on July 11 or 12, we are naturally led to believe that these two private documents were not without influence with respect to the declaration of the Assembly of July 24. If, in addition, we recall the many signs that Cardinal Gerlier had given for more than a year of his interest in the Jewish cause,[2] we are perhaps also justified in supposing that if there were in the Paris Assembly any expression of fears (as a result of the legitimate but utopian desire, held especially in the occupied zone, to dissociate the Vichy government as much as possible from German oppression), Gerlier's opinion must have been one of the most pressing and decisive.

Such a declaration may seem to us today to be very general and very weak. We are tempted to see in it scarcely anything but abstract, quasi-conventional formulas. It is difficult for us, from a distance and in a peaceful context, to judge what was advisable, useful, even possible to do in those tragic and confused circumstances. The assembled archbishops may have had more than one reason for judging that a thundering condemnation risked causing more evil than good by definitively removing any hearing they might have had with public

[1] See below, Chap. 13.
[2] See particularly below, Chap. 12.

authorities. They may have still hoped that someone in the government, perhaps even someone at the top, who had acted or allowed others to act only with reluctance, might listen to a voice that tried to avoid offending them. (We know that the "Pétain myth" was powerful at that time in the nation, that, in the misfortunes around them, it aroused great hopes and that the bishops were not immune to this.) They also undoubtedly foresaw, with good reason, that a more pointed form of declaration would meet with censorship and would consequently not achieve its goal. However that may be, and even if we judge such prudence to have been excessive or such a hope to have been too naïve, we cannot fail to understand, under those circumstances, that it was at the recent legislation about the Jews that this declaration was aimed. Readers were trained to grasp the slightest allusions, and those in authority in the Vichy government could not have mistaken the very clear meaning of this reminder.

So, if one forgets the circumstances, one could say that this was very little. It was not "nothing, nothing at all". This "very little" was very well understood—and, as we will see, very poorly received at Vichy, where it created a great disturbance.

"The remarks were admittedly general," J. M. Mayeur justly concludes, "but the reactions they aroused in the context of the times attest that they could not have passed unperceived."[3] A reflection by a wise and equitable historian, in contrast not only to the invectives of someone like Vladimir Rabi but also to judgments we would not have expected from a historian who is equally as wise: "Vichy was able to intern foreign Jews and work out a whole anti-Semitic legislation without any notable opposition, indeed, *with the blessing of the bishops.*"[4]

[3] Loc. cit., 154.
[4] François Delpech, in *F.Q.J.*, 203–4. (The italics are mine.) And several lines above: there was within Christian circles in France, "after the anti-Semitic

To continue following the thread of our story, we must now change the scene to Vichy. We are going to be present at a rather involved diplomatic episode following the anti-Jewish law of June 3, 1941, one composed of several acts. To read the authors who have recounted it to us, whatever might be their opinions or the sequel to their account, we might think at first that it resulted simply from an initiative by Marshal Pétain. In a letter dated August 7, "the Marshal, anxious to protect himself vis-à-vis the Catholic hierarchy, had asked for a report from the French ambassador to the Holy See on the attitude of the Holy See with respect to anti-Semitism and the Vichy legislation": so begins the account made of the incident by J. M. Mayeur.[5] Similarly, François Delpech: "Ambassador Léon Bérard, charged by Pétain to consult the Holy See . . . ";[6] or again, Guy Pedroncini: "The Vichy government had sounded out the Vatican with respect to the measures taken against the Jews."[7] The same abrupt introduction to the subject is given by Léon Poliakov: "Pétain even took the precaution of seeking information from the Holy See about the appropriateness of the Vichy measures",[8]

---

statutes of Vichy in October 1940 and in June 1941", neither any emotion nor any condemnation. These texts, which date from 1979 and were published in 1981, are reproduced in *Sur les Juifs* (1983), 214 and 215. Another error, and a severe judgment in consequence, although less polemical in tone, in Philippe Bourdrel, *Histoire des Juifs en France* (Albin Michel, 1974), 385: "No voice was raised when the statutes of October 1940 *and of June 1941* were promulgated, no voice to denounce that work of iniquity. The foremost moral power of traditionalist France, the Church, confined herself *to a silence that was either indifference or approbation.* Let us give preference to the first interpretation and conclude that there was a kind of unawareness, an inability to measure the fullness of the danger, a collective breakdown of intelligence and of the faculty of judgment." (The italics are mine.)

[5] Loc cit., 154–55.

[6] *Sur les Juifs*, 215. These words follow directly after the phrase pointed out above on "the blessing of the bishops".

[7] Cf. *F.Q.J.*, 30, n. 24.

[8] *Bréviaire de la haine, le IIIe Reich et les Juifs* (Calmann-Lévy, 1951), 57.

and from Fr. Georges Jarlot, S.J.: "On August 7, Marshal
Pétain charged Léon Bérard to consult the Holy See."[9] Similarly, Jacques Duquesne (who in addition confuses the 1941
statute of the Jews with that of 1940): "According to Xavier
Vallat, Pétain sought to find out, in 1941, the Vatican's point
of view on the measures taken, in October 1940, with respect
to the Jews. Léon Bérard . . . "[10]
The fact is incontestable. But we can then ask ourselves
why. And, according to the response given to this "why?"
the fact itself, and what will follow it, will take on rather
different meanings.
It is somewhat difficult to see how Pétain himself would
have come up with the idea of consulting "Rome" so as to
enlighten or appease his conscience. If this had been the case,
it is hard to understand why he took this step so late, once
the statute in question had already been promulgated, applied
and recently made still worse; also, in this case, we might
wonder why he chose for this purpose an intermediary whose
response, as we will see, shows that he had entirely accepted
in advance the position taken by the "French state" in the
Jewish question. Even if, as everyone indicates, it was a maneuver motivated entirely by self-interest, we might still wonder what the meaning of this maneuver was. Why, precisely
on this date, did Pétain write to Bérard? Was it because of a
wholly spontaneous desire to use Rome to protect himself?
Such an idea hardly seems to have been habitual to him.

[9] *Le Vatican et la Seconde Guerre mondiale* (Pedone, 1955), 220.
[10] Op. cit., 20. Similarly, after having indicated the protest "by four professors of the Catholic faculty in Lyons", Jean Chelini adds: "At the same
time, Vichy received the unexpected support of a report which seemed to
have the approval of the Vatican. As a matter of duty, and in order to avoid
the possible awakening of public polemics, the Marshal had asked in 1941
that Léon Bérard inform himself about the reactions of the Holy See." He
discloses the reply, "and, for months, Vichy was able to affirm the support
of the Vatican, in spite of the protest made by the nuncio in the face of this
fait accompli" (*L'Eglise sous Pie XII* [1983], 205).

Although Pierre Pierrard does not give a complete answer to the question, his approach sets us on the right track: "The major document—which Xavier Vallat received as a precious gift from the hands of the Marshal himself—was the letter addressed to Pétain, on September 2, 1941, by Léon Bérard, ambassador of France to the Holy See, the head of the French state having asked Bérard to inform himself as to the judgment that, from the Roman Catholic point of view, the Holy See might give about the French statute of the Jews. It was a reassuring text."[11]

It was a text that they wanted in advance to be reassuring. The ambassador did his work well; he honored the command with consummate skill. Except for what concerns a point of canon law on mixed marriages, everything in his text is so vague,[12] so sparing of personal names, so mixed with general considerations and historical allusions, drawn from unidentified sources, that it escapes any precise discussion. Moreover, in order not to expose himself to any official protest, the author took care to have it understood that his response to the Marshal was not a diplomatic document but correspondence of a purely private character.[13]

---

[11] *Juifs et catholiques français* (1970), 295–96.

[12] Following the passage quoted above (cf. n. 8), one can judge how satisfied Poliakov was to add: "The very precise reply of his ambassador: 'Nothing has ever been said to me at the Vatican which would imply any criticism or disapproval on the part of the Holy See of the legislative and regulatory acts in question' undoubtedly eased his conscience definitively." This was a reply from Bérard to Pétain, but was it the reply of an authority of the Holy See to Bérard? And had the latter even posed the question?

[13] See below, Chap. 7. It was this thesis that he would again defend when confronted with Vanino, the author of the work *De Rethondes à l'île d'Yeu*, as well as in his reply to a request for information made by Fr. Paul Duclos, S.J., who, in his benevolence, not perceiving or not wanting to perceive the ambassador's cunning, adds this reflection: "It is regrettable that he did not foresee the probable use that would be made of his report by a government under German control": *Le Vatican et la Seconde Guerre mondiale* (Pedone, 1955), 221.

Certainly the idea had not sprouted all by itself in the mind and heart of the old marshal to make "a precious gift to Vallat"! Obviously not a private sentiment but a political reason was behind the letter to Bérard. Whoever it was, in the top echelons of the Vichy government, who first whispered the idea to Pétain, it clearly seems to have set off a counterattack, and Vallat does not seem to have been the only or even the principal interested party in this maneuver. The government, that is, Darlan (who was all powerful after Laval's dismissal in December 1940), was seeking a reprisal, through the intermediary of the Vatican. Against whom, if not above all against the bishops? He hoped to place them in contradiction with Rome, presented as more tolerant, and Bérard had been charged to do what was necessary to accomplish this. Delpech here fortunately completes Pierrard's account. At the symposium in Lyons in 1978, proving more equitable than in the passage I quoted above, he recognized with fairness the existence and the importance of the episcopal declaration of July, toning down his sentence with a "perhaps": "Despite their discretion," he observes, "the repeated steps taken by Pastor Boegner and the declaration of the cardinals and archbishops of July 24, 1941, perhaps provoked a certain uneasiness in Pétain and Laval. Otherwise it would be difficult to explain why Vichy asked its ambassador to the Vatican to get information about the difficulties that the application of the statute might eventually raise on the part of the Holy See." Done, certainly not in order to modify his "realistic" politics in consequence, but in order to close the mouth of the French bishops by placing them in contradiction with Rome.[14]

Pastor Boegner, as I said above,[15] had written two letters on March 26, one to the Grand Rabbi of France, the other to Admiral Darlan (who was then vice-president of the Council).

[14] *Colloque de Lyon* (1978); taken up again in *Sur les Juifs*, 277–78. ("Laval" was a slip of the tongue. It was Darlan who was then in power.)

[15] See above, Chap. 4, n. 12.

He was concerned about the increasingly miserable fate of the "non-Aryans" being poured by Hitler onto our soil, by that of the political refugees called back by Germany as well as by the effects of the racial law of October 1940, about which one minister had said to him: "It is a law of defense; it will lead to terrible injustices, but it must be uncompromising." Without replying to Boegner in writing, Darlan summoned him to Vichy, where he informed him that another draft was being prepared: "I warn you", he said to Boegner, "that the first article is very hard." That was the law of June 3. Then, through the intermediary of Gillouin, Boegner informed Pétain of "the emotion felt in our churches", and he did so again in August, once again in agreement with Cardinal Gerlier, who also intervened one time more with the Marshal. "We know", as François Delpech writes very accurately, "that Pastor Boegner had gone to Cardinal Gerlier in September in order to ask him for a discreet but explicit intervention."[16] Alluding both to the declaration of the A.C.A. (Assembly of cardinals and archbishops) and to this new step taken by Gerlier, Boegner concludes his account with these words: "The Marshal, moved by the joint protests made by the Christian churches, called for Xavier Vallat . . . and stipulated moderation in the application of the law"[17]—which could scarcely have been more than a "pious wish".

Without entering into an indiscreet and in any case impossible analysis of consciences or into an attempt to determine the different responsibilities involved, there is no reason to

---

[16] But the author does not add that Gerlier, in fact, did intervene; and he says, two lines below: "The repeated steps taken by Pastor Boegner and the declaration of the cardinals and archbishops of July 24 . . .", forgetting that of Gerlier in September. This is why he can ask, on the following page: "But what did they do . . . from the Catholic side in September 1941?": *Colloque de Lyon*, 240. On that point, Boegner is positive: having promised him in August to intervene again, directly, with Pétain, Gerlier did so "several days later" (Marc Boegner, *L'Exigence oecuménique*, 149).

[17] Ibid., 146–49.

have the least doubt in the world about what Boegner reports here—nor about the accuracy of the reflections that he makes a little farther on: "What the Marshal learned about the disastrous effects of the racist measures caused him real suffering. He saw clearly that great injustices were being committed. But . . . he felt the painful sense of his own powerlessness to prevent these injustices or to repair them. Moreover, he was not surprised that the churches informed him of their indignant protest; it was their silence that surprised him." [18] The mentality of someone like Pétain cannot simply be merged together with that of people like Laval and Darlan; but he himself was incapable of entering into a truly Christian perspective; on the other hand, he had been caught up in a fatal system without really being able to escape it, and it is not surprising that he sought to justify, even with respect to the head of the Catholic Church, a policy with which he had gone along in the beginning but without seeing where it would lead him in spite of himself.[19]

In this sequence of events that I have tried to show, it is also undoubtedly necessary to take into consideration the letter that Rabbi Jacob Kaplan, then auxiliary to the Grand Rabbi Jacques Kahn, who had withdrawn to the southern zone, wrote to Vallat: "If a pagan or an atheist denigrates Judaism, he is certainly wrong, but there is nothing illogical in his manner of acting; while, on the part of a Christian, would

[18] Ibid., 149.

[19] On November 17, 1942, when he found himself forced to delegate to Laval the greatest part of his powers, he had this constitutional act followed by three secret conditions, the third of which was formulated like this: "You will respect the spiritual traditions of France by protecting them from all attack, particularly religious and philosophical convictions, the exercise of worship, the rights of the family, youth movements, respect for the human person." A kind of credo or political concern that does seem to have been as constant as it was sincere in him, but which was increasingly unable to involve any practical application, and the last point of which had already long been violated (cf. J. Duquesne, 21).

80   CHRISTIAN RESISTANCE TO ANTI-SEMITISM

not such an attitude seem inconsistent on the spiritual level
as well as ungrateful?"[20] He might even have asked more
precisely, in substance (I do not now have the complete text
of the letter in front of me), how, claiming to be Catholic,
he could reconcile his actions with that Catholic doctrine to
which his bishops had just called attention.[21] In his book *Pie
XII et le IIIe Reich*, in other respects so unreliable, Saul Friedländer showed, at least as a hypothesis, a very plausible connection between events: "It seems that the letter from Rabbi
Kaplan had caused some embarrassment to the Vichy government. . . . On August 7, Marshal Pétain, in consequence,
asked his ambassador . . . "[22]

To recapitulate: *June 3*: the new anti-Jewish law; *June 16*:
Chaine's text approved by Gerlier; *July 12*: Riquet's text sent
to the bishops of the occupied zone; *July 24*: declaration of
the A.C.A.; *July 31*: Rabbi Kaplan's letter to Vallat; *August
7*: Pétain's letter to Bérard.

Is not the very succession of these six dates telling? Without
claiming any certitude, we cannot fail to note a relationship

[20] Vallat replied to him through the head of his cabinet, Jarnieux, that there
was no anti-Semitism in the government's attitude, only the application of
a "reason of state". Kaplan's letter, having been circulated, contributed to
Vichy's uneasiness. Cf. *Pierre Pierrard interroge le grand rabbin Kaplan, Justice
pour la foi juive* (Le Centurion, 1977), 70–75. "Reason of state" was the
expression with which Boegner found himself confronted on every occasion,
from 1940 on, by all the ministers and high police officials to whom he had
recourse. (It was also the expression with which Fr. Dillard found himself
confronted by the censors of my article "La défense du Christ et de la Bible".)
(Cf. Chap. 8.)

[21] This second, more emphatic version, or perhaps this other passage from
the same letter, written eight days after the declaration by the A.C.A., would
testify more clearly still to the impact of that declaration. However that might
be, we also have reason to believe that the spiritual reaction of the Church,
under these circumstances, was able to help lift a certain number of Jews
from the docile passivity which they seemed to have imposed on themselves
in order to escape the worst. (Suggestions proposed by Charles Molette.)

[22] Saul Friedländer, *Pie XII et le IIIe Reich*, French trans. (Seuil, 1964),
92–93. Pierrard (cf. n. 20) does not make this connection.

between events that was close enough, precise enough to allow us to think that the text worked out by the Lyons theologians (supported by that of a Parisian theologian) was, at least in part, at the origin of that Vichy incident whose consequences we have yet to see.[23]

---

[23] If I have gone on at some length on the second point of this enumeration, it is because it has been the object of lively discussions and because it is something about which I have had personal knowledge.

Chapter 7

The Bérard Report:
Its Contents, Its Consequences

"We could go on at even greater length about the Bérard report", wrote François Delpech.[1] The ambassador's previous history sheds some additional light, and we can also try to offer a few more facts and put forward a hypothesis or two on the basis of what is known of the affair.

Léon Bérard (1876–1960), former secretary of Raymond Poincaré, representative and then senator from Basses-Pyrénées, several times Minister of Public Instruction, a praiseworthy champion of classical humanities, very cultured and very skillful in parliamentary debates, academician since 1934, was twice Minister of Justice in the Laval cabinets (1931–1932 and 1935–1936). A man of order, he soon joined the new regime in 1940. Even afterward he agreed completely with what could be drawn from the discussions at Montoire, and he was very open about this in his address to Pius XII when he delivered his credentials to him on December 9, 1940: "So we are disposed", he said to the Pope, "to fulfill our duties *toward Europe*. We know what these duties demand of us and that they could demand nothing contrary to our dignity and our honor. The establishment of lasting European order will be first of all a work of reason and intelligence. France will find her work and her employment in this." A speech of Lavalian commitment based on a Maurras foundation, a speech of a realist claiming to be moderate but who, like many

[1] *Sur les Juifs*, 295 (Colloque de Lyon, 1978).

actors in the first Vichy government, seems not to have had any suspicion of the reality.

Pius XII's response to the new ambassador, while maintaining the tone and reserved language required in those sorts of ceremonies, constitutes a reply that is no less clear and manifests quite a different orientation and sensitivity:

> In the midst of events and upheavals that are beginning to give some common features to the external aspect and spiritual physiognomy of Europe, events whose external development remains for the moment so obscure, . . . the French nation . . . contemplates in sadness its devastated countryside . . . , a sadness increased even more by the uncertainties of the future. . . . These words, well worthy of a saint and hero, come from Bernard of Clairvaux, one of the greatest sons France has given to the world and to the Church: "*Vinces spem tuam in Deo fortiter figendo et rei finem longanimiter expectando*" (Epist. 22, PL, 182, col. 137); "You will be victorious by fixing your hope firmly in God and by waiting with forbearance for the end of the trial."

This was to contrast, with as much clarity as strength, a Europe built on the victory of Hitlerian theories with a Europe penetrated by the Christian spirituality of France, and, at the same time, it was a resistance at least of a heart full of hope against the new "European order" that was beginning to impose its yoke. I do not know if these two speeches were known publicly during that period;[2] they were certainly not spread

---

[2] They were published in 1946 in *Documentation catholique*, the volume entitled *La Vie catholique, documents et actes de la Hiérarchie*, for the years 1940–1941. Charles Flory recalled in 1945, in *La Semaine sociale*, from Toulouse that "the first clandestine sheet that reached me . . . was a copy of this moving message in which the successor of Peter proclaimed that our country would revive as surely as day follows night." Fessard quotes, at the end of *France, prends garde . . .* , these words of Pius XII in his speech of June 29, 1941: "It is necessary to trust in God. . . . God can permit temporarily the malignity of men. But the triumph of evil will not endure. God's hour will come. The hour of freedom and joy, the hour which permits the resurrection of justice and peace."

by the official propaganda! Our reading of them today is enough to warn us that if, in August 1941, Bérard could write to Pétain that in his consultations in Rome he had not received any objection, it is because, in one way or another, the game had been fixed. It does not take much guesswork to give an explanation.

The request addressed by Pétain to his ambassador was dated August 7; Bérard's reply is dated September 2.[3] It was a "long memorandum", "long and detailed", in which the author, François Delpech tells us, "delivers a rather complicated demonstration". According to its first publisher,[4] it gives witness to the "quibbling and sophisms of the dialectician ambassador". Rather than a report, it is, for the most part, a historical dissertation and an argumentation. The essential, practical points of his inquiry and the conclusion for which Vichy was waiting are confined to a few lines that might be described either as giving a "very precise answer"[5] or, quite the contrary, as leaving us in the dark, depending on whether one is satisfied to take them as they are, in their apparent generality, or whether one also wonders to what precisely they apply, what were the questions asked and to whom they were asked. "As someone in authority said to me at the Vatican," Bérard writes, "he will start no quarrel with us over the statute for the Jews." That seems very clear, peremptory. But first of all, who is that someone? And, in the final analysis, does his nonquarrelsome disposition signify approval, pure

[3] There had been, in fact, a first, less lengthy reply: "I had the honor to address a first reply to you . . . "

[4] In *Le Monde juif*, 2 (October 1946): report on "the question and difficulties which the measures taken with respect to the Jews might raise". See also Jacques Nobécourt, *"Le Vicaire" et l'Histoire* (Seuil, 1964), 356–62.

[5] Léon Poliakov, 57, quoting this phrase of the report: "Nothing has ever been said to me at the Vatican that would imply, on the part of the Holy See, any criticism or disapproval of the legislative acts and regulations in question." The author gives in a footnote (345–47) "the essential passages of this report". See n. 22.

and simple? How can we know without any information about the discussion, the person interviewed, the points dealt with and the conclusion? Why, on the other hand, if Rome's agreement was so manifest, did Bérard strive at such length—and with such skill—to "reduce the possible opposition of the Holy See"?[6] Why would he still feel the need, as we will see, to resort to arguments drawn from history? Why would he invoke the famous "distinction between thesis and hypothesis", a distinction that, according to him, the Church would once more have to accept? And how is it that, at the end of so many efforts, he finds himself again forced to recognize that, with respect to the juridical definition of the Jew and to what results from it, "there is a contradiction between French law and the Church's doctrine"?

In his brief study on anti-Jewish legislation in France, Guy Pedroncini, in judging "the attitude of the Holy Office in this matter", refers solely to the Bérard report as if to a decisive authority. This report was published first in *Le Procès de Xavier Vallat présenté par ses amis* (1948, 500–509), then (in part) by Saul Friedländler, *Pie XII et le IIIe Reich* (93–98). The reader clearly cannot find in either of these two works any critical examination of this document. This is understandable, coming from friends of Vallat. As for Saul Friedländler, whose book falls rather under the province of pamphleteer literature, about which one critic has said that the method followed is nothing but a "falsification of historical truth as superficial as it is irresponsible"[7] and about which Alfred Grosser himself, in

---

[6] Cf. J. Mayeur, *F.Q.J.*, 254. Ibid.: Bérard "nonetheless gives a rather precise idea of where Rome stood . . . : rejection of the principle of 'racism'— which signifies a radical opposition to all that drew its inspiration from it—concern for the interests of the Church and therefore for Jews who were baptized or married to Catholics, acceptance of the state's right to impose a *numerus clausus*".

[7] K. O. Aretin, in *Merkur* (1965), 19:1192; quoted by Victor Conzemius, *Eglises chrétiennes et Totalitarisme national-socialiste, un bilan historiographique* (Louvain, 1969), 61; cf. 59–60. G. Pedroncini, *F.Q.J.*, 30, n. 24. V. Con-

his postscript to the French edition, observes with more restraint that "intellectual precautions should be taken in using this book as it is" (221), it is not surprising that he was in complete agreement with Bérard and passed over in silence the protests that he received. In 1964, in *"Le Vicaire" et l'Histoire*, Jacques Nobécourt published, among appended documents (356-62), the whole "Letter addressed to Marshal Pétain by the French Ambassador to the Holy See", but in his own account, he quoted it only in passing, the subject of his book being other.

In summary, then, in the part of Bérard's memorandum that deserves the name of report, we must ask ourselves whom the ambassador was addressing as well as what precisely were the questions he asked or perhaps avoided asking; in brief, what actually was the subject of discussion. There are many people in the Vatican, and many of them could be or could believe themselves to be authorities, in varying degrees, most of whom employ a discreet courtesy that (if it is in one's best interests not to want it) one must sometimes know how to break through. The ambassador was assured that "the Holy See had no hostile intention"; he was persuaded that it did not wish to "seek a quarrel". Such expressions seem more appropriate to the beginning of a discussion rather than to its

---

zemius, 53: the importance of the collection of *Actes et documents* (recently published) "is fully evident only when one compares it with the facile hypotheses on which some journalist-historians have feverishly constructed certain publications. Fr. Blet and his confreres have allowed the discussion to begin again on sure foundations; they have done their work in such a way that what was only a pastime for journalists may now become the object of serious historical research." (We should, however, be lenient with respect to the excess and lack of understanding shown by Saul Friedländer, an inexperienced author, using only very unilateral documentation, seeing that he has dedicated his work "to the memory of my parents, killed at Auschwitz".) One clarification already solidly documented has appeared in *Civiltà cattolica* (June 6, 1964), 437-54: Angelo Martini, S.J., "La vera storia e 'Il Vicario' di Rolf Hochhuth".

conclusion, and nothing can be deduced from them. Given what follows the second statement, it would appear to have been intended by some canonist as an introduction to two reservations, the only ones indicated by the ambassador, calling them a "twofold wish", a "desire". One was very general: "That the precepts of justice and charity might be taken into account in the application of the law", but as this was not a direct quotation, one might wonder if the words "in *the application* of the law" might not have been intended to soften a remark of an entirely different significance, all the more so since the phrase that follows aims at softening it still more: "My interlocutors seemed to me to be alluding particularly to the liquidation of businesses in which Jews possess some interest." The other "wish" concerns a point considered "delicate": "No disposition concerning marriage should be added to the law about the Jews."

There, it would seem, we have finally been directed to a specific subject that raises no real disagreement. Does this mean that, according to the mysterious interlocutor, the Holy See would have had been in agreement with the "ethnic" and not strictly the "racist" principles of the Vichy legislation? According to Bérard, such an agreement was self-evident; for what the Holy See condemned was solely, he implies, the very specifically nazi form of anti-Semitism. In any case, *nothing* in his report can assure us that the question was even asked. If he was able to enter into some peaceful discussion, there is nothing that permits us to see that this dealt with any subject other than a problem of canon law, with respect to Jews being baptized or married to Catholics—a problem that the Church considered to be essentially within her own competence. Perhaps it was to this subject, mentioned several times, that Bérard agreed to apply several more or less conciliatory words, whose meaning he might easily have stretched in order to give them quite a different importance in his conclusion.[8] We are reduced to

[8] When Bérard writes that the Holy See "has not received any complaint", this could signify, in this context, that no Jew, baptized or not, had yet had

conjectures. And how can we make ourselves believe that "the *precepts* of justice and charity" could be the subject only of a simple "*wish*"?

However, our ambassador must have realized that this all remained a bit scanty and that one could not fail to suspect something questionable about it. So he had to find still another interlocutor. This had to be a person who carried weight, able to cover the French legislation in litigation with his own un-disputed authority—and no longer in some vague, implicit, anonymous fashion but by treating things in depth and by a proper demonstration. What a curious tête-à-tête between our diplomat, in some supposed office of the Vatican, with this venerable, seasoned theologian, whose name for once is re-vealed to us: none other than St. Thomas Aquinas! Still more curious perhaps, the *Confirmatur* with which he follows it, through no less unexpected testimony from Ernest Renan, who, as a "good Thomist", relies on his great ancestor! Fran-çois Delpech might have let some astonishment break through in the face of this kind of "rather complicated demonstration",[9] so out of place in a diplomatic document. Yet in my opinion it constitutes, if not the most valuable support awaited by Vichy, at least one of the more substantial parts of Bérard's report.

The nuncio might have thought he could recognize here and there in this report the hand of Fr. Gillet, master general of the Dominicans. That is not impossible, at least with respect to some aspects of the history of doctrines—which does not signify that the two interlocutors were in agreement about

---

recourse to it against the French law with respect to marriage; but, in this general form, one could take it to mean that no one had protested to Rome against Vichy's anti-Jewish legislation—or something else again. On that legislation about marriage, which subsequently achieved a fortunate practical importance, cf. L. Poliakov, "Une singularité des temps jadis: les législations nazies et vichyssoises en matière de mariage interdit", in *Le Couple interdit, entretiens sur le racisme* (Mouton, 1980), 244–45.

[9] *Sur les Juifs*, 277.

the conclusions drawn from them. In fact, a "Thomistic" conversation might have taken place not in the Vatican but on Aventine, in the Santa Sabina convent. But whoever gave him the information, what Bérard retained of it was not Roman: it was purely the product of an old tradition that was at once Gallican and clerical, exacerbated by nationalism of the kind that held sway at that time around Maurras and that claimed to recognize in the anti-Jewish legislation of Vichy the "modern continuation of the old medieval precautions". It gave much space to a few texts of St. Thomas as well as to a severe bull by Paul IV dating from 1555. Now Xavier Vallat was blindly won over by this school, "proud", says Jacques Nobécourt,[10] "to proclaim himself reactionary and faithful to the France of the Ancien Régime and to the Church of the Counter-Reformation"—these two proclaimed fidelities being a bit simplistic and totally anachronistic. He would write again in 1942: "All the measures contained in the French legislation of the new state and many others that were more excessively severe were formerly taken at the request of those very religious authorities whom the Jews of 1942 now claim tacitly disapprove of the actions of the Marshal's government in this regard."[11]

Vallat had not invented anything. In the review *Nova et Vetera* from Freiburg (Switzerland), Abbé Journet had, in September 1941, refuted the "Thomistic" argument: one indication among others that this argument was circulating in anti-Semitic circles before Bérard received his orders from Vichy.[12]

[10] Op. cit., 358.

[11] Cf. L. Poliakov, 57; cf. above, n. 5. The author, whose criticism is usually more exacting, seems to grant that Bérard's letter to Pétain, taken as a whole, was exactly that "very precise response" needed to appease "his conscience, without doubt definitively". This text of Vallat appeared "in the sumptuous journal *La Légion*". Cf. Duquesne, 253–54.

[12] 225–31. *Cahier* 6–7 of the *T.C.*, appearing in May of the following year, would refute the argument of Bérard's dissertation, using this article by Journet. On the other hand, as M. Ruby observes, there was a "connection

Lacking the substantial material he had wanted to collect from his Roman conversations, Bérard, not being a cleric, had needed to combine in his report some information coming from other sources. He found it, ready made, in France itself. Certainly he could not very well reproduce a few extracts drawn from the coarse propaganda headquarters functioning in Vichy, but I believe I know one or two sources to which he could easily have had recourse in order to get, if not a solid lesson in Thomism, at least some well-chosen information.[13] I had sometimes met, even before the war, a certain number of excellent men whom I could call innocent, with minds as narrow as their hearts were large, living in a confined atmosphere. They were among those royalists who were sincere but not very enlightened Catholics, scattered heirs of the old traditionalist movement (in the sense that that term had toward the end of the nineteenth century), but then won over without any malice to the Action française movement, persuaded as they were of working toward the goal of saving the Church and France. How, under the heavy blows of the summer of 1940, were they not to become not perhaps totally allied to Vichy but at least fervent Pétainists? Was it not the only way for them to rush in order to change their anguish into hope? Now some of them frequented at that time a certain library, where it seemed to me they came to seek not so much a personal introduction to the variations of history or the depths of Thomistic theology, but a little bundle of facts and a little bouquet of texts capable, as they thought, of strengthening Pétain and encouraging Vallat in their saving work. Others,

---

between the publication of this *Cahier* 6–7 and the episcopal protests of the summer of 1942", and in return, *Cahier* 10–11, *Collaboration et Fidélité*, could, in citing these protests, find its support in the attitude of the episcopate, which would be "very important for its audience".

[13] The fact that he took his time in replying lets us put forward a hypothesis, one which, moreover, in no way contradicts that of the nuncio: he was able to write to France to request information. But he might also have received information in advance; he must have.

in other places, devoted themselves to similar research, not always with the same innocence. There was no need to run to Rome for that. It was a job that was essentially French, and typically Lyonese, we might add.[14]

Was the "Thomist" dissertation that was inserted in the Bérard report like a main course the work of one of these men who sincerely believed they were working for their little part in a national or even Christian regeneration, without the contamination, as they thought, of the detested occupying power's nazi ideology? I do not know. In any case, it reflects the atmosphere of such a milieu, and it looks a little strange in a diplomatic document.[15]

Let us reread what we might call the central page of the shrewd ambassador. He is very careful to keep from making an appeal or even simply an allusion to any Roman interlocutor whatever, even an anonymous one. So he does not expose himself to any very clear refutation:

> *We know from general history* that the Church has often protected the Jews against the violence and injustice of their persecutors and that at the same time she has relegated them to ghettos. One of her greatest doctors, St. Thomas Aquinas, has left some teachings that account for this attitude. He treated the Jewish problem in passing but in very clear terms in the *Summa Theologica*, question 10 of the *Secunda Secundae*, art. 9, 10, 11 and 12. Here is a resumé of his doctrine. It is necessary to show tolerance toward the Jews insofar as this concerns the exercise of their religion; they should be free from religious constraint; their children should not be baptized by force, without the

---

[14] See the "Bref aperçu historique de la loi historique concernant les Juifs", by Antoine Lestra, editor in chief of *Nouvelliste de Lyon*. F. Delpech, *Colloque de Lyon* (1978), 284.

[15] Bérard report, in J. Nobécourt, 358. Note the three expressions I have placed in italics. They belong to argumentation, not to inquiry. Being prudent, the ambassador is careful not to say, even vaguely, that he heard such comments in the course of his Roman inquiry.

consent of the parents. On the other hand, while forbidding any policy of oppression against the Jews, St. Thomas nonetheless recommends taking in their regard proper measures to limit their action in society and to restrict their influence. *It would be unreasonable*, in a Christian state, to let them administer the government and thereby reduce the authority of the Catholics. *From which it follows* that it is legitimate to forbid them access to public office; it is equally legitimate to admit them to the universities (*numerus clausus*) and professions only in a fixed proportion.[16]

If we did not have reason to believe that the government—whose only concern in the matter was to obtain a "reassuring" report—was ready in advance to receive it with closed eyes, providing that its conclusion was in fact reassuring, we might be tempted to say that its ambassador was making fun of it. Who could be made to believe that this class in "general history", as vague as it is elementary, with its totally anachronistic reminders, coupled with a light injection of Thomistic theology, would have been deemed necessary if its author had been able to allege the least sign of unequivocal approval on the part of one of the "representatives with much authority in the Church"? And, even more, who could be made to believe that any one of these "representatives with much authority" could have gone off to search for "some part" in the works of Ernest Renan, remaining "faithful to his *notebooks from Saint-Sulpice*", from which to authorize Vichy's anti-Jewish laws? Who could be made to believe that any one of them could have given in to such argumentation to the point of forgetting the formal condemnations pronounced against the anti-Jewish doctrines and policies (and not only in their strictly nazi form) now revived by Vichy?

Bérard's statement not only made appeal to anachronistic situations and theories but also failed to breathe one word about the injustice of a statute that with one stroke and

[16]Jacob Kaplan, *Justice pour la foi juive*, 56.

retroactive effect crossed out a whole body of earlier legislation of which all the French, Jews or not, had reason to be proud; much more, it wanted or claimed to be totally unaware of the real situation, which placed this "à-la-française" anti-Semitism (inscribed even more in the statute of June 1941 than in that of October 1940) in the wake of Hitlerian racism. Was the propaganda, organized by Vichy itself through official broadcasts, not one of the immediate signs of this? "It could be heard from loudspeakers, which . . . spread . . . declarations harmful to the Jews, who were held responsible for everything, accused of all possible crimes."[17] Was there not another sign in those "abominable collusions between the Vichy police and the Gestapo", well before the great roundups of 1942, in order to hand over to the victors the German Jews who, from 1933 on, had come to seek asylum in France?[18]

Jacques Nobécourt believed it possible to conclude that if Bérard's report did not "come directly from the Secretary of State, he at least gave an officially authorized 'side of the story'".[19] That, it seems to me, is to say a lot, perhaps too much. In fact, if the ambassador had been able to obtain from any personage at all in Rome a reply that was even slightly clear and favorable, he would not have taken so much trouble to "bring together the elements of a well-founded and complete report" obviously fabricated by himself or by one of his friends. "General" history and Thomistic theology having spoken, Renan having come to the rescue, the inquiry undoubtedly seemed to him for the most part sufficient. He sought a practical *Confirmatur* only in a comparison with

---

[17] Cf. Marc Boegner, *L'Exigence oecuménique*, 146–47.

[18] *"Le Vicaire" et l'Histoire*, 356.

[19] J. Nobécourt, 355. It is clear, on the other hand, that if the Holy See was able to condemn through diplomatic channels certain points of fascist legislation, that does not mean (as Bérard let it be understood) that in its eyes, without the Concordat, these points would have been worthy of approval.

"fascist legislation on the Jews", which our diplomat, moreover, admits to knowing only by hearsay (he promises to send the texts to Vichy when he is able to procure them); he knows only that Rumania was inspired by it in its own marriage legislation. But what he is anxious to observe is that, if fascist legislation met with an "unfavorable reception in the Vatican" and if the Holy See raised, "through diplomatic channels, a formal protest" against it, it was because it "violated the Concordat". Now such is not the situation in France, so the Holy See cannot make such a complaint against us. Undoubtedly, with regard to certain details, there are "in our legislation, which is still Napoleonic in its vigor, many dispositions that the Church cannot approve"; but they cannot constitute a serious obstacle to an agreement. In such cases, one resolves the difficulties by distinguishing the thesis from the hypothesis, a distinction that is "essential, full of wisdom and reason: it is in the 'hypothesis' that the arrangements for practice are organized". Here we see how the most serious matters for discussion are avoided by turning attention to diplomatic and canonical subtleties, raised by ancient or foreign legislation. Here we see how to confuse the issue.[20]

When Bérard's report reached Vichy, Marshal Pétain wasted no time in making it public, and the government took advantage of it in order to present its legislation as moderate and liberal. When, on September 13, at a reception at the Parc Hotel, the apostolic nuncio, Bishop Valerio Valeri, made some severe remarks to the Marshal on the subject of this legislation,

---

[20] If one wants, by way of contrast, an example of simple consultation and clear response (with respect to another subject): about the same time, Bishop Dellapiane, apostolic delegate to the Congo, at the request of two missionaries, questioned the Vatican on the moral value of the Resistance; the reply arrived by radio: "The Holy See could not disapprove a movement whose goal is the liberation of its country, which is a sacrosanct duty." René Cassin, *Les Hommes partis de rien* (Plon, 1974), 200; quoted by J. B. Duroselle, *L'Abîme*, 1939–1945 (Imprimerie nationale, 1982), 333–34.

Pétain replied to him, in front of the ambassadors from Brazil and Spain, that "the Holy See, while finding certain dispositions hard and a bit unfeeling, had not on the whole found fault with it". To this remark, made with assurance but whose terms betrayed a certain embarrassment, Bishop Valerio Valeri replied "sharply that the Holy See had already manifested its ideas on racism, which was at the foundation of the measures taken against the Jews", and that Ambassador Bérard could not have expressed himself "in so simplistic a manner". About which the Marshal continued, "jokingly, that the nuncio perhaps was not in agreement with his superiors".[21] Valerio Valeri, surprised and suspecting some intrigue, immediately informed Cardinal Maglione, Secretary of State, of this discussion, asking to be informed.[22] But around the twenty-sixth, I do not know under what circumstances, Pétain received Bishop Valeri again and "communicated to him the report itself". The nuncio judged it to be "more qualified" than the Marshal's remarks. He delivered to him, on the other hand, a brief note on the "the grave drawbacks, from a purely religious point of view, of the legislation in force, an attitude characteristic of that of Roman diplomacy, which bases its protest on canonical foundations". From which came, on the thirtieth, a new letter from Valerio Valeri to Maglione, accompanied by a report, in which he was able to specify certain things, having not only read at leisure but copied the Bérard report. On his part the Secretary of State, having received this information, informed the nuncio through a letter of October 31 that Bérard had in fact met with Tardini and Montini, but that if it were one of these men that he meant to use as a reference, he had misunderstood their remarks, which in no

---

[21] J. M. Mayeur, loc. cit. We do not, obviously, have a stenographic report of the nuncio's words and the Marshal's reply.

[22] *Actes du Saint-Siège pendant la Second Guerre mondiale*, V, no. 99.

way authorized "that unfortunate law".[23] In diplomatic language, it would have been impossible to put forward "a more formal denial".[24]

"Through the sureness and perspicacity of his judgment, Bishop Valerio Valeri proves to be like a light of foremost magnitude in the Vatican's diplomatic corps." Besides intending to use the Bérard report to protect themselves, Vichy perhaps dreamed of using it on some broader scale: it could have initiated the opening of negotiations for a new Concordat. It seems that some, at least, desired that; "but the nuncio,

---

[23] If he had really been able to use one of them as a reference, he would certainly not have omitted his name. That would have been more convincing than all his long, embroiled argumentations. (It is very clear as well that he did not consult Tisserant.) Cf. L. Poliakov, 345–47: "Even if we are still free to suppose that the diplomat from Vichy went to seek his information from prelates whom he knew to be favorable and that he interpreted them in a way that would least disturb the master he served, the fact nevertheless remains that such a report would have been unthinkable if its author had had to face formal and frank disapproval from the Pope." I do not see what these last lines can mean: it is clear that Bérard did not risk asking for an audience to go and receive that "formal and frank disapproval"! If the author had had at his disposal all the documents published today, he would undoubtedly have written his remarks in a different way. Yet he does say with good reason: "We do not agree that there was even a trace of anti-Semitism in the Pope's thinking."

[24] Actes . . ., VIII, nos. 165 and 189. For those incidents consecutive to the Bérard report, we are indebted for several details that complete J. M. Mayeur, loc. cit., to Abbé Charles Molette, director of the Archives of the Church of France. On the other hand, in his response, Maglione congratulates the nuncio. Mayeur observes that, according to the editor of the Actes, no Vatican document confirms the version that Bérard gave of his informal exchange of views. He adds: "In fact, the Secretary of State questions more the way in which Pétain presents the report than the report itself." It seems to me that to question this interpretation is at the same time to question whether the vague language in Bérard's report did not offer the Vichy government any meaning that would serve its purposes. Cf. Angelo Martini, S.J., Civiltà cattolica (June 6, 1964), 442–43. It is difficult to see why Delpech treats the repeated protest of the nuncio as "confidential" (Sur les Juifs, 295).

who did not believe in the stability of the regime, evaded the government's solicitations".[25]

Having received support from the Secretary of State, Bishop Valeri drafted a note of protest, which he charged Cardinal Gerlier to deliver to the Marshal.[26]

From the very first day, as can be seen above, the opposition between the orientation of the Vichy government and the thought of Pius XII was patent. The incidents provoked by the Bérard report emphasized this again.[27] From the summer of 1940 until the end of 1944, the nuncio never ceased to defend Rome's point of view, in union with his predecessor in Paris, Cardinal Maglione, who had become Secretary of State. After the liberation of the area, he would leave France, on December 23, 1944, in virtue of the decision made by the provisional government headed by General de Gaulle not to recognize any connection with the government stemming

---

[25] V. Conzemius, 37 and 136. The desire was especially that of Bishop Chollet. (Cf. J. Duquesne, 103–6. Hubert Claude, *Revue du Nord*, 237 [April–June 1978], 263.) Secretary of the A.C.A., and claiming at times to speak in the name of his colleagues, he was an embarrassment for the French episcopate. "That old man, cut off from his diocese", a refugee at Vénissieux, "suffered besides from an inadequate understanding of politics".

[26] F. Delpech was perhaps alluding to this step when he wrote, *F.Q.J.*, 204: "Rome charged the nuncio with getting the French bishops moving. But, besides the first protests and some isolated groups, there was no stir, no real protest before the 1942 roundups." This way of presenting Gerlier's protest (which shows the union between Rome and the French episcopate in the face of Vichy's claims) is at the very least curious. And the total oversight of the text of the A.C.A. (see above, Chap. 6) is equally astonishing. It is regrettable that these interventions were not more prompt and strong. But a systematic disparagement of the episcopate is no more the concern of objective history than certain apologies. Nor is it possible to see what allows Delpech to affirm that "the nuncio's step remained confidential"!

[27] When, a little after these incidents, Marshal Pétain, having published "Les principes de la communauté" in his collection *Paroles aux Français*, offered a copy of it to Pius XII on November 21, 1941, the Pope did not hesitate to express some explicit reservations. Cf. J. Duquesne, 20.

from the defeat.[28] But to show clearly that this general measure was in no way aimed personally at Bishop Valerio Valeri, to whom France was on the contrary very grateful, General de Gaulle, after consultation with Rome,[29] received him in a formal audience before his departure; in the course of the audience, de Gaulle decorated Valeri with the Grand Cross of the Legion of Honor, and at the conclusion had military honors paid to him.[30]

[28] "The express wish of the General is not to admit any diplomat who has been the representative of his country to Marshal Pétain": declaration of Tixier, new Secretary of the Interior, to André Latreille, technical adviser to his minister for questions with religious repercussions. André Latreille: *De Gaulle, la Libération et l'Eglise catholique* (Cerf, 1978), 15 and 21–22. Cf. Charles de Gaulle, *Lettres, notes et carnets, mai 1945–juin 1951* (Plon), 50; speech to the consultative provisional Assembly, July 28, 1945: "It is necessary, after more than five years, to leave a provisional and unconstitutional situation . . . "

[29] It is easy to believe that the Holy See, which did not know the reasons why the new French government wished to proceed to this change of nuncio, agreed to it only in return for some clearly apparent conditions. The negotiations were carried out, in Rome itself, by Charles Flory: he made it understood that it was solely a measure taken as a matter of principle, justified by the exceptional circumstances, and he found support particularly from Bishop Montini with respect to Pius XII. On December 5 or 6, the Pope decided to recognize *de jure* the new government and to accredit a new nuncio to Paris (A. Latreille, 45–46).

[30] Carlo Falconi, in his pamphleteer work on *Le Silence de Pie XII* ([Monaco: Ed. du Rocher, 1965], 376), did his best to mix the case of the nuncio with that of the French bishops, several of whom, newly arrived on the scene, then asked to resign: "De Gaulle asked for the resignation of a hundred or so Pétainist bishops; the nuncio Roncalli succeeded in reducing them to three; his predecessor to the nunciature, Bishop Valerio Valeri, however, had to return to Rome." Everything seems intentionally mixed up in this simple sentence. In reality (besides the fact that the role attributed to Roncalli is not correct), it was not a question of "Pétainist" bishops but of bishops suspected of having compromised themselves with the occupying forces; the complaint against them was not due to the initiative of General de Gaulle, who had only five of them referred to Roncalli (only three for the city itself; cf. Falconi, 19); finally, the case of the nuncio had nothing in common with that of the bishops about whom, rightly or wrongly, the authorities were complaining. The same confusion is found in Jean Chevalier,

"If the social isolation of the Jews could have had any meaning in a period of Christianity, it no longer had any, either for Christians or for Jews, in a neutral and secular state." Whatever judgment one might have had on centuries long past, this reflection by Joseph Folliet would have been obvious to anyone of good sense.[31] Xavier Vallat nonetheless persisted to the end in his illusion: nothing could shake his invention of a "Christian state", even when governed by someone like Darlan and submitted to the pressures of someone like Hitler. Again in December 1947, during his trial, he would shield his statute of 1941 under the authority of St. Thomas Aquinas, and even—would you believe it?—under that of St. Paul.[32] And, of course, his supreme argument would be the authority of the present Magisterium, whose thinking, despite its denials, was infallibly defined by Bérard's report, itself interpreted by the remarks of Pétain, in agreement with our national traditions:

As for my Thomist conception, I do not find it at all outdated. On the contrary, it is confirmed by a document subsequent to Pius XI, since it issues from our ambassador to his successor, and since that document expresses the same doctrine, which I find entirely normal. . . . I have been inspired by a doctrine,

---

La Politique du Vatican (S.C.P.P.), 257–58: "At the time of the Liberation, from August 1944, De Gaulle called for a change of nuncio and of a great number of bishops" (according to Paul Lesourd and Claude Paillot, Dossiers secrets de l'Eglise de France, vol. 2 [Presse de la Cité, 1968], 482). The attitude and activity of Bishop Valeri were always exemplary. "What struck me in this prelate", says Stanislas Fumet, who knew him well, in his Mémoires (Fayard, 1978), "was a profound sense of the human" (433). According to J. Duquesne (49), Bishop Valeri very early on advised the bishops to be prudent: "Do not get too close to Marshal Pétain. . . . Besides, that man has been outwitted."

[31] Joseph Folliet to Jean Toulat, in J. Toulat, Juifs mes frères (Fayard, 1968), 151–52.

[32] Despite the text to which Maurice Guérin took exception: "There are no longer Jews or Greeks or Gentiles."

let me repeat, which has a long foundation in our historical traditions and which finds its guarantee—and one need go no farther—in the very doctrine of the Church.[33]

Vallat's defenders were not entirely wrong when they said that the official anti-Semitism of Vichy was other than that of the nazi occupying forces. One can possibly distinguish, in the abstract, a Germanic line leading to Hitler and a French line leading to Vichy. But their origins are mixed, and consequently their conjunctions are numerous. Voltaire was French, but he indoctrinated Frederick II, and Hitler read Voltaire with delight. That is only one example. The expression *Christian anti-Semitism* has also been much abused. But if, as is only too true, many French of the Christian tradition sought security in the Catholic tradition, it is not from it that they received their anti-Semitism. The Rewbels, Comtes, Ménards and the Sourys, the Michelets, the Toussenels, paragons of modern anti-Semitism in France, were not at all Christians; they were no more Christian than were people like Schopenhauer, Wagner, Nietzsche and Chamberlain (English but settled in Vienna).[34] Neither was Maurras, as we know, when he wrote in *Anthinéa*: "The great historical periods of unrest are explained, for the West as a whole just as for the

---

[33] Quoted by J. Nobécourt, 208. Vallat will also say that, "in order to put his conscience at rest", he asked one of his collaborators, named Gazagne, to have contact with the most representative members of the French episcopate in order to "submit to them the principles" of his legislation. In fact, only one testimony will be cited: that of Archbishop Saliège. But all those familiar with the Archbishop and those who knew him closely during this period have challenged this verbal, indirect testimony, reported by a subordinate. They also observed that the remarks of the very disabled man were often incomprehensible. Cf. P. Pierrard, 296–97. To be just, however, we must repeat that if Vallat "remained blind to the outcome of the route on which the disciples of Rosenberg were leading the French Jews", still there was nothing "in common" between him and "the Baltic theoretician unleashed against Christ" (cf. J. Nobécourt, 208).

[34] See, in F. Lovsky, *Antisémitisme et Mystère d'Israël*, chaps. 8 and 10.

little village, by the heat of the Jewish and Syrian miasma, brought here two thousand years ago."[35] Someone like the obscure Labroue could write in Paris in 1942, in the service of nazi propaganda: "Our state anti-Semitism is inspired so little by confessional proselytism that it finds its most decisive reference in the Voltairian tradition."[36] From left or right, nationalists or racists, social doctrinarians or discoverers of pseudoscience, the modern anti-Semitic leaders are all at least close cousins. Drumont was closely dependent on Toussenel, he set the Semite in opposition to the Aryan, and *La Libre Parole* opened in 1895 a debate on "the Jewish danger considered from the point of view of race and not from the point of view of religion".[37] Shortly before the Second World War, when Léon Blum came to power, Vallat was indignant, "not that a Jew was the head of a *Christian* state, but of a Gallo-Roman country".[38] Around the end of the nineteenth century, a Fr. Constant was determined to "prove" the Jewish crime of "ritual murder" despite the wild denials, he said, "of the eighteenth century", failing to mention that these denials were those of a Pope, Benedict XIII, and of a future Pope, Ganganelli (Clement XIV). De Vries and Bishop Jouin, in the period before our last war, were racists, as was that German Pastor Johnsen who proclaimed: "Racist thought is our great hope."[39]

[35] *Anthinéa*, 5th ed. (Champion, 1913), 222ff. Representative Allard, in a speech to the Chamber, said in January 1903: "I make only one reproach against the Jews, that of having poisoned Aryan thought . . . with Hebrew monotheism."

[36] *Voltaire antijuif* (Paris, 1942), 8. In private, Hitler gave the *Règlement pour les Juifs* by Frederick II as his reference, "worthy of a cannibal", in Mirabeau's judgment.

[37] F. Lovsky, 330; cf. 274–77.

[38] F. Lovsky, 330–31.

[39] F. Lovsky, 327–30. Without discussing at all the historical studies devoted by Jules Isaac to Christian anti-Semitism, I believe it is impossible to agree that this anti-Semitism, explored in Christian antiquity to the Middle Ages and after, is sufficient to disclose to us "the profound—and too often veiled—

Such was the common background of the two anti-Semitisms then promoted to power, the French dependent on the German through the misfortune of defeat. The statute of the Jews worked out at Vichy was proclaimed to be both "typically French" and conformed to the tradition of the Church. This twofold title was wrongfully applied. It would soon be more fallacious still, when, in its wake and under its application, the "general union of Israelites in France" would be instituted, intermingling all Jews, baptized or not, patriots or stateless, not in order to fuse them together into a nation but to set them completely apart: to "represent from now on", as it was said discreetly, "the interests of the Jewish people with respect to public powers".[40]

---

sources of anti-Semitic hatred". (Cf. Jules Isaac, Genèse de l'antisémitisme, essai historique [Calmann-Lévy, 1956], conclusion, 330. The study pursued in this work up to the eleventh century already seems sufficient to the author to authorize such a conclusion.)

[40] F. Lovsky, 383–84; cf. 361–63.

Chapter 8

"Defense of Christ and of the Bible"

In October 1941, I had succeeded in getting an article of rather general appearance, entitled "Explication chrétienne de notre temps" [A Christian explanation of our times], into *Cité nouvelle* and later reproduced as a pamphlet.[1] It was the text of a lecture given to the Ecole des cadres d'Uriage, at the request of Hubert Beuve-Méry, who served there in the capacity of Prefect of Studies. The appearance of the article had been made possible by Fr. Desbuquois, editor of the journal, and Fr. Victor Dillard had written to me that he recognized his own thoughts in it. "I was surprised", he added, "at all you were able to say. . . . It is necessary to fight at this moment, for we carry a crushing responsibility, and we must use all the freedom that remains to us in order to write and to cry out."

Encouraged by this small success and by the sympathy of Fr. Dillard, whose lively energy I knew, I then conceived a slightly more ambitious project. Either following the

---

[1] A first edition appeared, under the title *Vocation de la France*, in the little collection of pamphlets entitled "Le Témoignage chrétien", which our house at Fourvière had founded before the war under the impetus of Fr. Décisier and which was under the direction of one of the professors, Fr. Emile Janot. As a result, the coincidence of this name with the *Cahiers* of Fr. Chaillet occasionally served as an alibi for the Lyons students who, when visited by the police, were able to show them the cover of inoffensive pamphlets. On the Uriage: J. Duquesne, 206–11. Cf. *Cité nouvelle*, October 25, 1941, p. 553: "It is to the Gospel that we owe our very idea of man. If we deny the Gospel, we are lost."

attempted declaration by Abbé Chaine or perhaps even a little before, I had drafted several pages to use in more or less private conversations, and I had given them the title "Defense of Christ and of the Bible", with the vague hope that such wording, which would not arouse suspicion of any intrusion into "politics", would allow it to get past the censorship barricade. The journal *La Chronique sociale*, where I had several friends, wanted it.[2] It had my pages printed, but the local censor was uncompromising. Then, both Frs. Dillard and Desbuquois tried to rescue my "Defense . . ." by appealing directly to the national censor in Vichy. A courageous attempt, total failure. I learned about it through a sad little note from Fr. Desbuquois and through a long, very beautiful letter from Fr. Dillard. (I have before me copies of these two letters, dated December 12 and 14.) The one from Fr. Dillard seems to me worth quoting:

Vichy, December 12, 1941

Dear Father and Friend,
I am coming from a final try with the censor for your article "Defense of Christ and of the Bible", and this time I am hopelessly beaten. I had made appeals at all levels, and finally I had a conference with all the directors, who are nice, intelligent types, knowing how to take their responsibilities, who have always been very decent to us, but who today were implacable. Perhaps I would have had more success in the matter if I had gone directly to the commission on Jewish questions. But I see that there was very little hope, and I have come away rather pessimistic about these processes.

I have the impression that we could have spoken about these questions several months ago, but the noose is tightening. "If

---

[2] According to François Delpech, it was *La Chronique sociale* that took the initiative in asking me for this article. Undoubtedly he is right (*Colloque de Grenoble*, 157). On the disputes with the Vichy censor during this period: Paul Droulers, *Colloque de Lyon*, 222. Around the same date, the fine article written at Mongré by Fr. Jean Daniélou, "Culture française et mystère", which appeared in *Esprit*, was extensively censored.

we let this article go by," they said to me, "we would immediately have a reaction from the occupying power." For it is
that which is obviously the cause. There could be even less
doubt about it since all polemics are forbidden between the free
zone and the occupied zone, and since your references to Montherlant, for example, could not get by.

I objected that the question was serious, that it was the very
freedom of the Church that was at stake. They replied that they
had indeed taken this into account, but that they could do
nothing about it, that some public declarations by the Cardinal
himself on this question had been censored and that the pastoral
letters from the bishops themselves could not escape censorship.
I pointed out that they could nevertheless not keep us from
speaking in the pulpit. But I wonder if we will be able to do
that much longer.

It would be good to keep the Cardinal informed, and if it
were possible to obtain an official declaration from him on the
Jewish religious question, I believe that it could get by while
things are still as they are. The future does not belong to us.

I am all the more distressed because for over a year I have
begged Fr. Desbuquois and others to take a position in *Cité
nouvelle* or in *Renouveaux*. It seemed to me then that this was
our duty. Now it is too late.

Do believe, dear Father, that no one is to be accused here.
Conscience matters are cruel, but I have the impression that
each is doing his duty. We must pray for France.

Very fraternally yours in O.L.

P.S.—If the censor authorizes it, I am to give a lecture here in
January on "Bergson and Catholicism". I would very much
like to know in this regard the truth about Bergson's conversion,
baptism and last wishes. Are we to believe Raïssa Maritain's
article?[3]

---

[3] Cf. *Journal de Raïssa*, published by Jacques Maritain (D.D.B., 1963), 271:
"New York, January 5, 1941. Bergson died yesterday. . . . They wrote to
us from France that he had been baptized and that he did not want to announce
this publicly out of sensitivity toward the Jews handed over to persecution
during these recent years." In a note, from Jacques Maritain: "This informa-

Would you agree to come to Vichy, if the case arises, to speak of your article in a private meeting to a Catholic Action group?[4]

Our Provincial at that time, Fr. Joseph du Bouchet, who had already received sympathetically the confidential memorandum of April 25 of which I have spoken in Chapter 2,

---

tion was not accurate. . . . Raïssa explained all that in the second of her articles in *Commonwealth* (January 17 and August 29, 1941). Cf. also *Henri Bergson, Essais et témoignages inédits*, collected by A. Béguin and P. Thévenaz (Neuchâtel, 1941)."

Bergson's testament, February 8, 1937: "My reflections have led me closer and closer to Catholicism, in which I see the complete fulfillment of Judaism. I would have converted if I had not seen for years the tremendous wave of anti-Semitism building, which is going to break over the world. I wanted to remain among those who will tomorrow be the persecuted ones. But I hope that a Catholic priest will, if the Cardinal Archbishop of Paris authorizes it, be able to come and say prayers at my funeral. . . . If this authorization is not granted, it would be necessary for me to speak to a rabbi, but without hiding from him and without hiding from anyone my moral adherence to Catholicism as well as the desire that I expressed first of having the prayers of a Catholic priest." Cf. *Auguste Valensin*, unpublished texts and documents (Aubier, 1961), 296–97 and 307–8. René Violette, *La Spiritualité de Bergson* (Privat, 1968), 517–29 and 544–46. There is the interesting essay "Bergson et le Judaïsme" in Vladimir Jankélevitch, *Henri Bergson* (P.U.F., 1959), 255–85.

Here is an example of the way in which the collaborationist press greeted Bergson's death: "Bergson tossed aside? And why not, if you please? If only for the alibi that he so often furnished for the worst Jews, Bergson should never have had the right to write and teach in French": *Le Cri du Peuple* (quoted by F. Lovsky, 369). France (in appearance the only one who had the right to express herself) sank into ignominy.

[4]Fr. Dillard, from 1940 on, "resolutely measured the danger of nazism and the battle. The London radio called him 'the only courageous man in Vichy'." J. Duquesne, 64, who quotes this passage from one of his sermons, given at the Saint-Louis church in Vichy on February 1, 1942, with respect to the German attack on Russia: "It would be pointless to hope for the victory of one paganism over another; we French do not have to wish or hope for any victory by force and violence, for it is not with force that one fights blind beliefs." On Dillard, see also Michel Riquet, *Chrétiens de France dans*

wrote to me, on December 18, an encouraging letter in this regard:

> As soon as I learned about the incident provoked by your article, I immediately made known to Fr. Desbuquois my desire to be familiar with it. Which is to tell you how much your package corresponded to my affectionate curiosity. I am very sincerely grateful to you for having thought yourself to satisfy me. What I have read surpasses my expectations. I liked it as soon as I saw your fine title. And after having read it, I am more than ever convinced that, for the honor of God and Holy Church, such ideas must succeed in being published. —We have just had a first failure; but I remain persuaded that the final word has not yet been spoken, and, one way or another, such truths must be heard.
>
> Thanking the good worker for Holy Church and the Society, I repeat, dear Father, my very devoted affection in Our Lord.

The wishes of my Provincial were to be realized at least in part during the following year, in June 1942. How did *La Vie spirituelle* learn of my rejected manuscript, and how did it come to publish this "Defense of Christ . . ."? I no longer

---

l'Europe enchaînée (S.O.S., 1972), 75. In another sermon in the same church, he said: "We are thinking of the eighty thousand French who are in the process of being held up to ridicule with a yellow star." When it was a question of the S.T.O. (Service du Travail Obligatoire), he protested publicly: "Here they are, asking [the J.O.C. (Jeunesse étudiante catholique)] in the name of civil obedience to go furnish manpower to the foreigner! How can we believe that it is not being taken in by the deception of the 'relief'?" He afterward left, using another name, as a specialist worker in order to give spiritual help to the deported youth. The police tracked him down, and he was interned, then transferred to Dachau, where he died. (Cf. Victor Dillard, *Suprême témoignage* [Paris: Spes, 1945].) One could compare the analogous position of several members of the J.O.C. who left for Germany to help their comrades from the S.T.O. (Cf. Bishop C. Molette, *A propos de quelques cas chez les jeunes du S.T.O. de résistance spirituelle jusqu'au martyre* [Angers University Presses, 1987].) Dillard had been asked to leave Vichy in 1943 by Pétain because of his preaching (Droulers [*Colloque de Lyon*], 219).

remember. For a long time I even thought I had never known, but now I prefer to accuse my memory.[5]

The other three authors of the stillborn declaration of June 1941, however, had not remained inactive. Abbé Chaine, unrelenting, had organized, on another model, a collective work, distributing to each of us our own task, and on June 9, 1942, our team obtained, thanks to the active interest of our archbishop and chancellor, an Imprimatur in good and due form, signed by Bishop Rouch, the vicar general, for a little book that appeared in October through the L.U.F. (Library of the University of Freiburg, Switzerland): *Israël et la Foi Chrétienne*, by Henri de Lubac, Joseph Chaine, Louis Richard and Joseph Bonsirven. Two of Fr. Chaillet's closest collaborators, Louis Cruvillier and Germaine Ribière, a disciple of Fr. de Montcheuil, had allowed us to establish clandestine relations with several Swiss friends, among whom our most effective supporter was Abbé Charles Journet, the future cardinal, professor at the major seminary of Fribourg. Little by little, copies of our little book slipped secretly into France, right up to the end of the Occupation years. My contribution had changed its title; it was "Un nouveau front religieux" [A new religious front].[6] According to Jean-Marie Mayeur, the book's effect "during and after the war was considerable".[7]

So this was the third, belated effect of Abbé Chaine's initiative.

With respect to this Fribourg book, François Delpech made the following curious reflections at the seminar held in Grenoble in 1976:

[5]The journal was at that time published in Lyons, at the Editions de l'Abeille, substituting for Editions du Cerf.

[6]The few historical additions hurriedly introduced later for a new publication in the collection entitled *Affrontements mystiques* (Ed. du T.C., 1950) are entirely inadequate.

[7]In *F.Q.J.*, 169. See also F. Delpech, *Sur les Juifs*, 284.

The aborted project of the declaration of the theological faculty at Lyons refers only to the rights of man and to the principles of French law. . . .[8] The articles in the first *Cahiers du T.C.* . . . do not neglect this aspect of things, but they stress the exigencies of the Faith. This is still more clear in the book . . . *Israël et la Conscience chrétienne* [sic], which extends and deepens the positions taken by *T.C.* But . . . here it is not, or not only, a question of biblical fraternity and respect for the chosen people *but rather of a defense of the Church threatened in her Jewish roots, in a perspective dear to Maritain and Fr. de L. Is this perhaps because the return to the Bible is more recent and the weight of the institution heavier?*"[9]

One wonders what such antitheses can really mean when they are referring to three texts coming from exactly the same milieu and, even more precisely still, to a great extent from the same authors. As if the same subject could never be approached from more than one perspective! As if there were some contradiction in considering the issue, according to the circumstances, sometimes from the viewpoint of law, sometimes from that of faith, and as if the "biblical fraternity" excluded a "defense of the Church", the latter finding itself absorbed, according to a cliché that one would not expect to see used in such a context, by the "weight of the institution"? And what is the purpose of this "return to the Bible" here, undoubtedly judged too recent (if we really understand this mysterious allusion)[10] to have

---

[8] Here, a prudent parenthesis: "But as we have only the incomplete and rather uncertain text of Archbishop Guerry, we cannot use it as an argument." In fact, these professors did not forget that they were priests of the Catholic Church, and it was in the name of their Faith that they were expressing themselves in a final part. It was, moreover, completely natural that Archbishop Guerry did not reproduce it, for it no longer constituted a fully valid argument for the legislator in a country containing numerous unbelievers. The text reproduced by Archbishop Guerry is perfectly accurate.

[9] F. Delpech, *Sur les Juifs*, 284.

[10] The author seems to have forgotten, at the very least, that two of the four signatories were professors of Sacred Scripture in higher education and had no need of any "reorientation" to effect a "return to the Bible".

allowed the authors of the book in question to shake off the "weight of the institution", so that while seeming to take up the defense of the persecuted Jews, it was in reality the cause of their "institution" and its weight that they intended to defend?[11]

Gaining confidence from the twofold approval of Fr. du Bouchet, I took still another, quite unexpected occasion to speak a few words of warning publicly, in France itself and in a semiofficial milieu, taking the inevitable precautions. I had been invited by Abbé A. Millard, director of chaplains for the Chantiers de la jeunesse (youth camps), to speak at the congress of chaplains held in Sainte-Baume, from April 14 to 17, 1942. General de la Porte du Theil, director of the Chantiers, was to come. The theme of the congress was "the sense of the Sacred", and the opening lecture was given by Fr. Paul Doncoeur, S.J.; of very pure inspiration, it kept to a level that avoided any risk of dispute. Fr. Forestier, O.P., general chaplain, then took the occasion to stress the fact that "there is something more tragic in our times than in authentic paganism. Paganism was waiting for Christianity. . . . The neopagans have . . . rejected it, loathe it. They no longer hear the call of beatitude. Now", he continued, "it is with them that we must work; it is a problem of practical pedagogy." The title announced for my lecture was "Internal Causes for the Dimming and Disappearance of the Sense of the Sacred". In the introduction, I warned my audience: "Such a subject is risky. To treat it sincerely and with any chance of profit, we have to avoid watering it down. An examination of con-

---

[11] Undoubtedly my criticism goes beyond its goal in seeking to put a little coherence into a reflection that was too quickly expressed to be coherent. Does not the author himself then say that the writings of which he has just spoken manifest, conjointly with those of "Protestants of various persuasions . . . , a common return to the sources"? Yet even so, I am even more hesitant to criticize this strange page since it is not in any way a matter of a personal conflict, the author concluding with these words: "Be that as it may, these texts are essential."

science is very likely to be useless if it is not, at least in some regards, disagreeable. . . . But we should not confuse it with denigration." Having given this precaution, I was able in what followed to slip in several rather clear reflections: "Today, when the essential doctrine of the unity of the human race is attacked, mocked by racism, do we not sometimes experience a pang of anguish when we see it so weakly defended?" Or again:

> This Old Testament, which once formed the very basis of reli-
> gious teaching (as the long series of "prophecies" on Holy Satur-
> day still gives witness), this "holy history", which was later
> learned by everyone, . . . is hardly ever taught any more, is
> hardly ever preached any more. . . .[12] In the face of powerful
> movements that present themselves as totalitarian conceptions
> of the world and systems of life, what action can be based on
> a doctrine whose statements too often remain abstract . . . ,
> fragmentary, inorganic, without internal fullness?

Nearing the end, I turned to Péguy, who could not fail to be well received in this setting of camp chaplains, but in order to quote a long page that was not at all according to the taste of the day, and from which I repeat here only the final words: "There must be some reason why, in the country of St. Louis and Joan of Arc, in the city of St. Geneviève, when one be-gins to speak of Christianity, everyone thinks it refers to Mac-Mahon, and when one is preparing to speak of the Christian

---

[12] In this cursory summary, I had in mind the recent situation created by the influence of the victor—but one made possible by our overly abstract theological education and our overly brief biblical formation. Now that our religious past has become the object of many an ill-considered criticism, it seems only fair to me to recall what Fr. Michel Riquet wrote in 1975 about his education in a free college at the beginning of the century: "Contrary to a stupid myth, we were encouraged early on to read the Bible in the translation of Canon Crampon, while the books of Abbé Fouard on Jesus Christ and the apostles got us used to situating the Gospel in its Hebrew context. It was exactly the opposite of what Maurras preached": *Un chrétien face à Israël* (Laffont, 1975), 14.

order, everyone thinks it refers to the sixteenth of May."
Many in the audience, if not all, picked up this impertinent
allusion; it prepared them to understand that it was necessary
to avoid, in the effort to restore the sense of the Sacred, "the
double peril of slipping into the profane and of a sacrilegious
surrender to a 'sacred' usurper". I was then able to close with
an exhortation to examine "the background of biblical revelation" and to base our behavior on "the twofold and unique
Revelation" that, inspiring "the whole life of the priest, the
consecrated man", must make men "perceive a mystery there
and understand that this mystery is, in the final analysis, a
mystery of love".

These "daring statements" (such banalities hardly seem to
be "daring" today) did not cause me any trouble. The speaker
who concluded the congress even recommended that the audience meditate on my lessons. And the *Bulletin des aumniers*
published my whole lecture (for internal use) along with several others, in August 1942—without, I imagine, going
through any censorship office.[13]

Shortly after this gathering of Chantiers chaplains, where
I had found myself—very quietly—confronted by Fr. Doncoeur, another occasion presented itself for a new "confrontation", which was unavoidable but equally unsuccessful
in turning him to face the tragic reality. Fr. Doncoeur had
just published a little book, *Péguy, la Révolution et le Sacré*,
which did not lack for style: the best of his chivalrous Christian
ideal was mixed there with an exaltation of that "national
revolution" that he still saw through his dream—even more
illusory then at the end of 1942 than it had been in the first
two years of the new regime.[14] He could not keep from

---

[13] *Bulletin des aumôniers catholiques, Chantiers de la jeunesse*, 31 (August 1942),
27–39.

[14] The naïve, but at times admirable, spirit of the young camp leaders,
which I had noticed in the early days, had gradually fallen. Marcel Pacaut,
who traced "the life in a youth group" from November 1942 to May 1943,

admiring, in contrast to the carelessness that had lost France, the virile virtues that had charmed him in Germany during the years before the war. He thought he could still discern them in their pure form, at least in the top ranks of the conquering party. This vision seemed to blind him—although I am sure it was not so—to the horrors of the nazi Occupation, which at that time were only growing worse. The "cult of the leader" that he had propagated since 1940, in opposition to the "chimeras of democratic liberalism", for the foundation "of a new world" was an ideal full of ambiguities which he did not sufficiently take into account. A few expressions from Péguy, drawn from a totally different context, served as his support. His apostolic zeal, the purity of his heroism and his gifts for leadership assured him of a potentially dangerous influence over some of the youth, leading them farther than he himself would have wished. So the publication of his book had aroused some agitation. The *Cahiers de notre jeunesse*, the new organ of the A.C.J.F., founded quite recently to replace as much as possible publications that had been banned and themselves subject to easily offended censors, judged it mandatory to react.[15] The reaction threatened to be strong and to overshoot its mark; so when they appealed to me, I did not hesitate long to take charge of the requested review. I was basically in agreement with those making the request, and I

---

gave a rather dismal description of it: he noted there a "lack of thought" and "indifference toward an institution and activities the first idea of which had not been totally devoid of value". "Nothing", he concludes, "was able to arouse enthusiasm except, at times, the remarks of some of the chaplains": *Mélanges André Latreille* (Lyons: Audin, 1972), 365–74.

[15] Albert Gortais, secretary general of these *Cahiers*, had indicated their tenor by writing in the first number: "Let us stop making the public confession of the French community." Quoted in J. Duquesne, 33. On January 26, 1941, at the forty-third session of the National Council of the A.C.J.F., he had presented a report on "Les jeunes au service de la communauté française: l'A.C.J.F." [The young in service of the French community: the A.C.J.F.]: this report had been published in *Cité nouvelle*, February 10, 1941, 224–42.

hoped in that way to avoid too loud an explosion, which would have aggravated dissensions that were already too regrettable, and without any compensating value. So here is what I wrote on *Péguy, la Révolution et le Sacré*, in the February 1943 number of the *Cahiers de notre jeunesse*:

> This little book merits attention because of the importance of its subject, the personality of its author and the evident nobility of its inspiration. All those who, during this troubled era through which we are passing, have not abandoned their special task as men, which is first of all to reflect and to judge, would profit from reading it. We must congratulate the author, convinced as was Péguy that "the frightful lack of the Sacred" in the modern world was the profound cause of our misfortunes, for having tried "to collect the most humble vestiges" of this Sacred, "as one collects in the course of an excavation the least fragments of marble in which the letters of an ancient inscription can still be discerned", so as to guide us from there, as if by a mysterious Jacob's ladder, to the Being whose "splendor surpasses all images, and who at last makes sacred, by his presence, all that we have loved and venerated here below". His goal and his method thus defined seem excellent in all respects. We only regret, for our part, that instead of having brought back from his exploration in search of "the wick that still burns" a certain mystique of the leader (elements of which would be difficult to find in our national tradition or in Christian tradition), he did not make a greater effort, after have spoken so well of the family and work, to discern in the people of France the many of the "vestiges" of the sacred that it still preserves from its Christian past. That effort might have saved him from a tendency, which for us was excessive, to hypnotize himself about our present degradation. It would also have allowed him to direct his analysis of the Sacred along a slightly different route and to show us more clearly how, among the various analogous notions that history offers and that theology sifts out, the difference is not only in its object but also, principally and by that very fact, in its nature. From this point of view, has not what we could call the Christian revolution consisted precisely in transforming (or rather in completing the transformation of)

a pagan idea, a pagan sense of the Sacred, which we might sum up in the word *taboo*, into a totally different sense and idea? It has not only shifted or completed their objects; it has interiorized and moralized them. Without doubt, religion remains something besides and more than the moral, and the sense of the Sacred cannot be reduced to a simple sense of duty; but it is now impossible for us to recognize the least trace of anything authentically, respectably sacred in a sense that does not take such a transformation into account. Undoubtedly there were still in paganism many human (let us even say divine) elements of permanent value, which would be saved by Christianity and which we must retain or rediscover. Péguy said, and Fr. Doncoeur is right in repeating: "A certain innocent and unfortunate paganism did not have the gods it merited." But, as Fr. Festugière explains very well in the work he recently devoted to holiness, and as Péguy himself also understood, that part of the ancient heritage is the fruit of a reason that, piercing the mist and shaking off the chains of superstition, sensed the God of justice and goodness, the God who was "before us": the only true God who, after having made himself known to Abraham, then to Moses and the prophets, was to reveal himself fully to us in his Son. We are sure as well that there is no fundamental disagreement between the author and us. But if these and other analogous distinctions had been clarified, it seems to us that this would have dispelled completely the ambiguity in the atmosphere into which the reading of this little book plunges us, and we would have been able to enjoy with unalloyed appreciation the admirable pages for which any Christian reader would be grateful to Fr. Doncoeur for having provided such a benefit.

I believe that in this way I succeeded, in this delicate matter, in calming the minds of many young friends without failing in what we all owed to Fr. Doncoeur.[16] The latter, far from being angry about it, was shortly after the Liberation to give

[16] On the *Cahiers de notre jeunesse*: J. Duquesne, 140–41. On the A.C.J.F. before and during the war and Occupation: A. Michel, "Les mouvements de jeunesse catholique et le nazisme dans l'entre-deux-guerres", *Colloque de Biviers*, September 1984.

me a warm welcome, both in Paris in his room at *Etudes* and at his center for the Spiritual Exercises at Troussures. But of course the article was not likely to save the poor *Cahiers* from shipwreck; they were soon to be suppressed by the censor.[17]

[17] In its *Cahier* 15–16, 2d ed. (April 1943 in Lyons, December in Paris), the *T.C.* would publish a fine text by Fr. Doncoeur, drawn from his pamphlet of 1931: *Qui a brûlé Jeanne d'Arc?* ("Les voiles se déchirent", in the new ed., 1:278–80). Nothing prevents us from supposing that the ever-good Chaillet put a little gentle malice into it.

According to Fr. Xavier Tilliette, who knew him very well, Fr. Paul Doncoeur "was by temperament a born leader, a trainer, an energetic professor. . . . In 1940, it was normal that he place his confidence and his hopes in the victor of Verdun. [But] nothing was more abhorrent to him than resignation and surrender. Perhaps he let himself be carried away for an instant by the heroic spectacle of nazi youth singing and surging into the June sun. . . . He encouraged everyone he could to hasten a moral renewal; he was in no way interested in politics." "He was an admirable writer; he could describe places and beings in an almost tangible way. . . . He translated and edited the *Spiritual Exercises* for Orante; his version, made from the Latin text, has not been surpassed. . . . [All his gifts] found a multiple use and a kind of synthesis in a devotion to Joan of Arc. He founded in her honor the *Cahiers Sainte Jehanne*"; he studied firsthand and edited the minutes of her process. "His veneration of the Maid was a kind of patriotic reflection of his devoted love for our Lady, *terribilis ut acies ordinata*. He wrote a little masterpiece, *La Vierge Marie dans notre vie d'hommes*. . . . He spent his last years at Troussures, venerated as a patriarch." See a more complete text in the *Cahiers Paul Doncoeur*, 1985.

Chapter 9

Relations with Bishops and Superiors

Les Cahiers du Témoignage chrétien were not the earliest of the clandestine publications inspired by the Christian faith during this time of the Occupation. Other, slighter papers had preceded them. As far as we know, the first pamphlet calling for resistance was written and distributed at Brive, even before the Armistice and appeal of June 18, by Edmond Michelet, in agreement with Fr. Maydieu, O.P., and under the inspiration of Péguy. In the name of their Catholic Faith and of love for their country, Robert d'Harcourt, Paul Petit and undoubtedly others, took similar initiatives—but their papers would be short lived. D'Harcourt would just barely escape the Gestapo; Michelet would be deported; Petit would be arrested February 7, 1942.

Close friends with Claudel and Massignon, Paul Petit distributed from the end of 1940 several clandestine writings that would later be gathered together under the title *Résistance spirituelle*. We had seen him for a few days in Lyons in 1941, at Fourvière and at the home of Paulus Lenz-Médoc. After his arrest, he was subjected to thirty months in a cell and was finally beheaded with an axe, on Hitler's orders, in Cologne, on August 22, 1944, the day of the liberation of Paris. During his trial, in October 1943, he had been able to declare to his judge that he loved Germany and the Germans, among whom he in fact counted many friends, such as Theresa Neumann and Gertrude von LeFort (he had translated her famous *Hymns to the Church*). He had been able to affirm that he had never written anything against the authorities of the Occupation, that in his clandestine "journal" he had condemned the assassination attempts against them and that he had done nothing except for "moral reasons".[1]

But the true older brother of the *Cahiers* was *La Voix du Vatican*. From the very first page of the first *Cahier*, this spiritual filiation was recognized, and in the pages that followed, Fr. Fessard continued to echo this voice. It had been at first a very unassuming, typed sheet, coming from the Jesuit college in Avignon and distributed to a few friends. The first one reproduced a broadcast from Vatican Radio, picked up on July 3, 1940.[2] Soon the paper was mimeographed, then, from October on, printed by a small press in Marseilles run by Jules-Xavier Perrin, who also became the principal distributor. It spread rather quickly, in various regions of the unoccupied zone, and its influence was not negligible. The French broadcasts from Vatican Radio, entrusted to a Belgian Jesuit, Fr. Mistiaen, were sending out texts and news that could not be found in our newspapers, and their tone was often very energetic. Despite pressure from Germany and the constantly renewed protests of its ambassador to the Secretary of State, Mistiaen was able to remain at his post during all those years of the Occupation. (There was only one period when it was wisely interrupted.) It was strongly supported by Leiber, a German Jesuit, secretary and good friend of the Pope, as well as by Fr. Wladimir Ledochowski, the Polish superior general of the Society. The Secretary of State, Cardinal Maglione, handed on the most characteristic passages of his broadcasts to Pius XII. In March 1943, a scrupulous censor, having

[1] Cf. *Paul Petit, 1893–1844* (Paris: Imprimerie du Compagnonnage, 1970), "La France continue" (13 numbers).

[2] Likewise in Paris, during 1941, several students brought together by Fr. Michel Riquet had "the letters from the bishops of Germany . . . and the broadcasts of the Vatican Radio directed against nazism" duplicated in order to spread them: M. Riquet, 67. In Avignon, Canon Louis Ruy (a close friend of Maurice Blondel), Fr. Jean Roche, Robert Maddalena, etc. In Marseilles, Fr. Perrin, O.P., and Fr. Eymonet, S.J.

wished to restrain Mistiaen, asked the latter to leave and return to England; but the Pope, advised of this, changed censors. It was truly the thinking of the Church at her center that *La Voix du Vatican*, as a faithful relay, transmitted from Marseilles.[3]

In their study entitled "La Voix du Vatican, 1940–1942, Batailles des ondes et résistance spirituelle" [The voice of the Vatican, 1940–1942, battles of the waves and spiritual resistance],[4] François and Renée Bédarida noted with respect to the English author Robert Speaight, who had devoted a pamphlet to the Vatican broadcasts, "the satisfaction of a Catholic in a Protestant country in being able to affirm, at least in the battle against nazism, that the Vatican was on the side of the Allies". Yet a certain French secularism, coming to the aid of campaigns led against the memory of Pius XII, for a long time looked with scorn upon this too-Catholic enterprise. The historians of the Resistance were most often unaware of it; it did not appear in any catalogue. Jacques Nobécourt has nevertheless shown that it is thanks to this publication that those in France, during the worst times, could know of Rome's radical opposition to the anti-Semitic theories of nazism and of Rome's relentless condemnation of the gods of race and blood.[5] François Delpech also recognized that "during the

[3] From the end of 1940 on, the adviser of the German ambassador came to protest up to two or three times a week. But Cardinal Maglione held firm. A fearful censor had wanted to have the final formula of the broadcasts suppressed: "Courage and confidence, God is watching over you!" but Maglione and Ledochowski would not give in. On March 12, 1941, Maglione wrote to the general that the Pope read "with true consolation" the testimony received from correspondents of the French Vatican Radio. Cf. Paul Duclos, *Le Vatican et la Seconde Guerre mondiale* (Pedone, 1955), 34–36.

[4] In the *Revue de l'histoire de l'Eglise de France*, 64 (July–December 1978), 224–25. Cf. 241. See also the further information provided by P. Blet, 65 (1979), 220.

[5] *"Le Vicaire" et l'Histoire* (Seuil, 1964), 211. Along with Vatican Radio, Nobécourt also cites *l'Osservatore Romano* and *Civiltà Cattolica*, which the Pope likewise controlled. These organs "created the climate in which

whole war, the teaching of the Popes inspired numerous Catholic writers", while adding: "The calling into question came later"[6]—but it is permissible to think that this "calling into question" could do nothing to change this fact. The words of Fr. Mistiaen contributed a considerable part to it.[7] They truly expressed the thinking of Pius XII and gave the whole of his texts, which otherwise reached France only in mutilated and falsified form due to the cuts made by the press. They were a light and a support for many, thanks to the courage and competence of those who, despite all the interference, succeeded in picking up La Voix du Vatican to spread it.[8]

One might say that the fundamental union of mind and soul between Mistiaen on the one hand and Fessard and Chaillet on the other was perfect. All three wanted above all to spread the thinking of the Pope. This was why, if the "Témoignage" [Witness] planned by Chaillet took, very happily and for quite good reasons, the name "Témoignage chrétien" [Christian witness], it was nonetheless a profoundly Catholic witness. In the radio message addressed to the world

---

pontifical texts, such as the Christmas message of 1941, took on very concrete meaning. The furor of the authorities of the Reich was enough to prove that they had understood them."

[6] Sur les Juifs, 295.

[7] Mistiaen's tone, from September 1942 on, also took on at times that of a homelist. So under the title: "Ne trahissons pas nos frères [Let us not betray our brothers]": "Our Lord Jesus Christ always showed an immense respect for each man in particular and for all men in general. He bent over the flocks that belonged to his dear people, to the people of his race, to all those of his race from whom has come the salvation of the world, to whom his mother, his friends, his apostles belonged. He did so with an infinite love for these Jewish people. . . . Those who refuse in their heart to recognize the dignity of all the children of God commit a sacrilege" (R. Bédarida, 224–25).

[8] La Voix du Vatican pointed out the passages of the Pope's speeches that the press suppressed, and in the following days, the announcer on Vatican Radio took them up again and commented on them. P. Duclos, 36. It quotes Péguy (entire poems) against a "diabolical propaganda". (Cf. Roger Voog, Colloque de Lyon, 137–48, additional information by Renée Bédarida, 155.)

on August 24, 1939, Pius XII had said: "Empires that are not founded on justice are not blessed by God. It is through force of reason and not through force of arms that justice is affirmed. A policy freed from morality betrays the very ones who want it." Everyone understood, observes Charles-Roux, that this referred to Hitler and his imitator, Mussolini.[9] It seems that one of the principal sources for the Pope's speeches during the war years and especially for his Christmas messages may well have been a Frenchman, Fr. Delos, O.P., author of the thesis *La Société internationale et les principes du droit* (1929), of ten masterful courses to the Semaines sociales de France and contributor along with Bishop de Solages and Fr. Fessard to the meetings of the Fribourg circle.[10] "The Vatican Radio", Bishop de Solages would say in 1942,[11] "has spoken a great deal since our disaster . . . , but those who manage to hear and listen to what it says are rare. The Pope's Christmas message of 1941 was to be rebroadcast, and at the end of a few sentences, the rebroadcast was stopped. . . . The voice of the Pope was muffled."[12] But the "modest Catholic bulletin" generally

---

[9] *Huit ans au Vatican*, 327.

[10] Cf. Joseph Robert, "Courants théologiques chez les dominicains", 1930–1939, *Colloque de Biviers*, 1984.

[11] Lecture at the cathedral of Montauban, May 14, 1942. In *Discours interdits* (Spes, 1945), 79–80, cf. below, Chap. 13.

[12] In his Christmas message of 1942, Pius XII would mention "those hundreds of thousands of persons who, by the sole fact of their nationality or their race, have been doomed to death by a progressive extinction". A little after the remarks by Bishop de Solages that I have just recalled, on June 29, 1941, the Pope was already mentioning as well "the unspeakable sufferings and persecutions which the very solicitude for those who are suffering does not allow us to reveal in all their distressing and moving detail". He would nevertheless mention once more, on June 2, 1943, in his speech to the cardinals, "the anxious supplications of all those who, because of their nationality or their race, are overwhelmed by the greatest trials and most acute distress, and at times even destined, without any personal fault, to measures of extermination". And in a secret letter to his confidant, Bishop von Preysing (the one among the German bishops with whom his correspondence was the most frequent), the letter of August 30, 1943, we can read: "We are leaving

scorned by historians transmitted that voice to some of the
faithful, and, even outside official texts, each of the broadcasts
that it recorded was, even more than one could at times recognize, in all truth *The Voice of the Vatican*.

In November 1941, the *Cahiers du Témoignage chrétien* was
going to take over, thanks to the collaboration between Fr.
Chaillet and Louis Cruvillier, to which I alluded above (Chapter 3). A former militant of the A.C.J.F., companion of St.
Francis, disseminator of *Temps nouveau*, a "born organizer",
Cruvillier dreamed of making a great clandestine periodical
out of *La Voix du Vatican*, which he was distributing. As soon
as he understood Fr. Chaillet's plan and measured its scope,
recognizing a mind and spirit in perfect fidelity to the Holy
See, he abandoned his own dream and gave himself over
entirely to it.[13]

---

to the pastors, according to each location, the care of evaluating if, and in
what measure, the danger of reprisals and pressure, as well as perhaps other
circumstances due to the length and the psychology of the war, warrant
restraint—despite the reasons for intervening—so as to avoid greater evils.
This is one of the reasons for which we ourselves are imposing limits in our
declarations. Our experience in 1942, in letting pontifical documents be reproduced freely for the use of the faithful, justifies our attitude, as far as we are
able to see."

A number of facts, known from texts published today, give the whole
reason behind these reflections of Pius XII. (See also, among others, his letter
to Cardinal Faulhaber, of January 31, 1943, in V. Conzemius, "Le Saint-Siège
et la Seconde Guerre mondiale", *Revue d'histoire de la Seconde Guerre mondiale . . . ,* 128 [October 1982], 84.)

[13] Cruvillier brought together the forces of "the 'patron', the theologian-
writers, the leaders in Lyons and also the printers" (R. Bédarida, 69). He
recruited the teams of distributors; he himself made the rounds of the bishops;
he discovered the traps, exposing himself, and was soon tracked down by
the police and finally forced to go over the Swiss border; it was then that he
obtained for us the support of Cardinal Tisserant (Rome) and of Abbé Journet
(Fribourg). See also M. Riquet, 80. On the true or supposed or distorted
activity of Cardinal Tisserant, then secretary of the congregation for the
Oriental Church, whom the nazis held to be one of the most dangerous men
in the Curia, see Xavier de Montclos, 109–118.

During the year 1942, my Provincial, Fr. du Bouchet, was able to see the wish he had addressed to me fully granted through the series *Cahiers du Témoignage chrétien*, which, from the beginning, gave most of its space to the fight against anti-Semitism. These clandestine *Cahiers* were not always, in the early months, very well received. But a certain distrust in the face of anonymous pamphlets coming from who knows where is understandable; in a confused situation, maneuvers of any kind were feared at first sight. But mistrust and misunderstanding were not always fundamental hostility, far from it, and in many cases they were not long in fading. The *Cahiers* had, in Rome itself and in the French episcopate, more actual sympathy than was at times supposed.

Yet the exceptional situation in which we found ourselves demanded a division of tasks. Even there where the best personal understanding reigned, the concern not to betray oneself demanded that this not be spelled out or even that it be completely silent, by mutual understanding. With respect to the founding of the *T.C.*, it has been written that "Cardinal Gerlier would never be officially told" about it; such an expression does not make much sense. Was it necessary to request a formal audience with him in order to draft an act of foundation, armed with his approval and certified by a notary, ready to be offered to police searches? "He only knew", it has even been added, "that the publication came from his diocese." That pays little respect to his perspicacity, when he was in constant and trusting relations with the principal person responsible. Was it necessary besides to give him, for no particular reason, the name and address of the printer? Under such circumstances, which recent historians (and not only foreign historians) have difficulty imagining, a confidence that remains general and barely whispered, a gesture half-made but clearly perceived—any more precise indication being avoided in order not to compromise anyone—could create an understanding as profound as any official notification whatever.

It has also been said (granting perhaps too much credit to

some witness who was at times too impassioned to be always entirely fair) that, knowing that the clandestine publication of the *T.C.* had its principal source in his diocese and even in his city, the Cardinal had had on occasion, "in private, some rather severe words for its authors". That is quite possible—although I never heard the least echo of it. It does happen that one argues incidentally with one's best working companions, especially when nerves are tense from the anxiety of danger. That did not keep the Cardinal from having the highest esteem for Fr. Chaillet, from considering him always as one of his best and most trusted advisers and from working very closely together with him on more than one occasion— even after those terrible years. If the founder of the *T.C.* had had his center, not in Lyons, but in Toulouse, and if it had been in Toulouse as well that he had worked at "l'Amitié chrétienne",[14] it is very probable that he would have at times been subjected to more rebuffs than he ever had to endure in Lyons. (It is no secret to anyone that the Archbishop of Toulouse and the rector of the Catholic Institute of that area were in admirable agreement on all essential positions and that there were nevertheless collisions between them.) One must accept only with great reservations certain complaints or reflections, at times given even by people of exceptional merit but whose judgments were not always very sure or by historians who were not always conversant with the facts.

When in 1941 Louis Cruvillier made his long journey across the southern zone in order to organize there the distribution network for the *T.C.*, he found the warmest reception from Cardinal Saliège; other bishops would also prove to be very favorable to this task, which Fr. Chaillet himself declared "audacious"; but their encouragement could not be shown in public. From the first *Cahier*, the *T.C.* was addressed to the apostolic nuncio as well as to a number of bishops. Clearly they could not reply to a dispatch lacking name and address:

[14] See below, Chap. 10.

it is impossible to draw any conclusion about their sentiments. Some were opposed, others simply timid. Those who were suspicious at first were rather quickly able to perceive the perfect Catholic loyalty of the *Cahiers*; several were happy that the *Cahiers* were able to serve as substitute for them, to make known frankly what they themselves were not able to cry from the rooftops. As the situation of the Vichy government evolved, a kind of tacit agreement between a part of the episcopate and the *Cahiers* grew closer.[15]

On the other hand, the Jesuit community at Fourvière, from which the *T.C.* did in fact start, was never the center of ferment that some accounts have described or let one believe. Right in the beginning, when the German army entered Lyons, many of us went on foot into the mountains of Ardêche to escape being taken prisoner. Soon, once the demarcation line was established, the life of the scholasticate took up its normal course again, and theological studies were pursued there as usual. The artificial euphoria of the national revolution fed the dreams of some; others thought that the necessities of the war would dissipate the virulence of nazism and that in any case its propaganda would hardly touch the mind of the French, even though from the autumn of 1940 on, the staff room offered several attractive publications to our eyes . . . which, however, soon took flight. Whether to avoid disputes or to guard against indiscretions, events were rarely discussed. When Fr. Chaillet arrived in our house at the end of December, he came quite simply to resume his courses, and he was very careful not to gather around him a group of sympathizers to talk with them about his progress and his plans. He did not transform our Jesuit house into a "citadel" or a "fortress", as it has sometimes been designated in metaphors that are too warlike. Only three or four were taken—more or less—into his confidence.

[15] At the same time as several bishops, fooled by the official propaganda, became more and more hostile.

As for our successive religious superiors, provincials and rectors, I can affirm, speaking only from my direct and personal experience, that their attitude, taking into account the differences of their temperaments, was the same that Fr. du Bouchet had shown toward me, which I described above: whether it was a question of Fr. Décisier, who was at first my Rector, then my Provincial, or of Fr. Charles Chamussy, who succeeded him as Rector at Fourvière. Both, moreover, willingly followed the advice of Fr. Fontoynont, who had great moral authority with them and who was completely behind the most uncompromising spiritual resistance.[16] To protect their communities, they had to be extremely prudent, to the point of not wanting to know anything that might compromise one of us if they were one day subjected to a police interrogation. The first of the two never questioned me about anything in detail: this was not only benevolence; it was wisdom. If, for example, I asked his permission to be away two or three days to go and see someone who needed me, that formula was enough for him, and he understood perfectly that it had to be enough. (Actually, it was to go and look for the manuscript of a *Cahier*, at the home of someone who had had to flee from his usual place of residence; for, except for the increasingly secret rendezvous with Fr. Chaillet, my task was to read through the manuscripts carefully in order to organize each *Cahier*, then, after having confided it to one of our young emissaries, to correct the proofs after they had been printed and returned to me.)[17] When I informed his successor, Fr. Chamussy, one day that I was going to be away for a while as an extra precaution, he did not ask me

[16] With respect to Fr. Chaillet, Renée Bédarida likewise says, 44: "His rector, Fr. Décisier, feigned ignorance, but in fact he encouraged him discreetly. Fr. Chaillet thus had complete latitude. He did not hold back." Chaillet's superiors, knowing his religious soundness and his exceptional qualities, placed great confidence in him.

[17] In the last year, this duty was only intermittent, a single emissary having been given the secret of my retreat.

the place of my refuge (it was at first at a rectory in a neigh-
boring diocese); but on his side, without telling me, he
watched over me through the intermediary of an employee
of the prefecture, who was in a good position to know the
lists of suspects and projects and the orders for arrest coming
from the Gestapo. It was thanks to him that, after a return
to Lyons, I was able to leave again in time, without even
passing through the house, thereby just barely escaping the
net that shortly after picked up M. Richard at the university
seminary in order to deport him.

It must be stressed: even if those who have written about
those tormented years have done so with a view untroubled
by some not quite extinguished passion, they have not always
taken into account the conditions in which the Church was
living at that time in France. It is not possible for them, in
fact, to rediscover the trace of all the bonds that were more
numerous than one might think between the various categories
of her members and that have not left any written attestation.
Silent understandings, secret conversations, confidential papers immediately destroyed: all that of necessity escapes their
investigations. It is also difficult to reconstruct completely the
distribution of roles, which, through friction and varied trial
and error, often ended in developing on its own. The rigid
distinction between an official Church and the underground
world of "Resistance workers" offers the historian a conven-
ient framework, but in many cases this does not correspond
to the much more complex and fluid reality. In principle, the
entire episcopate agreed to the texts from the double Assembly
(north and south) of cardinals and archbishops; the language
of these texts was often weakened by the twofold necessity
of obtaining a morally unanimous consent as well as not giving
rise to unjustified interpretations that would have ruined their
effect with the men in power. It could hardly have been otherwise. However, as J. M. Mayeur has observed, "a critical reading of the protest of the churches must not mask the major
fact: through the declarations they made and the positions

they took, the churches, acting as a substitute in a country deprived of political life and freedom, spoke, in the silence of the constituted bodies and social authorities. Public opinion at that time, in France and in the world, could not mistake it." [18] Some bishops were able to add their individual protests to these collective texts; others simply reproduced them, according to their means, using if necessary typewritten sheets, which could reach only a rather limited group of readers. Some both spoke and acted with tenacious energy, such as—to cite only one, but if space permitted, how many others should be cited—the bishop of Nice, Msgr. Rémond, to save the numerous refugee Jews within the territory of his diocese, when the Gestapo suddenly replaced a rather lackadaisical Italian police surveillance. Others, without making any grand declarations, acted with great courage, such as the Archbishop of Bourges, the future Cardinal Lefebvre. As Archbishop Guerry, who was at that time Archbishop Coadjutor of Cambrai and secretary of the A.C.A., also remarked with good reason, "The deeds and words that . . . affirmed the independence of the Church were not quoted anywhere, nor could they have been"; similarly, censorship prevented the publication of texts that called to mind "the doctrinal principles opposed to nazi doctrine", principles more than once enunciated, but "only in a few words, because any amplification was in advance doomed to suppression", even "in the general unity of Semaines religieuses". [19] In this regard, the *Cahiers du T.C.* contributed greatly to spreading a teaching that had thus been suppressed. But by and large, it can be said that they played a twofold role: first by stimulating (without slipping into criticism) the zeal of our pastors; then, more and more, by depending on them to speak with increased authority. There was thus something like a twofold osmosis.

From the summer of 1942 on, the bond between our pastors

---

[18] In *F.Q.J.*, 170.
[19] *L'Eglise catholique en France sous l'Occupation*, 339–40.

and the *T.C.* was often stronger. In fact, as Jacques Nobécourt has written,

> In the proclamation of doctrine, the multiplication of works of mutual aid, clarity of language, solidarity too in the face of attacks directed against the Jews and against the Catholic Church, from then on the French episcopate spared nothing. Their prudence was exercised with respect to the person of the head of state, the legitimacy of his government, but in spite of all the references to St. Thomas Aquinas,[20] the steadfastness of its defense of the French and foreign Jews was unquestionable.[21]

Archbishop Guerry again wrote:

> When one interprets a document of the hierarchy, equity demands that it not be compared to a document composed in hiding and under the protection of anonymity. On this subject, allow us to reject the error that consisted in setting the "religious" theologians in opposition to the bishops! The religious had their role, and how useful and beneficial it was: they forcefully affirmed, in secret documents that circulated beneath the veil of anonymity, truths that needed to be recalled. Among them, the theologians of the *Cahiers du Témoignage chrétien* rendered the Church an invaluable service: some of them were discovered and deported for having rendered, with noble courage, a splendid witness to the truth; some paid for their love of the truth with the sacrifice of their life. But however important their role may have been, and without accepting moreover all their positions, we cannot without injustice and without error misunderstand or fail to recognize the role that the pastors, at grips with the occupying authorities or in relation with the government, had to play in broad daylight, through public decisions that involved, along with themselves, the Church, their clergy and all their faithful people and risked at every instant provoking a religious persecution similar to that which so many other nations have known. This will be better

---

[20] An allusion to the Bérard report and to Vallat's theories.

[21] *"Le Vicaire" et l'Histoire*, 213. On the question of the government's legitimacy, cf. below, Chap. 13.

understood when we show how and why the interventions of the hierarchy were efficacious. The writings of theologians cannot replace the actions of the pastors.[22]

Despite the slightly apologetic and even somewhat critical tone of this page, and whatever may have been certain particular cases, it seems to me that it corresponds rather well, as we will see, to what the "theologians" in question whom I knew best thought about the two respective duties, which were not opposed but complementary and imposed by the circumstances.

[22] Op. cit., 344–45. With respect to Pius XII, many writers and journalists still repeat the gross errors that have been spread against him: they seem completely ignorant of the important scholarly publication of the *Acta Apostolicae Sedis*, which has revealed the actions of the Pope during the entire war. This was still noticeable later in the press campaign with respect to the visit of Kurt Waldheim to John Paul II.

The secret and daring activity that Pius XII deployed during the first months of 1940 could be known only gradually in the course of the period after the war. See the account that Xavier de Montclos has recently made of this, *Les chrétiens face au nazisme* . . . (Plon, 1983), 199–205. The Pope had agreed, at the risk of compromising himself, to place himself in direct contact with the German civil and military Resistance (at the highest level) in order to serve as its support before the London war cabinet, and this on two occasions. The attack of the Wehrmacht on May 10 in the east abruptly put an end to the arranged plan, which had been going well.

Pierre Fernessole, *Pie XII et la paix du monde* (Beauchesne, 1947), 74–99, had already drawn up a long list of actions and words by the Pope with respect to nazism.

Chapter 10

The Spirit of
the *Cahiers du Témoignage chrétien*

Fr. Chaillet never intended to trade his profession as a theologian for a profession as editor of clandestine publications. If he came to found the *Cahiers du Témoignage chrétien*, it was due to the urgency of a situation that threatened Christian souls, confronted with the most pressing demands of their Faith. More generally, it was to raise the cry that served as Fr. Fessard's title for the first *Cahier: France, prends garde de perdre ton âme!* [France, take care not to lose your soul!] But even before the war, from the autumn of 1938 on, during his first years of teaching theology at Fourvière, he had begun to organize assistance in the Lyons region for those who had fled Hitler's Germany, first of all by filling the post of secretary for a "Comité de secours aux chrétiens réfugiés" [Council of assistance for refugee Christians], for which Cardinal Gerlier was honorary president and Pastor de Pury, vice-president. This council was soon doubled in size in order to meet the immense needs (the influx of Jews expelled into France after the German victory had increased so much) by a "council of assistance for emigrés". Its center was in Lyons, 26 rue Victor-Hugo; a "juridical counsel" (to which Dean Garraud, from the law faculty in Lyons devoted himself), a "work and housing" committee and a "clothing" committee were in operation there. It was a work of mercy, in the service of physical needs; from 1941 on, the *Cahiers* were in a parallel way a work of mercy, in the service of souls. As Jean-Marie Soutou has well shown, the two works were not only parallel, they were organically linked, complementary, indissociable.

On the other hand, an interconfessional work of the same kind owed its origin to the joint initiative of Gilbert Beaujolin, Protestant, and Olivier de Pierrebourg, of Catholic origin. Under the name of l'Amitié chrétienne [Christian friendship], it had succeeded in federating in some way various groups that had been set up by Protestants,[1] Catholics and Jews, all with a similar goal. I never knew the details of exactly how this fusion took place. In any case, l'Amitié chrétienne received earnest support when Fr. Chaillet returned to Lyons in December 1940. The primary, official goal recognized by this convergence of efforts was essentially to come to the aid through legal means of foreigners in distress—most often these were Jews—dispersed throughout the country or concentrated in camps. But, "with the progressive intensification of emergency regulations" aimed at the French Jews themselves, and the more the police forces of the occupying authorities penetrated into the so-called unoccupied zone, l'Amitié chrétienne also became increasingly a screen for an important clandestine service for the persecuted, and soon its ramifications stretched across all of southern France. It was publicly sponsored by Cardinal Gerlier, Pastor Boegner and the Jewish consistory. After *Temps nouveau* had been suppressed by Admiral Darlan, it had installed its "general quarters" in the old offices of the weekly, on rue Constantine, in the Terreaux district. Along with Fr. Chaillet, the central team consisted of Abbé Alexandre Glasberg, Jean-Marie Soutou, Joseph Rovan, Germaine Ribière and André Weil; it worked in liaison with many others, notably Fr. Braun, S.J. I will have more to say later about Germaine Ribière, national director of the Jeunesse Etudiante Catholique Français (J.E.C.F.), who had remained

---

[1] What precise connections the principal Protestant association, "the Cimade", had with the others, I am unable to say. On the dedication of the Cimade in the camps: Madeleine Barot, *Colloque de Lyon*, 295–303.

in Paris up until about the end of 1940. Abbé Glasberg belonged to a Ukrainian family; after becoming a priest, he came to complete his theology studies at our Lyons faculty, where I had him as a student, and he was curate for the Saint-Alban parish, whose pastor was Abbé Remillieux. Through his inventive charity, his organizational gifts, his stamina and an unparalleled courage, he worked miracles.[2]

In the autumn of 1942, Glasberg, condemned to death in his absence, had to flee far from Lyons. Chaillet already had to wander from shelter to shelter, keeping secret rendezvous with one here, another there. With Germaine Ribière and Jean Rovan on site, l'Amitié pursued its task.[3] But in November came the invasion of the southern zone (I can still hear the sound of the tanks rolling over the banks of the Saône while we were celebrating the annual opening of the Catholic faculties at the church of Ainay). As early as the following January 17, Gestapo agents "went to swoop down on l'Amitié chrétienne, to arrest its directors, to close its premises". Fr. Chaillet, having arrived at the fatal moment, was among those caught.[4]

---

[2] Jean-Marie Soutou sketched a portrait of Abbé Glasberg soon after his death (1983), March 22. He recalled Glasberg's unflagging and very ingenious dedication in helping the refugees, stateless people, any people who were "excluded", for thirty-five years, his combination of gentleness with a tumultuous temperament. See also Anny Latour, *La Résistance juive en France* (Stock, 1970), 52–53. I have not been able to read Nina Gourfinkel, *Aux prises avec mon temps*, vol. 2, *L'Autre Patrie* (Seuil, 1953) (a "romanticized account": R. Bédarida), in which Glasberg is described by the name "Père Elie".

[3] On l'Amitié chrétienne: R. Bédarida, 128–33ff. J. M. Soutou, in *F.Q.J.*, 249–53. F. Delpech, *Colloque de Grenoble*, 162–64 and *Sur les Juifs*, 203–9, 231–32. M. Riquet, 79. If the times had permitted, it could have been called l'Amitié judéo-chrétienne, and in fact it was one of the origins of that association. (See also Jean Toulat, *Juifs mes frères* [Fayard, 1968], 139–40, 153, 242–43.)

[4] On the activity of l'Amitié chrétienne in Lyons during the summer of 1942, cf. below, Chap. 11. On these different events: R. Bédarida, 133–37. Chaillet's main refuge at this time was in Savoy.

In a still unpublished speech at the annual conference of the Alliance israélite universelle, on June 25, 1979, Jean-Marie Soutou recalled this day of anguish:

> During the arrest of the directors, all were anxious to know whether the Gestapo was about to have at their disposal evidence concerning, not the humanitarian action of l'Amitié, but the clandestine and Resistance activity of the *Cahiers* (*du T.C.*) and other movements in which the members of l'Amitié chrétienne were lively collaborators.
>
> The catastrophe was just barely avoided thanks to Fr. Chaillet and Joseph Rovan.
>
> The former, in the room where Klaus Barbie had had the whole team confined before the interrogation, managed to chew and swallow all the gravely compromising documents that he was carrying under his soutane. He was facing the wall, his rather massive neck betrayed the movements of his jaw, and they feared at every moment that the guard would notice it. Nothing came of it.[5]
>
> The second, Joseph Rovan, defying the curfew, at the peril of his life, succeeded in getting into the premises of l'Amitié chrétienne during the night and in retrieving the false identity cards and other documents that would have allowed them to establish the close relationship that existed between l'Amitié chrétienne and the Resistance movements. In the morning, the curfew lifted, he was able to transport everything to a safe place.[6] He was

[5] The "they" was first of all Soutou himself (who would be detained for three weeks at Fort Montluc). The whole group was transported from rue Constantine to the Terminus de Perrache Hotel, the general quarters of the Gestapo. Not even suspecting any personal connection between this priest who had come to ask for a few blankets for a charitable cause and either of the two people responsible for the underground Amitié and *Cahiers*, they released Chaillet in the afternoon, "with hard slaps in the face and kicks". He came by to tell me of his adventure at Fourvière, after having gone to the archbishop's offices.

[6] Shortly after the Rovan exploit, the Gestapo installed itself on rue Constantine. It was the day it was open to the public, and Jews coming to seek papers there were going to fall into the trap. Ingenious and prompt, Germaine

later to be deported to Dachau, where he was the incomparable companion of Edmond Michelet.[7]

Just as with l'Amitié chrétienne, it was in a general way in full agreement with the ecclesiastical and religious superiors to whom we were responsible that Fr. Chaillet and his confreres pursued the enterprise of the *Cahiers du T.C.* While each of the collaborators might have his particular points of view, the spirit of the *Cahiers*, like that of l'Amitié, was always that manifested in the fight initiated by Fr. Fessard against anti-Semitism. Priests and laymen, Catholics and Protestants, carried on this fight, particularly in the following *Cahiers: Notre combat* [Our battle]; *Les Racistes peints par eux-mêmes* [Racists as described by themselves]; *Antisémites* [Anti-Semites]; *Droits de l'homme et du chrétien* [Rights of man and of the Christian]; *Collaboration et Fidélité* [Collaboration and fidelity]; *Les voiles se déchirent* [The veils are torn]; *Puissance des ténèbres* [Power of darkness]. (The first in the list was from December 1941, the last, from May 1944.) All one has to do is glance through these *Cahiers* to see that they quote above all texts emanating from the Catholic hierarchy (one of the *Cahiers*, entitled *Défi, l'ordre nouveau en Pologne* [Challenge, the new order in Poland], was entirely written by Cardinal Hlond) as well as from the Protestant churches, and that they never held to any other line but that of entire fidelity to the Christian faith and its demands.

They were not a political enterprise. To be more precise about their spirit, I would first of all borrow a page from *Cahier* 10–11, *Collaboration et Fidélité*, which was printed and distributed in November 1942:

Ribière disguised herself as a cleaning woman and, "armed with a scrubbing rag, began to wash the stairs of the building for hours: she was thereby able to warn visitors before the fatal moment". Cf. R. Bédarida, 135–37.

[7] Cf. Joseph Rovan, *Contes de Dachau* (Julliard, 1987).

The *Cahiers* give witness for those Christians who are fully conscious of their present responsibilities; who, caught up in the tragedy of their times, perceive the immense danger of seeing stifled that Christian spirit which formed them, of seeing enchained that Christian freedom of spirit without which no power will be able to save the soul of France—or even its body. The danger of the progressive magic appeal achieved through nazi propaganda, which finds too many conscious or unconscious servants among us. The danger of daily lies and camouflages from the press, radio and cinema. The danger of silences imposed by a censorship dominated by the occupying or controlling power. Perhaps it will be said that the nazi error is not the only one and that there are other dangers. We do not argue with this. But the freedom of word and pen to denounce these other dangers remains intact. There are even many ways of combating them that only make them worse. Our *Cahiers* bear their witness where no voice can make itself heard publicly, where temptation is the most immediate or most all-embracing. —They keep strictly to the Christian level. They do not give any "political" orders, because it is not at all their business and because Christian fidelity, alone and directly, is not enough to determine political options. If, in the present state of confusion of minds and distress of consciences, faced with the spinelessness of too great a number from whom one would expect more dignity, they feel united to all those who are not resigned to letting France be debased, it is because patriotism is a virtue; it is because Christian fidelity and national honor are intimately connected. But the *Cahiers* are not for all that departing from the only field that is theirs. We affirm—and no one can seriously deny it—that any economic or political "collaboration" with the nazi power, in circumstances where collaboration signifies subjection, carries with it a closely related danger of subjection in the realm of culture. Now nazi "culture" is fundamentally anti-Christian, and neither the repeated declarations of the nazi leaders nor their renewed actions are in the least reassuring. We therefore want to show all Christians and also all those who, without being believers, are attached more than they think to the principles of a Christian civilization that, *on this level of the spirit*, the duty is to oppose and to organize resistance to nazism.

The more strongly nazism brings its domination to bear over France, the more important it will be that this spiritual resistance become lucid and firm. We are simple Christians. We do not speak in the name of any authority. We are seeking honestly to inform consciences. We are reporting verified facts and authentic documents. We are recalling doctrinal directives that have come from the leaders of the Church. Doing so, we are fulfilling the duty that any believer, engaged in temporal life, has to bear witness to his Faith, to protect it from corruption, to defend it when it is threatened. It would be a great error, the fruit of great cowardice, to put off doing so under any circumstances until one had received an official mission. The *Cahiers du Témoignage chrétien* are the testimony of numerous and varied Christians who, without ulterior political motives and without claiming in any way to involve the hierarchy, are deeply committed as Christians.[8]

As we know, the *Courrier français du Témoignage chrétien* was founded in 1943, not to replace the *Cahiers* but to join them so as to find "a greater echo within the majority of people in France". The young people, both workers and students, very especially needed clarity of vision in the numerous practical problems posed by "collaboration", the S.T.O., the "battle against communism", the appeal to violence, terrorism, life in the "underground", preparation for liberation and for their future. Some were afraid at the time that the *Courrier* might have difficulty keeping to the pure line of the *Cahiers*. Some of us were worried that it might lapse into a certain secularism, letting itself be led to give ill-founded advice, to follow debatable trends.[9] Nothing of the sort. From its first editorials,

---

[8] *Témoignage chrétien, Cahiers et Courriers*, complete reprint in facsimile (Paris, 1980), 1:186–87.

[9] Cf. Renée Bédarida, *Les Armes de l'esprit* (Editions ouvrières, 1977), 214–17, who perhaps exaggerates a little the liveliness of the "discussions and confrontations". Under the influence of Mandouze, a new arrival in the group, and of Marcel Vanhove, a militant C.F.T.C. (Confédération Française des Travailleurs Chrétiens), and contrary to the opinion of Germaine Ribière

the *Courrier* clearly declared that its spirit would be the same as that of the *Cahiers*, "a spirit of French and Christian fidelity", fighting against nazism in the name of "that which Christians must defend to the death, their credo".[10] It was well able to maintain this line. I will quote two excerpts, drawn from numbers 3 and 4, which give several explanations judged at that time to be necessary:

> [*Courrier du Témoignage chrétien*, no. 3, 1943] No one will be surprised that, in a country that numbers more than eighty dioceses, some differences occur. Despite a few discordant voices, we continue to think that the letter of the cardinals and archbishops in February and the declaration of the cardinals in May constitute in an unparalleled way the most authoritative and trustworthy documents and express the moral unanimity of the episcopate. . . .
>
> In this respect, it would be good to recall a few elementary truths, which some seem to forget today even though they are a part of the current teaching of the Catholic Church.
>
> Recognition of a power is one thing; obedience to all the measures decreed by that power is another. In other words, one should not confuse the regime with its legislation. The Church of France has protested against many of the laws of the Third Republic without revolting against it. Anyone who today would consider the government of Vichy to be absolutely legitimate, without any distinction (anyone blind enough to believe it to be fully sovereign), would not be right to conclude that he owed it obedience in everything, without question. Such an abdication of conscience will never be approved by the Catholic Church. . . . Anyone who gives an unconditional oath to a

---

and several others, a certain autonomy tended to assert itself for the *Courriers* in order to "orient the journal toward temporal forms of engagement in the service of social justice and human dignity". The *T.C.* nevertheless remained from beginning to end without a single note that could have made the Church disavow it. But there was not at that time any rupture in the group of directors. "Despite a certain more or less perceptible reluctance, Fr. Chaillet ended in approving this important turning point."

[10] *Cahiers et Courriers*, 209 and 217.

man or a regime and who thereby binds himself in advance to
believe that he would not have the right to regain his freedom
under any circumstances, such a man is mistaken and abdicates
his dignity as a man. An oath only adds a more sacred bond
to a duty; it can never create an obligation in opposition to that
duty. The application of the principles we have just recalled is
certainly delicate, and it demands prudence: these principles are
nonetheless unquestionable, they are nonetheless particularly
necessary to recall today and, as long as Christianity lives, they
will never allow themselves to be barred by statute.

Complaints have been raised on many sides against "anonymous", "noncommissioned" theologians who have given suspect advice. Obviously we cannot defend texts with which we
are not familiar. But if this refers at times, as all would have
us believe, to well-known texts that we have quoted, the names
of their authors are perfectly well known by their ordinaries,
and it is only with a play on words that one can speak of
anonymity in their regard. As if, under the reign of terror in
which we are living, with the Gestapo at all our doors, those
who recall the truth could display their names as do those who
flatter the powers of the day! . . . Careful observers are not
fooled. The Church of France, in union with the universal
Church, with all her soul rejects Hitlerism, with its cruelty, its
tyranny and its lies. The French clergy is in profound sympathy
with the people of France. It suffers with them; it hopes with
them. Through an ever-growing number of its members, it is
in the first ranks of those who are fighting against injustice and
who are actively devoting themselves to their hunted brethren.[11]

[11] Ibid., 223–90. Several bishops had been disturbed at seeing "theological
advice" increase. Two such pieces, which M. Luirard cites in *Cahiers d'histoire*,
vol. 14:2 (1969), 198–99, did not come, as far as I know, from the quarters
of the *T.C.* and were not spread by it. One is entitled "Consultation donnée
par un groupe de juristes et de théologiens; notes sur quelques observations
techniques concernant le problème du gouvernement" [Advice given by a
group of lawyers and theologians; notes on a few technical observations
concerning the problem of government]; another (or perhaps it was another
part of the same piece) was based on the well-known work by Abbé Jacques
Leclercq: *Leçons de droit naturel, l'Etat et la politique* (Spes, 1960); besides, what

[*Courrier* . . . , no. 4, 1943] The Church usually acts quietly. She does not like aggressive manifestations. She does not anticipate the hour of the "non-possumus". She detests polemics. She fears that her declarations might be exploited for means other than her own. She tolerates everything that can be tolerated. She binds herself to long-standing patience. As a constituted organism, she practices a loyalty that goes well beyond what is imposed on simple citizens. Until she has evidence of the contrary, she hopes for some ground of understanding. She encourages as far as possible the desire for reconciliation. But when it comes down to what is essential for her to say and do in order to prevent her mission from being betrayed, one can be sure that this will be said, this will be done.

The tragic events that have been transpiring in France over the past three years have shown this to us once more. The Church has not remained indifferent in the face of measures of persecution taken against the Jews or in the face of the progressive invasion of the Hitlerian poison into French souls or in the face of the forced requisitions and deportations. The texts that our *Cahiers* have published have repeatedly attested to this. Particularly on the subject of deportations, in the most restrained terms, the judgment has been pronounced: they are contrary to the law; they are unjust; no one is bound by conscience to submit to them. Many things can be added to this minimum judgment: one cannot refuse to understand it. One cannot pretend that it has not been pronounced.[12]

M. Luirard quotes does not seem to me to represent anything heterodox. Still others circulated. Cf. above, Chap. 9, n. 15.

[12] *Cahiers et Courriers*, 236. We note two essential themes on which *Cahiers* and *Courriers* together insisted in opposition to the writings of communist obedience or inspiration. First: "Pour le maquis contre le terrorisme" [For the underground against terrorism], an article from the *Courrier*, no. 10 (which would be reproduced in *La Gazette de Lausanne* in July 1944); second: "We will not overcome him [Hitler] if we effect only a reversal of forces without overcoming within ourselves the spirit of hate, the spirit of vengeance and everything that resembles them" (*Courrier*, no. 9 [Christmas 1943]). But the growing autonomy of the *Courrier* was to set the stage for conflicts, which Fr. Chaillet had to suffer until after the Liberation. But that was no longer the clandestine *T.C.* (see Epiloque).

When all is said and done, I had only a little firsthand knowledge about the enterprise of the *Cahiers* and the *Courrier*—and about the participants (compartmentalization was the obligatory law)—and I must restrict myself to a few personal memories. So let me simply call to mind here a few names—first of all, those of two senior men, who, each in his "zone", helped us with their advice: in Paris, Fr. Jules Lebreton[13] and, in Lyons, Fr. Victor Fontoynont, about whom I have said a few words above. In December 1941, *Cahier* 4 of *Rencontres*,[14] on "the Christian meaning of history", published his brief article "The Destiny of the Jewish People", according to chapter 11 of the Epistle to the Romans; he concluded with these words from St. Bernard: "If you molest them, you risk wounding the Lord in what he holds most precious!" From the first day, Fr. Chaillet had found in him the firmest moral support, and in both of them prevailed the concern to focus the effort of the *Cahiers* on the battle against anti-Semitic racism. Fr. Fontoynont was also the guide and confidant of Germaine Ribière, disciple of Fr. de Montcheuil, who had become a "Resistance" worker because she knew what the nazi action would be with regard to the Jews. He called her "Joan of Arc". For the four following years, with a courage equal to her skill, she carried out many a rescue, silent, ever present, gifted with an extraordinary flair that allowed her more than once to help l'Amitié as well as the *T.C.* to escape catastrophes, to save numerous human lives— and always maintaining in her refusal to compromise the purity of the Christian ideal that she had learned from Fr. de

[13] M. Luirard, 208, quotes this passage from the Lebreton consultation: "The German authorities expect much more from us than fidelity to the terms of the Armistice; they expect a collaboration that would demand from us an alliance and, in the future, an assimilation of their moral and political concepts that would grow deeper every day. The government does not have the right to let itself be led into a collaboration that would bring indispensable help to the triumph of an unjust cause." See below, Chap. 13.

[14] *Rencontres*, December 1941, 105–12.

Montcheuil. Among my confreres who greatly contributed to the distribution of the *Cahiers* in one zone or the other, I would cite Fr. Pierre Ganne (who was also a writer, as well as Joseph Hours), Frs. Robert Hamel, Henri Chambre, M. A. Dieuzaide, Gonzague Pierre, Jean Minéry, Jacques Sommet (there were also many others), adding the names of some priest friends, Edouard Duperray (then curate at Lyons), Henry Jenny (future archbishop of Cambrai), J. M. Chalamet, M. Sanial (archpriest of Tournon), who each distributed four hundred *Cahiers* and a thousand *Courriers* and provided me for several days with an invaluable refuge, and so on, and two (among still others) who were victims of their dedication: Robert Ploton and François Boursier (the latter tortured to death in the frightful carnage of Saint-Genis-Laval in 1944). Finally, among those with whom I was most closely associated in Lyons: Louis Cruvillier, Adrien Nemoz, Robert Maddalena, Alphonse Drogou, the three Miguet brothers—and Fernand Belot, who had made in advance, very explicitly, the sacrifice of his life.

As all the preceding shows, the enterprise of the *Cahiers* was conceived and conducted—under unprecedented forms imposed by a situation that was itself unprecedented—in a way completely in conformity with religious obedience as with fidelity to the hierarchy of the Church. Obedience and fidelity have never meant the denial of all initiative or a fear of any responsibility. Besides, the essential idea of these *Cahiers* was always to spread an awareness of the acts coming from the authority of the Church, most especially from the papacy, from various episcopates, from the Holy Office—to say nothing, for example, of *La Voix du Vatican*.[15] This could be done

[15] The same spirit guided, among others, Fr. Michel Riquet, when he asked Fr. Maydieu, O.P., to gather together the passages selected from radio-broadcast speeches by Pius XII into a pamphlet, which was secretly distributed by one of the groups that also distributed the *T.C.* Cf. M. Riquet (1972), 64–66 and 79–80. R. Bédarida, 203–5 (on Robert d'Harcourt).

in full unity with similar testimonies coming from Protestant churches, without ever having to sidestep an issue, on that ground, in view of false agreements. And the total religious independence, desired from the first by Fr. Chaillet, was, despite several solicitations and offers of support, maintained until the end.

"These 'free-lance' Resistance workers always behaved like sons of the Church."[16] It was "the power of these 'noncommissioned' Christians not to be alone in their combat, for this took place in permanent reference to the Church".[17]

Besides, the *Témoignage chrétien* founded by Fr. Chaillet never claimed to have a monopoly on spiritual resistance. "From the beginning," André Latreille has written quite accurately, "a significant proportion of Catholics" had taken the same position.

> Remembering the teaching of Pius XI against totalitarianism and fearing the insidious contamination of the nazi leprosy for the French soul, finding again in the words of Pius XII everything that would extend that teaching and form the legitimate basis for spiritual resistance, not feeling bound by any diplomatic behavior on the part of the Holy See that would imply in any way an approval of the regime's principles, these Catholics participated in movements aimed at liberation not only of their country but of humanity itself. . . . Some [among them] were

---

[16] Renée Bédarida, foreword to the reprint of the *Cahiers* (1980), 15. This expression "free-lance" does not imply any assimilation with the groups of F.T.P. (Francs-Tireurs Partisans).

[17] F. Delpech, in *F.Q.J.*, 220. From Switzerland, Louis Cruvillier had several *Cahiers* sent to Cardinal Tisserant, with whom Count de Leusse had put him in touch; these were in turn handed over to Cardinal Maglione and to Pius XII. Tisserant would distribute them through copies or through summaries. He would send Cruvillier words of encouragement, which the *Courrier* would publish under the signature "a Roman friend". Beginning on October 9, 1943, Cruvillier would write in Switzerland a Christian bulletin of information, from which the *Cahiers* and the *Courrier*, thanks to a secret network, would produce news. His activities, known or suspected, would earn him a few difficulties with the Swiss police.

monarchists and committed conservatives. From Lieutenant
Estienne d'Orves, shot in 1941, to Gilbert Dru, massacred in
Lyons on July 27, 1944, Catholics were constantly represented
in the French Resistance, and often they were even its leaders.

What Latreille remarks more particularly in the *Cahiers du
T.C.* was that they vigorously formulated "the doctrinal
foundations of their attitude", and that they were very open
to the outside, with their numerous references to other Catholic countries suffering under nazi oppression, their special
investigations about Alsace-Lorraine and Poland, and so on.[18]
Let us add that the *Témoignage chrétien* always maintained
its independence with regard to London,[19] as well as its specifi-
city in relation to other Resistance movements. The position
that the first number of the *Courrier* insisted on calling to mind
in June 1943 remained its position to the end: "We are and
we remain totally independent from any political movement,
whatever it might be." When invited to become a part of a
"United Front of Resistance", it was necessary to explain once
again: "Insofar as we are Christians, our message transcends
that of patriotic Resistance movements and is directly opposed
to nazism as a doctrine. The movement of the *Témoignage*

---

[18] André Latreille, *La Seconde Guerre mondiale* (Hachette, 1966), 235.

[19] As we know, "General de Gaulle had very quickly determined as an
objective the organization and unification under his authority of the entire
Resistance in France and in the empire. A whole series of emissaries had
come from London to enter into liaison with the movements" (A. Latreille,
237). For my part, I explained to a brother of General de Gaulle who had
come to pay me a visit at Fourvière that, whatever might be my esteem for
the General and my sympathy for a "free France", I could not enter into any
bond with it, having placed myself, in conformity with my vocation, on the
level of a spiritual resistance to nazism. He seemed, moreover, to understand
me very well. Later, an English parachutist came to offer me a sum of which
Fr. Chaillet might have need; I refused, explaining (very briefly) why. Perhaps
(though I do not believe so) this was an agent provocateur, as I happened to
receive others—so easily spotted that they seemed to me to be dead give-
aways.

chrétien absolutely cannot be placed on the same level with other resistance organizations."[20]

When, in 1947, I came to Berlin—which, except for a few quarters on the periphery, was nothing but an immense field of ruins—and was received on Saturday, August 30, by Bishop von Preysing, the confidant of Pius XII, who had not ceased to encourage him in his firm resistance, we embraced each other with emotion. "From our two sides," he said to me, "*we led the same fight.*" Against the same adversary, with the same spiritual weapons. One of our *Cahiers* had quoted this declaration by the Bishop of Berlin:

> No doubt is permitted us: we are Christians, engaged in a hard battle. Against us stands the religion of blood. Everywhere, from the scornful rejections of the doctrine of Christ to the passionate and open hatred, everywhere signs of the struggle break forth. A fire rolling with affirmations borrowed either from history or the present sweeps over us. The end purpose of the battle is clear: it is the suppression and expulsion of Christianity. A clamor of joyous victory is being raised from the ranks of anti-Christianity.

Now, the adversary seemed destroyed. But it always returns, in other forms. The struggle must always be resumed, with the same weapons, outside of us and within us.[21]

---

[20] *Courrier* of the *T.C.*, no. 2 (1943). The same article went on to say that if a Christian took part in a Resistance movement, "he must always be inspired by the demands of his Faith". Cf., in *Antisémites*, April–May 1942 (reprint, 119): "If we do not have the authority to speak in the name of our churches, . . . we know at least that *our personal witness* as Christians is a faithful echo of the judgment of our hierarchical leaders about anti-Semitism, that it responds to the unequivocal demands of Christianity and to the integrity of the message of Jesus Christ." When that was written, Fr. Chaillet knew very well that (in addition to official episcopal texts) he had the friendly support of Cardinal Gerlier.

[21] On the history of the *Témoignage chrétien*, cf. Renée Bédarida: *Les Armes de l'Esprit, Témoignage chrétien* (1941–1944), with the collaboration of François Bédarida (Editions ouvrières, 1977).

Témoignage chrétien, 1941–1944, *Cahiers et Courriers*, entire reprint in facsimile (Paris, 1980). Two volumes. (Work published by subscription by Renée Bédarida and Adrien Némoz, in an edition of two thousand copies.)

Chapter 11

The Roundups of the Summer of 1942:
The Lyons-Toulouse Connection

We know what an atrocity the summer of 1942 was for refugee
Jews in France, whether interned or not. I will make hardly
more than an allusion to it simply in order to situate a personal
event—a minor event, which had scarcely any consequences
and of which no written trace has been left. However, it
reflects a certain climate at that time, and it seems to me to
be the sign of an understanding that was closer than ordinarily
believed, both between the activity of the Lyons group of
l'Amitié chrétienne and the *Cahiers* and that of its archbishop,
and between the two leaders of the Toulouse and Lyons dioceses, particularly with respect to the Jews.

In Paris, the great roundups had begun on July 16 and 17.
On July 22, the cardinals and archbishops of the northern
zone, in an emergency gathering, drafted on site, without
waiting for a text to be proposed in advance for their consideration, a protest of about a dozen lines. "Deeply disturbed,"
they wrote, "we cannot stifle the cry of our conscience. It is
in the name of humanity and of Christian principles that our
voice is raised in a protest for the indefeasible rights of the
human conscience", and they addressed to Marshal Pétain
their "anguished appeal" that "the demands of justice and the
laws of charity might be respected". The text was delivered
immediately to Pétain by Bishop Chappoulie, secretary of the
A.C.A., and each bishop received the charge of communicating it to his clergy. The nuncio at Vichy, Bishop Valerio
Valeri, judged it at first to be a little weak ("*piuttosto platonica*"),

but it was followed by a discussion, in Paris itself, by Cardinal Suhard with Laval.[1]

It was on August 2 that the operations began in the unoccupied zone. The first batch of Jews packed into the camps of the southwest was loaded onto trains by the French police to be delivered to the Germans. The first public episcopal protest, on August 23, was that of Cardinal Saliège, in the diocese from which this first delivery had been effected.

From the time Hitler first rose to power, the Cardinal Archbishop of Toulouse had proved clairvoyant. On April 12, 1933, at the capital, he had declared:

> If I have agreed without hesitation to speak at this time, before this moving assembly, in this place where I do not usually appear, it is because it seemed to me that I have a duty to fulfill, the duty of bringing my profound sympathy to all those who suffer, and whose suffering makes them in my eyes sacred beings. Persecution awakens deep within our human souls that instinct of fraternity that Christianity has placed there like a seed always ready to flower and never weary of bearing fruit. "Who suffers but that I suffer with him?" In those words, Paul of Tarsus expressed not only his great heart but also the purest spirit of the Gospel. And through conviction, I am, I cannot fail to be, of that same spirit. Through conviction also, through my living Faith, which is that of the Church, I am an unaccustomed being who does not, who cannot take part in injury, in the injustice that is affecting his fellowmen, whatever be his religion, whatever be his race. Not only do I feel struck by the blows that are falling on the persecuted, but my shudders are all the more grievous as I find misunderstood and ridiculed, not some confused ideal, some cold and abstract idea (I would

---

[1] *Actes* . . . , 8:610 and 621. J. M. Mayeur, *F.Q.J.*, 157. Text of "Adresse à M. le maréchal Pétain" in P. Bourdrel, 599. "This letter is rather brief . . . , it is very clear, very frank; it is courageous, but it was not published, although they had asked it to be circulated. . . . I do not have to consider the reasons why this letter was not published . . . , it was obviously a question of prudence": F. Delpech, *Sur les juifs*, 299.

be lacking in the sincerity and respect I owe you if I did not reveal the whole of my thought to you), but that living, personal Being whose breath has crossed and carried the whole history of Israel, Yahweh, he whom I call "the Good God", the Just One par excellence, whose action never ceases to manifest itself through this irrepressible aspiration for the kingdom of justice which, like the firmament or the waves of the sea, shapes and raises humanity.

The Israelites will understand me, and others too. I could not forget that the staff of Jesse has flowered in Israel and has given there its fruit. The Virgin, Christ, the first disciples were of the Jewish race. How could I not feel bound to Israel like a branch to the trunk that has borne it!

Moreover, I recognize only one morality, one that is universal, and in every man I see I respect the eminent dignity of human nature. Catholicism cannot agree that belonging to a specific race places men in a position of inferior rights. It proclaims the essential equality of all races and all individuals. Any difference in the scale of human values based on the sole principle of blood, or race, is unknown in a universal religion like Catholicism. "He is of another race; I am permitted anything against him": we condemn this principle of violence, of injustice, this morality of sovereign force, destructive of the rights and duties of the human person. . . . And now, to sum up my deepest thought, I take the words of a great Jew who became a great Christian: "There is among you now neither pagan nor Jew, neither Scythian nor barbarian; all are but one in Jesus Christ". [2]

In his pastoral letter for Lent in 1939, the Archbishop had again denounced "the new heresy of nazism, which shatters human unity and places a superhuman value in what it considers to be privileged blood". [3] Right after the debacle, on June 30, 1940, he had written to the members of his diocese: "Our humiliations and our misfortunes are only beginning." [4] On

[2] *Bulletin diocésain de Toulouse* (1933), 311–12.

[3] Quoted by P. Pierrard, *Juifs et catholiques français* (Fayard, 1970), 272.

[4] Letter "on what is to be learned from the ordeal". It ended with these words: "To those of you who have the opportunity, I would advise reading chapter 12 of the Epistle to the Hebrews."

May 17, 1942, General de Gaulle had addressed to him "in all confidence" a secret letter in which he expressed to him his fear that one faction of our episcopate, giving "the appearance" of being too closely linked with Vichy, might have to submit to grave consequences "after the Liberation".[5]

Written on August 20, Saliège's letter "was immediately given to the priests, who were participating at that time in a priests' retreat". The regional prefect, aware of this, "wired the mayors to inform the pastors of the government's will" that they not have it read.[6] It spread quickly nonetheless and shook public opinion powerfully, and it still remains famous. It deserves to be.

Other protests soon came from other dioceses, "seeming then to follow each other from Sunday to Sunday" (as if all had been prompted only by the one from Toulouse). Moreover, as the one from Marseilles included a rather bad-sounding sentence, the Lyons protest—which contained nothing of the sort—was linked with it, saying that it had a "related tone". In reality, things happened a bit differently. But let us first recall a few facts, some of which are well known.

On August 17, Cardinal Gerlier received the visit from the Grand Rabbi Kaplan, whom the Grand Rabbi of France, Isaiah Schwartz, who was absent, had delegated to go to him. Kaplan made known to Cardinal Gerlier scenes that he had just

[5] It is reproduced by Charles-Louis Foulon, "La France combattante devant la persécution des Juifs", in *F.Q.J.*, 337–38. Nevertheless, said de Gaulle, "I will keep from expressing any complaint."

[6] The prefect had obtained two minor amendments: "scenes of terror" became "moving scenes"; "horrors" became "errors". Some pastors did not read the letter, but a firm reminder from the Archbishop imposed a reading of it on the following Sunday. Details in J. Duquesne, 256–57. J. M. Mayeur, 160. It was read over the microphone in London on September 2. Cf. *Actes . . .* , 8:638–40. On the origin of the Saliège letter, the news received from the camps at Noé and Récébédou, see the details given by Bishop de Courrèges in *Rencontres, Chrétiens et Juifs*, 28 (1972).

witnessed at the station and informed him of the arrests of Jews in the city: whether coming from the camps or seized at home, all were being directed toward the east. . . . Gerlier, who had just returned to Lyons, intended first of all an immediate step with respect to the regional prefect Angeli, who was a powerful person, for Cardinal Suhard had already had the protest of the A.C.A. carried to Vichy, and he knew that he himself did not have much credit there: he was already considered there to be something like the "official defender of the Jews". But the Grand Rabbi Kaplan insisted. He informed him of the vastness and the horror of the operation in process: it was not a question, as rumors had it, of an "ethnic regrouping in Poland". The Jews, in reality, were being dispatched to Germany in order to be exterminated; Kaplan had obtained from Isaiah Schwartz precise, secret but reliable information. Deeply distressed, the Cardinal immediately called Pastor Boegner. By the next day, the eighteenth, he had come to an agreement with him: each of the two would write to the head of state, one in the name of the Protestant federation, the other in the name of "all the archbishops of the free zone".[7] On the nineteenth, he sent his own letter to Pétain. After having declared himself in solidarity with the protest coming from Cardinal Suhard, he expressed his own feelings about it and appealed to what he hoped still to be the "personal sentiments" of the old Marshal; he told him of his "pangs of anguish" in the face of "everything in the kind of treatment already suffered or anticipated, as also in the material organization of the convoys, that failed to recognize the essential rights of every human being and the fundamental rules of charity".[8]

---

[7] We note in passing that from August 6 on, in Paris, various people shared their feelings with Pétain, among whom was Fr. André Arnou, S.J., of l'Action populaire.

[8] Cf. Jacob Kaplan, *Justice pour la foi juive* (Le Centurion, 1977), 83–94. It is the nearly word-for-word reproduction of his "Notes for the Central Consistory", written after the conversation, which would be published in 1984 in his little book *N'oublie pas* (Stock), 139–68.

Although the inspiration behind this step is usually recognized, it has been criticized on two counts. First of all, there is at least the implication that it was an outpouring of the heart, not the solemn protest that was required. But they are forgetting that the Cardinal had begun by affirming his solidarity with the official protest coming from Paris. Persuaded with good reason that by renewing that protest he would only aggravate the government without obtaining anything, he tried rather—the final argument or the final illusion?—to touch the heart of the one who, alone, would perhaps be capable of attempting the saving gesture. And besides, this letter of the nineteenth did not "remain without effect: the number of convoys of deported people leaving, which had until then been accelerating, slowed down at that time". The Grand Rabbi Kaplan himself assures us of this, according to what he later learned from Serge Klasferld, author of the *Mémorial de la déportation des Juifs de France*, and according to the summary of a conversation between Laval and a Gestapo leader, dated September 2, 1942: "Laval wishes to be spared new demands in the Jewish question, for he has some difficulties with the Church and in particular with Cardinal Gerlier."[9]

It has been observed in the second place that, avoiding the subject of "extermination", he only referred to "anticipated treatment", and this restraint has been found rather "strange". This would be to forget that, even deeply distressed as he was by the revelations of the Grand Rabbi Kaplan, the Cardinal did not have any proof to put forward: to speak too clearly would be to risk a refutation that would put an end to any possible intervention on his part. Undoubtedly, in Vichy, all were not without at least a suspicion of what this "anticipated treatment" meant: in this case, the Cardinal's allusion would be perfectly clear to them.

[9] In *N'oublie pas*, 146. This last text had been published by Georges Wellers in *Le Monde juif* of July–September 1980.

Here, some brief, general information, too often overlooked, is necessary.

"I wonder", Daniel Mayer recently wrote, "at those who tell us that they did not know that the Jews would suffer any particular fate. But after all, the German Jews had been suffering that particular fate since 1933, [and] it was enough to have read *Mein Kampf*. But no one at that time believed it."[10] That view seems too simplistic. Neither the racist persecution in Germany nor the remarks made in *Mein Kampf* announced a whole plan of extermination to people of that time. Hitler took all his plans seriously—although he took care to hide the passages most threatening to the French in the only authorized French translation of *Mein Kampf*[11]—but the plan of exterminating the Jews did not figure in it, at least not clearly, and undoubtedly he had not fully conceived of it at that time.[12]

---

[10] In *F.Q.J.*, 380. See also the entire book by Léon Poliakov, *Bréviaire de la haine*.

[11] Cf. Gabriel Marcel, *En chemin, vers quel éveil?* (Gallimard, 1971), 147: "The pacifism to which a number of intellectuals at that time subscribed seemed to me illusory and dangerous; . . . it could only be exploited by the predatory powers for their own advantage, as Wilhem Foerster was to show in a conference I attended in 1937, if I am not mistaken." The French did not imagine that, having become head of state, Hitler would want to pursue his dream to the end. Nor did they know the whole of *Mein Kampf*. The translation of the entire book, prepared by Nouvelles Editions latines in 1934, was immediately seized at the request of Hitler's Munich publisher and pulped.

[12] But the French would have been more seriously disturbed if they had paid more attention to an article by the director of *Etudes*, Fr. Henri du Passage, who, having had a copy of the forbidden translation in hand for several hours, analyzed, with quotations from vivid texts, the racist, anti-Jewish, anti-Christian, pagan myth in *Mein Kampf* (*Etudes*, April 20, 1934, 219:204–20); he wondered, in conclusion, if Hitler had let himself be led astray by his "totalitarian" logic. Another Jesuit, Fr. Pierre Delattre, a correspondent for *La Croix*, tried to alert public opinion. D'Harcourt increased the warnings: *Juifs et chrétiens devant le racisme* (French trans. by Faulhaber, Sorlot); in 1939, in *Ambitions et méthodes allemandes*, he cited *Mein Kampf*, giving a definition of Hitlerian peace: "A peace supported, not by the peaceable, generous female palms, but founded by the two-edged sword of the

The first idea he expressed seems to have been to get rid of them by sending them to Palestine, which was the reason for Eichmann's surprising discussions with the World Zionist Organization and the Haganah—but England had opposed it. In November 1938, Goering had alluded to a possible deportation to Madagascar. From 1939 on, a Jewish reservation was organized in Poland: this was the "Polish Madagascar" to the south of Lublin, where by April 1940 around two hundred thousand Jews had already been gathered. The French defeat once again awakened the idea of making Madagascar a Jewish state. Did Hitler already have ulterior motives? "It would be impossible to emphasize enough the difficulties involved in penetrating the ultimate secrets of the nazi enterprise."[13] In any case, on July 31, 1941, Goering ordered Heydrich to take all measures necessary for a "final solution". The first camp of systematic extermination was installed at Chalmo (Poland) in December 1941. On January 20, 1942, at Wannesee (near Berlin), Heydrich set down for the principal agents the broad lines of the plan appointed by Hitler.[14] But rumors of all that

---

victor on a people of the Lord, forcing the universe to submit to the service of a superior culture"; he would explain Hitler's tactic: "To arouse Germany but make the rest of the world sleep . . . , one hand seizes the goal while the other offers the olive branch"; "The hegemony of Europe", he would say, "is for the Third Reich the way of world hegemony", and he would quote these words of an official journal: "The only danger to peace would arise from a determination by democracies to oppose by force the forward progress of events" (11, 17, 20, 45ff.). D'Harcourt had been thanked for his action by a handwritten letter from Cardinal Pacelli, then Secretary of State. But such warnings were rare and seldom heard. Cf. Raymond Aron, *Mémoires* (Julliard, 1983), 60–66, 131–58, 247. Léon Noël, *Les Illusions de Stresa* and *La guerre a commencé quatre ans plut tôt* (Ed. France-Empire, 1975 and 1979).

[13] Annie Kriegel, "La Résistance communiste", in *F.Q.J.*, 365f. Cf. F. Lovsky, *Antisémitisme et Mystère d'Israël*, 372–78.

[14] On January 30, 1942, Hitler announced, in a still ambiguous way, the "destruction of Jewry". "The hour will come when the greatest enemy of humanity will have finished playing a role for at least a thousand years" (quoted by *Antisémites*, April–May 1942). Again on April 21, 1943, Ernst

followed spread only slowly, and many did not want, were not able, to believe it.

In August and September 1942, reports arrived at the World Jewish Congress about a large-scale world extermination. From July 4 on, the *Université libre* had reported the killing by "gassing" of those deported. At the end of October, the "trio of directors" of the "Jewish language group" learned that "eleven thousand Jews deported from France had been gassed on their arrival" and finally published this news on November 20 in *Unser Wort*.[15] On December 3, Visser't Hooft, who was not moving rashly, wrote to the Red Cross: "In Poland, in a single locality, six thousand Jews are shot every day, and that has been happening for weeks."[16]

In 1943, the truth penetrated here and there, but still without spreading everywhere. "An insane rumor", a member of the Foreign Office had declared in August 1942.[17] The first of those to escape from Auschwitz were thought to be mad.[18] Everything that began to be recounted seemed to many to be wartime propaganda, ridiculous exaggeration. The neutral press did not dare say anything; even the Allies were hesitant. "People had no place in their minds for this unimaginable horror; the blindness nearly everywhere was stupifying."[19]

Jünger, in Paris, wrote: "Apparently those shootings [of the Jews] are no longer taking place, for now they have gone on to gas" (*Journal de guerre et d'Occupation*, trans. H. Plard [Julliard, 1965], 223); cf. October 16, 1943 (p. 280; but we might wonder if there has not been an error in the date [1943 instead of 1942?]).

[15] A. Kriegel and W. A. Visser't Hooft.

[16] W. A. Visser't Hooft, *Le Temps du rassemblement, Mémoires*, trans. from English (Seuil, 1975), no. 23: "L'extermination des Juifs européens", 211–19.

[17] Cf. Xavier de Montclos, *Les Chrétiens face au nazisme et au stalinisme* (Plon, 1983), 139.

[18] Examples in F. Lovsky, 379–80; in Anny Latour, 144–46.

[19] Two basic works are informative: Georges Wellers, *L'Etoile jaune à l'heure de Vichy. De Drancy à Auschwitz*. Preface by Jacques Delarue, postscript by Fr. Riquet (Fayard, 1973). Eugène Kogon, Hermann Langbein, Adalbert Ruckel,

The illusions in France were persistent. When the great round-ups began in 1942, it was at first believed that only foreign Jews or even only adult Jews would really be threatened with being sent to work camps. When the Grand Rabbi Kaplan came to warn Cardinal Gerlier, the latter apparently still believed that it was a question "of an ethnic regrouping in Poland".[20] Dannecker had decided that only a "transplantation of Jews would be spoken of",[21] and everywhere clever camouflages were invented, more effective, at least at times, than one would believe: at least with those who were not witnesses and who, in the depths of themselves, did not want to know.

The *Cahier du T.C.* entitled *Défi*, devoted to Poland, which appeared in January–February 1943 and was nearly unreadable, filled as it was with so many horrors, but which was perfectly well informed (it was the work of Cardinal Hlond), published without hesitation:

> The "general government" has become a ghetto where all the Jews of Poland and Germany have been gathered and where the Jews from all occupied countries are now being led. . . . Anyone leaving the ghetto is shot. Exhaustion from work, hunger, cold and sickness furnish it with a rich harvest of the dead. Sometimes the Gestapo go in and massacre them. Mass shootings and poisoning by gas are the daily order. . . . *A total of more than seven hundred thousand Jews have been brutally assassinated on Polish land, and there is no possible doubt about Hitler's plan for a complete extermination of the Jews on the European continent.*[22]

Nevertheless, it seems certain that Laval himself and his men knew everything: he was not particularly anti-Semitic,

Les Chambres à gaz secret d'Etat, trans. from German by Henry Rollat (Editions de Minuit, 1983). Cf. Anny Latour, 144–45. Léon Poliakov, *Bréviaire de la haine*, chap. 5, "Les exterminations". Cf. André Brissaud, *Hitler et l'Ordre noir* (Perrin, 1969), chap. 16.

[20] Kaplan, *N'oublie pas* (Stock, 1984), 140.

[21] F. Lovsky, 387.

[22] *Cahiers et Courriers*, 1:230. Cf. R. Bédarida, 155.

but he accepted the work that the victor imposed on him in the hope that France would have a better fate at the time of the peace treaty.[23] "When I returned to power (February 18, 1942), I had to make decisions and take responsibilities." Organized by the French authorities, the deportation of the Jews, children included, became, as the German Heinrichsohn announced on August 13, "a permanent action".[24] For a long time, despite everything, "part of the French Jews, a good many Christians and many legalistic or simply reasonable leaders failed to realize that Vichy France was in the process of handing over its prisoners to the executioners".[25]

I was aware of the Grand Rabbi Kaplan's visit to Lyons only much later, through an account that he gave of it in his moving book *Justice pour la foi juive* [Justice for the Jewish faith]. It is understandable that his revelation deeply grieved the Cardinal and that the latter had taken the action I have just recounted. The horrible events that were occurring had not left him inactive. Several have recounted what he did there for months with his friends in l'Amitié chrétienne. I would like to add a personal memory.

---

[23] But Laval had said to Boegner, on July 27, 1940, at Vichy: "The Jews have done so much harm in the country that they need a collective punishment." Cf. M. Boegner, *L'Exigence oecuménique*, 134–35: "The long conversation that I had with P. Laval in September 1942 . . . confirmed the thought he had expressed to me on July 27, 1940." On Laval's return to power and his policy of racial collaboration: J. B. Duroselle, 338–42.

[24] Cf. in *F.Q.J.*: Kupfermann, 31–56; J. Delarue, 68–69; M. Moch, 260; G. Ribière, 394.

[25] F. Delpech. It is advisable to make a rough distinction, in the nazi evaluation, between the "submen", such as the Gypsies (all to be exterminated)—the inferior races, such as the Slavs, exterminated as much as possible behind the lines of the German armies or destined for slavery—and, at a slightly higher degree, the Latins. The Nordics, pure Aryans, were the creative men, while the Jews, their antagonists, were degenerate, though formidable, for they were destructive and decadant: an "antirace", said Rosenberg; "a germ debilitating humanity", said Hitler (quoted in *T.C.*, *Antisémites*, 3).

As far as I remember, it was around August 10. Fr. Chaillet had come to see me to tell me what the Archbishop wanted:

1. To receive as quickly as possible detailed news from the southwest, where most of the camps of Jewish foreigners were located.

2. To consult with the Archbishop of Toulouse with a view to a joint intervention: the union of the two archbishops would give more weight to their public protest. (The convoys of Jews taken by the police in the Toulouse region were beginning to pass through Lyons.) So I was sent as an emissary. I had to leave immediately for Toulouse.

I still have a vivid memory of the impressions from that hard trip in slow, crowded trains, of my unexpected arrival in the antiquated hotel on rue Perchepinte that the Archbishop had taken over from a Jesuit residence, the warm, serious welcome in the room where Archbishop Saliège was sur-rounded by his close associates for the evening meal. The atmosphere was heavy, tragic; shortly after my arrival, mes-sengers came to bring the latest news from the camps. The Archbishop was then carried, like an inert mass, to his office, and, according to the prudent discipline of the times, the door was closed on the two of us alone. Fatigue increased my anguish. The conversation was difficult: in his almost total paralysis that day, Archbishop Saliège could not manage, de-spite persistent efforts pursued with a patience I admired, to pronounce the least intelligible word or even to handle the large pencil that was supposed to take the place of his voice.[26] But we understood each other even before we began, and as I spoke, the quick flashes of his glance were all that I needed to convince me of it. I had a table of the latest information. Now, the plan was sketched out: each of the two prelates and also some others in the Toulouse area would prepare a speech;

[26] M. Boegner, 161, on his visit to Saliège (in 1942?): "He could scarcely make himself heard with hoarse cries, in which I had the greatest difficulty in grasping a few syllables."

the text of it would be written, and a copy would be transmitted secretly to the pastor of each parish in the diocese; this would be a solemn "pastoral letter", read in the pulpit on the same Sunday as the Archbishop read it in his cathedral. So, as we saw above, the police would be faced with a fait accompli; all censors would be caught unawares.

This is, in fact, what took place shortly afterward. The Toulouse protest, the most forceful of many, took place on Sunday, August 23. Others, undoubtedly set off at least in part by it, would follow. The Lyons protest was read and disseminated under the same conditions as that of Toulouse on September 6. This delay was perhaps due to the considerable practical difficulties of recruiting the numerous voluntary and trustworthy messengers needed to carry the Archbishop's text and order to each of the parishes in his large diocese, but even more, probably, to the exhausting days during the last two weeks in August, particularly around the end of the month, when, "in the tragic night at the Vénissieux camp"[27] and then through Lyons itself, the great roundup of Jews took place on the twenty-sixth, twenty-seventh and twenty-eighth, with the bitter debates about saving the children, in which Gerlier was closely involved, and his lively discussion with the prefect Angeli.[28] But, contrary

[27] Jean-Marie Soutou, who was with them, points particularly to the courage and the presence of mind of "Abbé Glasberg and Charles Lederman, thanks to which the gates of the camp were forced open, emergency regulations provided for in the telegrams from Vichy were applied as broadly as possible, and finally, the children were saved. . . . No one knows how many there were in the end. There were three crowded gas generators; that is all I can say. . . . Only one father and one mother refused. . . . Those people . . . who were separated from their children were not unaware of what was waiting for them, even if they did not know the whole horror in detail. But whoever saw their expression at the moment of separation . . ." (stenographic text, March 12, 1979; cf. *F.Q.J.*, 250–51). Cf. M. Boegner, 151.

[28] *Colloque de Grenoble*, 169–70ff. After having reported these appalling facts, M. Ruby, in a less than clear passage, writes: "This was the moment when anti-Semitic propaganda redoubled in France in an attempt to justify Vichy's attitude." Xavier Vallat, judged to be too lukewarm, was replaced in the spring of 1942 by Darquier de Pellepoix (imposed by Germany).

to an opinion that has since been voiced, he was in no way a kind of belated follower, trying to water down the whole affair; quite the opposite.[29]

"Archbishop Saliège had never shown excessive confidence in collective decision or actions. Moreover, he thought that it was necessary to act strongly and openly, to fire up public opinion and not the government, which was quite powerless in this matter. The occasion presented itself for him to act alone. He seized it." These pertinent remarks by Jean Guitton[30] do not contradict what I have just stated. The initiative of an agreement beforehand between Lyons and Toulouse did not come from Toulouse but from Lyons; and if Saliège had little confidence in collective declarations or actions, which always risked being weakened at least in their form, he had no objection whatever to two *concerted* actions.[31]

The protest by Théas (Montauban) came on August 30; those by Gerlier and Delay (Marseilles) on September 6; that by Moussaron (Albi) on September 20, and likewise that by Vanstenberghe (Bayonne). On September 15, those by Théas and Gerlier were quoted on the London radio. That of the National Council of the Reformed Church was read in the churches on October 4. Those by Saliège and Gerlier (and the Reformed Church) carry the note: "To be read in the pulpit without commentary." (I have not verified this in the others.) This group of letters gave rise to a great stir in the

[29] If Théas' letter was able to be read one Sunday before Gerlier's communiqué, it was because (in addition to the Cardinal's exhausting days at the end of this August) in the large diocese of Lyons all the parishes could not be alerted and served in secret, like the little diocese of Montauban, by three people, for whom this was already a feat. Cf. M. R. Gineste, in *F.Q.J.*, 229; R. Bédarida, 126. On Théas: André Latreille, "Un évêque résistant, Mgr. Pierre-Marie Théas, évêque de Montauban", in *Revue d'histoire ecclésiastique*, 75 (1980), 290.

[30] *Le Cardinal Saliège* (Grasset, 1957), 163–64.

[31] Moreover, I had come before a man who had already made up his mind.

country.[32] To put a stop to its effects, Vichy had an article signed "Saint Julien", taking up once again Léon Bérard's "Thomist" argument, printed in *Le Grand Echo du Midi*; *La Croix* (Fr. Merklen and Alfred Michelin) had refused to include it; likewise *La Dépêche*, whose editor, Maurice Sarraut, replied: "I want to be able to look the Archbishop of Toulouse in the face."[33] The article, which appeared on September 3, was followed the next day by an "advisory note" sent by Vichy to the press and disseminated over the whole country. In it we read that "this whole disturbance has been kept alive behind the scenes by the adversaries of the national revolution; it is a political maneuver that must be thwarted and into which Catholics must not let themselves be drawn." *Cahier* 10–11 of the *T.C.*, which appeared in November, would publish this official note, as well as a refutation of the article, under the title "Tartuffe 1942", and it would be good to recall its position once more:

> The agents of Hitlerism in France do not go to very much trouble when it comes to inventiveness. For more than two years, they have always used the same argument, the same tactic: all spiritual resistance to the invasion of nazi paganism is denounced as a maneuver of political opposition to the government of France. We will not cease to protest against equivocation or to restore the truth. Our *Cahiers* are not and do not wish to be anything but an echo of the Christian witness.[34]

[32]J. M. Mayeur, in *F.Q.J.*, 157 and 163. "The present-day reader of these declarations might be tempted to note their limitations. An overly critical attitude would be an anachronism and would not give a true idea of the feeling of those at that time."

[33]J. M. Mayeur, 161.

[34]Reprint, 1:214–16. This *Cahier*, *Collaboration et Fidélité*, gives the text of the episcopal documents as well as a letter from Bishop Kolb, General Vicar of Strasbourg, to the regional prefect of Clermont-Ferrand; but there was still no knowledge of the protest by Bishop Vanstenberghe (Bayonne), published on September 20: an indication of the difficulty in communicating between the two zones. With respect to this latter text: H. Amouroux, *La Vie des Français sous l'Occupation* (1961), 421–22.

Several common expressions among three of the episcopal letters (those of Saliège, Théas and Gerlier) have led some to suppose that one of the three was the source of the other two. In reality, it seems rather that the three drafts were written independently of each other. Their common elements might have come from a secret letter sent to several bishops by Fr. Chaillet, who informed them of certain facts, begging them to intervene. He may have managed shortly before, through the network of l'Amitié chrétienne, to obtain a note from some Vichy departments showing what the Germans were doing. This is not impossible; it may even be probable. I have no precise memory about that, and I do not believe that this problem has ever been cleared up.[35]

After these pastoral letters (and the Boegner letter), the "task of l'Amitié chrétienne", as Jean-Marie Soutou says, "became easier" (in the sense that it found more who were willing to act in complicity); its members "have only very rarely been betrayed. . . . We keep", he concludes, "a shining memory of that great devotedness and generosity from which we benefited. . . . We found unexpected support even among the officials charged with carrying out the roundups" (June 25, 1979).

Our bishops were actively supported by the Holy See. Already, on April 15, Bishop Valerio Valeri had organized a secret meeting with Gerlier, Liénart and Piguet, Bishop of Clermont-Ferrand. In August, he protested to Vichy. Marshal Pétain, less confident than in June 1941, reportedly said to him: "I hope that the Pope understands my attitude in these difficult circumstances"; to which the nuncio is said to have

---

[35] Cf. F. Delpech, *F.Q.J.*, 222–23, following a conversation of Fr. Chaillet with F. and R. Bédarida in 1965. Given the similarities of expression in these two letters, I wonder today if one part at least of my mission to Toulouse was not to carry verbally this Chaillet document to Saliège. A mere hypothesis. Cf. Bédarida at the symposium of March 1979, Center for Contemporary Jewish Documentation, 222–23.

replied: "It is precisely that which the Pope cannot understand." The nuncio's intervention was suppressed by the censor, but it was known by the Allies and disseminated by their radios; in France, the October number of the clandestine journal *Combat* gave news of it.[36] The nuncio made a quick trip to Rome to explain the situation. Once more, however—an unbelievable thing!—Vichy tried to obtain at least some backing from the Vatican through the intermediary of its ambassador. A severe reply from Maglione to Bérard cut it short. Several episcopal letters from France were reported in *l'Osservatore Romano*, in *Civiltà cattolica* and on Vatican Radio; according to Jean Toulat, it was even "at the express request of Pius XII" that Vatican Radio broadcast Saliège's letter twice and made comments about it on six consecutive days.

In its August 20, 1942, issue,[37] the clandestine journal *La Voix du Nord* published an article by the Catholic Natalis Dumez, former secretary to Abbé Lemire:

> In a remarkable pastoral letter, through his courage and nobility and through a loftiness of thought that has made him a great witness to eternal truths, the Archbishop of Toulouse is denouncing this new order, commended by Hitlerian collaborators. . . . He is defending the dignity of the human person.

[36] "At the moment when France rose up in horror, . . . at the moment when Bishop Valeri, the apostolic nuncio, protested to Vichy in the name of Pius XII and the human conscience . . .": quoted by G. Wellers, 405. Cf. L. Landau, *Revue d'histoire de l'Eglise de France*, 59:1 (1973), 244, referring to *Actes du Saint-Siège*, 3:2 (1967), 738. I have not been able to find all the specifics about the dates and exact terms of these various facts. Cf. J. Nobécourt, 212–13.

[37] The letter from Saliège was read on August 23; if there was not an error in the 1978 reproduction, this number of August 20 (no. 37) was thus late in appearing, as frequently happened. In any case, it was written very shortly after August 23, for Natalis Dumez was arrested in September. In number 40, dated September 20, other writers would point out several other letters by bishops. Cf. *Revue du Nord*, 60: 238 (July–September 1978), 636–37, article by Marc Sueur.

> ... This attitude has received the highest approval of the
> Church. ... History will prove that the Archbishop of
> Toulouse has been the courageous interpreter of the great voice
> of the papacy.

This last affirmation was dictated to the author only through
a comparison with the famous "toast of Alger" pronounced
by Cardinal Lavigerie, as was later known, at the request of
Leo XIII; however, in substance it was just: facts have shown
that Saliège's letter responded to the desire of Pius XII. "History" has also nonetheless shown that this Toulouse letter, so
quickly spread through secret networks, was worthy of the
fervor with which it was received.[38]

[38] We also note in this regard a recent reflection by Cardinal Joseph
Ratzinger: "Bureaucratic structures . . . end in producing texts that have been
a bit smoothed out, in which personal positions are dulled. . . . In my country,
Germany, an episcopal conference already existed in the thirties. Well, the
truly vigorous documents against nazism were those produced by the bishops
personally. The texts of the conference were often a little softened."

—N.B.: How the "Letter of H. E., the Most Rev. Bishop of Montauban,
on Respect for the Human Person", dated August 26, 1942, was distributed
to the clergy of the Montauban diocese: "On August 26, 1942, indignant
about the measures taken in France against the Jews, Bishop Théas, Bishop
of Montauban, wrote his very energetic letter on 'respect for the human
person'. He asked me if it was possible to reproduce it on the Gestetner
machine that I had at the social secretariate. I undertook the distribution. A
friend and a young officer from Lorraine, the father of six children, agreed
to help me, and we left on bicycle across the roads of the district. We brought
it to all the parishes, and, on the following Sunday, the letter was read
simultaneously all over the diocese. The immense joy that I felt at having
thwarted prefect, censor and police compensated greatly for the fatigue of
kilometers traveled in record time and in the month of August! From that
date on, Bishop Théas put me in charge of hiding Jewish children and adults
in the convents of the district or in individual homes, as well as of procuring
false papers for them and all the services we were able to render them" (Mlle.
Marie-Rose Gineste to R. Bédarida). The diocese of Montauban was quite
small, while that of Lyons was very vast (it comprised at that time the two

departements of the Rhône and the Loire), and organization and time were needed to distribute the letter to all the parishes.

A local director of the "General Commission for Jewish Questions" (Commissariat général aux questions juives, or C.G.Q.J.) in Toulouse, horrified by Saliège's pastoral letter, called for "an energetic interdiction [*sic*] of the Nunciature as a punishment for the impropriety of such a manifestation" (cf. Marrus and Paxton, *Vichy et les Juifs* [Calmann-Lévy, 1981], 191).

Chapter 12

Concerning Cardinal Gerlier

In several of the preceding sections, I have had, and will have subsequently, occasion to speak of Cardinal Gerlier, of his feelings, his activities during those years of the Occupation. I would merely like to add here a little further information, to stress a few characteristics, to point out a few myths, to show the injustice of certain reproaches that have been made against him and that are still today addressed in good faith against him.

Jean-Marie Soutou, who knew Cardinal Gerlier very well and also knew very well the clandestine work he did for the Jews (having collaborated closely with him), wrote me on October 30, 1984: "For years, my wife and I have been unable to touch these subjects except with our closest friends. I am forced to do so when told that I must leave some lasting trace of my testimony. What impels me most strongly is the growing distortion of memories about Cardinal Gerlier's actions." In the same letter, Soutou sent me the stenographic record of one of his interventions at a symposium of historians of the Resistance: "Particularly", he said, "about what I think of Cardinal's Gerlier's attitude, on which subject I have been made to say negative things that were not at all my true opinion".

Too great a contrast has been drawn between the respective behavior of the two prelates, Saliège and Gerlier, in their relations with the Vichy government. Certainly their temperaments were not the same. However, in order better to understand their respective attitudes, one thing must not be forgotten. In a France cut in two (or even in four), the Archbishop of Lyons was in a peculiar situation. Lyons, the city next in importance after Paris, would have undoubtedly been chosen as the capital if it had had the necessary hotels. Gerlier, on the other hand, was the only cardinal in the unoccupied zone. He therefore found himself to be the official representative at least of the Church to the government. He used as best he could this situation and the obligations it entailed in order to make Vichy hear the voice of the Church, in conditions that seemed to him the only ones possible or the only ones giving any hope of being effective. That the results were meager, disappointing, is obvious; but he should not be reproached for this. Could someone else have obtained more? In his relations with those in power, he never gave up anything of his independence, and his "loyalty" did not keep him from fighting against projects or from protesting against acts that the Church was to condemn. In one instance, at least—and one with weighty consequences—he obtained, in union with his colleagues, a success: in imitation of the totalitarian states, and urged on by a press in the service of the occupying forces, the French state wanted a "uniform regimen for youth": he backed away. It is easy to take to rhetoric in setting diplomat and prophet in opposition, but that must not excuse one from looking at things a little more closely. We still admire the "sly Auvergne man" of Toulouse, who takes out his counterinsurance, in September 1942, by affirming "once again his perfect loyalty with regard to the Marshal and those in power in the country": it is not logical to reproach a similar declaration by the "Lyons lawyer"![1]

At the Lyons symposium in 1978, André Latreille expressed several provocative reflections on this subject, which I would

[1] In *F.Q.J.*, 256, J. M. Mayeur observes with good reason that Saliège no longer "wanted to be used by resistance workers of communist allegiance and on the other hand reaffirmed his loyalty with regard to the established power".

wish simply to corroborate by recalling a number of well- and less-known historical details:

In the confusion of memories and impressions, people remained attached to a word or gesture that had particularly struck them, or else they forgot to take into consideration actions that might well have carried far more weight. At the time of the Liberation, people no longer remembered that Saliège had been a Pétainist like everyone else in 1940, and it was due to his declaration in favor of the Jews that he enjoyed the position of national hero. Cardinal Liénart was regarded to be quite on the side of the Resistance because he had said that leaving for Germany was not in conscience obligatory, but no one remained more of a marshalist than he or more sensitive to the threat of "Bolshevism", whose development would be favored by a "civil" war. On the other hand, with regard to Gerlier, people only thought of the famous "Pétain, he is France", instead of honoring him for the fact that he "covered up" some of the activities of the spiritual Resistance . . . , that he received certain information from the Lyons Resistance workers through the intermediary of his secretary, Bishop Maury . . . and particularly that, in 1944, he stood up to the Germans with such rash courage that the latter thought to stop him, even to have the militia kill him. In any case, according to M. Umbreït, the authorities of the occupying forces said that he was not the Primate of the Gauls but the "Primate of de Gaulle" . . . At the very least, he was among the first French bishops to perceive "the dangers of governmental gifts and clerical politics" in the first months of the Vichy government.[2] Through his sincere affection for the Marshal, he hoped to encourage him to resist the pro-German leanings of the members of his government and in the first place the projects for a "uniform regimen for youth". He

[2] Already in July 1940, a rather suspect "clerical" trend began to stir at Vichy; rumors circulated that an agreement was being prepared between "the French state" and the Holy See; the Cardinal immediately made known his opposition to such a project, letting the minister Alibert know that Rome could only reject it. (Cf. Pastor Marc Boegner, *L'exigence oecuménique*, 134–35.)

always refused to speak of "collaboration" and to give the least, even purely verbal support to the hypocrisy of the "fight against communism". That required great moral energy of him, and it broke his heart: as he increased his interventions, in 1944, in order to obtain the liberation of prisoners from Fort Montluc, among whom were at least two of his priests, the chief of the Gestapo proposed to free them in exchange for a declaration condemning communism: he refused.[3]

At the same symposium, André Latreille gave detailed information about the circumstances under which Gerlier spoke the words that have more than once been claimed to symbolize his consistent attitude under the Occupation, and he restored their precise content. It was in November 1940:

> I have heard [he tells us] from a firsthand witness (Abbé J. Gay) of the incident that the famous words "Pétain, he is France"—for which the Cardinal was later so reproached—were whispered to him by a war veteran, at the moment he entered the Lyons cathedral where he was celebrating, in the presence of the Marshal, a solemn service in memory of the dead from both wars. The master of ceremonies, overwhelmed by the influx of people, war veterans with flags and decorations, people from all social classes and of all inclinations, and by the atmosphere of intense emotion that was reigning in the immense nave, quoted these words to him, which he had just heard from a veteran. Gerlier, used to improvising and to integrating into his speeches expressive phrases, emphasized these words, not, however, without modifying them, through a reflex of prudence, by inserting the word *today*, which limited its scope: ". . . and Pétain, today, he is France". . . . A modification that most people at that time and too many historians since have not taken into consideration.[4]

---

[3] *Colloque de Lyon*, 592 and 593; cf. M. Ruby, 385, 388, 391–92. Similar blackmail was tried in vain with Suhard on October 29, 1943 (cf. Guerry, 294) and with Boegner, who asked for the liberation of four pastors, among whom was Roland de Pury (*Exig. oecum.*, 165–68).

[4] A. Latreille, ibid. Similarly, *De Gaulle, la Libération et l'Eglise catholique* (Cerf, 1978), 33. This speech is reproduced in *La Vie catholique, documents et*

There was another detail in this speech that was certainly not unintentional, and that François Delpech has fortunately recalled: the Archbishop of Lyons called for unity among the French "without distinction of race"—an appeal that the audience could not have failed to grasp.[5] Nor should we forget that at that time France counted, according to a title by Henri Amouroux, "forty thousand Pétainists", that people were persuaded everywhere in Lyons that there was a secret understanding between Pétain and de Gaulle,[6] that there was a distinction made between the Marshal and his government, that it was even against his government (that of Laval or that of Darlan) that Gerlier intervened to the Marshal, that he stopped seeing him—and soon stopped even citing his name—from October 1942 on; that he was one of the best informed of the bishops, from the beginning, about the danger of the

---

actes de la Hiérarchie, 1940–1941, 69. "For Pétain is France, and France, today, is Pétain. To lift up the wounded country, all France, Monsieur le Maréchal, is behind you." Around the end of the Occupation, during a friendly conversation with Jean Lacroix, Gerlier would say how much he regretted this eloquent expression: "What I could tell about that! I have been endlessly reproached for it, and will be reproached for it until I die." This was not only, Lacroix observes, "the weariness caused by those reproaches, but the expression of an evolution and an opening that were going on endlessly" (Colloque de Grenoble, 337). Let us also observe that the historical situation had become quite different, and that they were very far from the "today" of 1940. Later, he was able to take the criticism with good humor: invited to the banquet of the Lyons fair, which was celebrating the return of Herriot to his city, he made a laudatory toast to the latter which he concluded with these words: "In short, the fair is Herriot, and Herriot is the fair!" (I did not hear it, but all Lyons repeated it.)

[5] F. Delpech, Sur les Juifs, 238.

[6] The rumor even circulated that an airplane was secretly commuting between London and Vichy! Such was also at first Claudel's state of mind, and although he soon called himself "naïve", he nevertheless never denied his "Ode to Pétain": Fumet, who remarks on this (439), considers the final verses to be "very beautiful" and thinks that they imply this conviction about an understanding between the two leaders. "It was difficult in Lyons", he adds, "to doubt Pétain's strong orthodoxy".

advantages that Vichy was offering to the Church; that, if there was fawning on all sides, as ridiculous as it was odious, with respect to those in power, it was not in any case the Cardinal Archbishop of Lyons who went, in his zeal, to the point of proposing one day to the schoolboys that they "follow the Marshal like the Hebrews followed the luminous column in the desert": it was the Prefect of Lyons.[7]

It is a little surprising to read today, from the pen of one of the best-informed historians of this already distant period, these words, which are apparently intended to be lenient toward Cardinal Gerlier: "He dissociated himself several times from the Maurras trend."[8] If anyone had no need to "dissociate" himself from such a trend, it was indeed he! From the summer of 1940 on, it was enough, without any further knowledge, to pass by the esplanade in Fourvière from time to time as I happened to do in order to see who among the many who had "withdrawn" from the capital came to seek comfort from the Archbishop. The former president of the A.C.J.F. was true to form, very far from any Maurrasian accommodation![9] There was no mistake about this in Vichy. When the General Secretariat for Youth was created, he was immediately concerned and had obtained the choice of a secretary and an assistant (Lamirand and Garrone) disposed to respect the pluralism of "movements"; but a less reassuring

[7] Laffont (1977). H. Amouroux, *La Vie des Français sous l'Occupation*, 439: "Victor of Verdun, leader of the French state, wise man whose speeches constituted a civil catechism, Philippe Pétain was all that for a long time in the eyes of many of the French in the unoccupied zone." Let us also note that it was one of the bishops most criticized for his "loyalty", judged to be excessive, who on January 23, 1941, called the fanatics back to propriety: "The respect due to authority does not demand that we deify the one who personifies it" (Archbishop Feltin of Bordeaux, quoted by J. Duquesne, 48).

[8] Op. cit., 238. He had presided over a demonstration against racism and anti-Semitism in 1938 (Marrus and Paxton, 155).

[9] We know that the A.C.J.F. had played a rather active role in the dissensions that would end in the condemnation of the Action française.

"charter for youth" was soon promulgated. In union with his present successor at the A.C.J.F., André Colin, the Cardinal protested, at first personally (December 2, 1940), then with the A.C.A. from the southern zone (January 6, 1941), and when things got worse, again on July 24, 1941.[10] It was with his support that, beginning in September 1940, Stanislas Fumet, assisted by Louis Terrenoire, revived *Temps présent*, which now became *Temps nouveau*;[11] it was he who had Fumet come to Lyons, who blessed him beforehand, who, through his warm welcome encouraged writers and readers.[12] The astonishing survival of the journal until August 1941 is undoubtedly explained by a certain concern by the government not to provoke a new conflict with him.[13] It is already known that he was an active supporter of Fr. Chaillet, through whom he also backed, at first discreetly and then explicitly, l'Amitié chrétienne. When, later, Louis Richard, P.S.S., was arrested by the Gestapo at the university seminary of Lyons and deported (for his frankly admitted ties to the *Cahiers* of the

[10] Let us also recall, in addition to his defense of private schools, his repeated interventions for the freedom of unions as well as to obtain pardon for communists condemned to death (according to J. R. Tournoux, *Pétain et de Gaulle* [Plon, 1964], 294).

[11] Terrenoire was the editor-in-chief; Louis Cruvillier provided the distribution, "covering the zone in every direction".

[12] Stanislas Fumet, *Histoire de Dieu dans ma vie*, 426–27, 436, 437. Cf. Riquet, 75. *La Croix du Rhône* denounced the "good Christians who are bad citizens" and asked in an accusing tone: "Why are Catholic journals like *Temps nouveau* so cautious with regard to the national revolution and the Marshal?" (May 21, 1941). One historian, poorly informed about Lyons matters, quoting these lines, thought it possible to say that this journal had been published "under the authority of the Archbishop". This might mislead the reader. Rather, it would be more accurate to consider this a shot directed at the Cardinal, whose encouragement and protection of *Temps nouveau* could not be ignored by the editors of this journal, which was independent of the archdiocese (cf. J. Duquesne, 166).

[13] Such is at least the hypothesis of Ruby, who is well informed about the incidents in Lyons during this period.

T.C.),[14] rumors circulated in police circles that this was a warning meant for the Cardinal (as had already been the case when Chaillet had been consigned by Vichy in 1942 to a supervised residence). One must be a little better informed on this subject than several historians of that period believe themselves to be.

To keep to what directly concerns the Jews, Gerlier "maintained excellent relations with the consistories; he knew President Helbronner (who would die as a prisoner in a concentration camp) very well", "when the central consistory withdrew to Lyons, he welcomed it warmly, and he helped it in its efforts for the benefit of the refugees. The juridical advisers of the consistory, André Weil and Mme. Kieffé, often went to see him to ask his help and advice."[15] As early as December 1940, informed through l'Amitié chrétienne of the miserable conditions in which twenty thousand foreign Jews had been packed into the Gurs camp improvised for Spanish refugees (and members of international brigades), he had approached, after having put together a dossier from a serious inquiry, the Vichy government through his envoy Archbishop Guerry. His message was addressed to the Secretary of the Interior, who at that time was Peyrouton: Guerry was received by the head of the cabinet, who listened to him closely; Peyrouton even had an inspection of the camp made, and the doctor in charge of it was forced to recognize the accuracy of the Cardinal's information, which corroborated a similar representation made by Pastor Boegner; but no perceivable improvement followed. Delpech, who reports the fact, concludes, with a note of reproach, "Gerlier and Guerry let the matter drop, as did Pastor Boegner as well."[16]

The Cardinal's position was not easy. At precisely the same time that Fr. Chaillet, accompanied by Abbé Glasberg, came

---

[14] See above, Chap. 10.
[15] M. Ruby, 383–84.
[16] F. Delpech, *Sur les Juifs*, 273.

to urge him to intervene in this way, President Helbronner was on his way to the Archbishop to beg him not to do anything: such a gesture, he said, could only make the situation worse by giving rise to similar internment measures against the "French Israelites". "I am dumbfounded", Glasberg supposedly recounted; "Chaillet and I left saying: 'One more battle lost, and in a completely unexpected way!'"[17] The account apparently stops there. But, as we have seen above, the one Gerlier listened to in the end was not Helbronner, who represented French Judaism: it was Chaillet supported by Glasberg.

Later, at the end of the summer of 1941, when it was a question of a new statute for the Jews, the Cardinal had a meeting at Vichy with Xavier Vallat. It was, says Michaël Marrus,[18] "a kind of warning against the anti-Semitic policies of Vichy". But why judge that, in speaking of justice and charity, he "was speaking the language of Léon Bérard"? These two words were neither the invention nor the property of Bérard, whose report, moreover, seems to have been later than this Gerlier-Vallat confrontation.[19] Such a purely verbal

[17] *Colloque de Grenoble*, 203. A similar incident was to occur in Paris in 1942. Cardinal Suhard, after his protest in the summer of 1942 against the persecution of the Jews, had received the visit "of high Jewish authorities", coming to thank him "but also to beg that he not renew his solemn protests so as not to bring about harsh reprisals on the numerous Jewish families who were still in hiding". Yet he intervened twice again with Abetz, on February 7 and 19, 1944, against the many arrests and the conditions of the interned and deported, then on August 13, to tell him of his increased anxiety about their fate (Guerry, 111–13). One might wonder if it would have been better to disregard the fears of the rabbis, to think also what he would have done if he had truly *known*. Today we know. But who are we to judge?

[18] In *F.Q.J.*, 259.

[19] On June 27, 1942, the Council of the Protestant Federation of France would set before Pétain "the unanimous desire to see an effort made in a spirit of justice and understanding to find a solution of the Jewish problem, the importance of which none of us fails to recognize" (cf. *F.Q.J.*, 168). Would the word *understanding* be less suspect of overshadowing the word *justice* than the word *charity*?

comparison is all the more invalid since that Bérard report was anything but a "warning": it was rather a reply to the bishops and an attempt to justify, in opposition to them, the anti-Jewish policies of the government.[20] On January 21, 1942, through a public letter addressed to the Grand Rabbi of France, Gerlier would express again "the grief and indignation" he felt at the thought of the "hideous persecutions of which our brothers of Israel are the victims on our soil": "At this time of Christmas, Christians think with deep feeling of the gift that the people of God have made to humanity, and they know that if the Child Jesus returned to live in France, it is in the camp at Drancy that he would wish to live, with his unfortunate brothers."[21]

Gerlier certainly did not challenge, with respect to the Jews, the existence of a problem for which the French state must find a solution. He was not the only one to see it. Fr. de

---

[20] One might wonder if Gerlier's remarks, reported without any reference, do not in reality come from Vallat, chosen and transcribed by him for his own defense and more or less diverted from their end. The text is ambiguous besides: Gerlier seems, in the same conversation, to be speaking before the law of October 1941 and then after that law.

[21] Entire letter reproduced in Philippe Bourdrel, *Histoire des Juifs en France* (1974), which also reproduces his letter to Marshal Pétain of August 19, 1942 (598 and 600). Aimé Pallière, who was in Lyons during these years of the Occupation, wrote to Abbé Jules Monchanin (then in India) around the end of 1945: "Cardinal Gerlier has shown the most touching and courageous solicitude for the poor hunted Jews. The attitude of the Catholic and Protestant clergy in the face of the persecutions is one of the only comforting memories of that frightful period of the war. I must say, however, that unfortunately it has not always been understood and appreciated according to its true worth. The rabbinate, on the other hand, did give a public expression of its gratitude" (private letter). F. Delpech, 288, makes a rather scornful allusion to "some gestures made by Cardinal Gerlier toward President Helbronner and the central consistory, which had withdrawn to Lyons"; and the episcopal Assembly held at Lyons on June 16, 1942, having declared, in regard to the sacking of the synagogue of Nice, that it "renews its former protests against these unjust acts of violence and expresses its sympathy to the victims", he asks with suspicion: "Had it already protested?"

Montcheuil did not deny a "duty of vigilance" on the part of the public authority. In an address to Darlan, on November 16, 1941, the National Council of the Reformed Church specified that a "problem" was "posed to the state by the recent massive immigration of a great number of foreigners, many of whom are of Jewish origin, and by hasty and unjustified naturalizations". The "theses of Pomeyrol" (Protestant, September 1941) recognized that "the state is faced with a problem to which it has to give a solution".[22] To pursue this word *problem*, even to its use by the most ardent defenders of the Jews, would be unrealistic, and to suspect all those who recognized the existence at that time of a Jewish problem of opening the door to anti-Semitism would be quite wrong. Did not François Delpech himself point out, without the least hesitation, the "difficult problem of integration that is posed by the Polish immigration into France"?[23]

There were always, as we know, a reciprocal consultation

[22] See the complete sentence, quoted by Pierre Bolle, in *F.Q.J.*, 181–82. Other texts quoted by J. M. Mayeur, 167–68. Cf. above, n. 19.

[23] *Sur les Juifs*, 168: "Polish Jewish immigration into France", Franco-Polish Symposium of Religious History, Lille, October 1981.

I will not go into here the much-discussed subject of the "Jewish problem" or the "Jewish question", in its multiple and changing aspects. All I want to say is that the reproach that was made against Gerlier (as well as against de Montcheuil and Chaillet!) of having used this word, which is to say, of having recognized a fact, is unjust and even absurd. J. M. Mayeur has not fallen into this fault. The problem then referred to resulted in practice from a particular situation at that time. The simple *Histoire des Juifs de France de 1789 à 1860*, set forth by Patrick Girard (Calmann-Lévy, 1976), allows us to glimpse through an example the complexity of the "Jewish problem", or rather the Jewish problems—profoundly renewed but not disappeared since then. As for the "mystery of Israel", it is in faith that we must meditate on this, and I make no allusion to it here. It is the grandeur of the Jewish people to be a unique case in history, from which springs this enigma about which Jewish intellectuals never cease to question themselves, as witnessed, for example, once again at the twenty-fifth annual symposium organized by the French section of the World Jewish Congress, from December 1 to 3, 1984, seeking "what might be the axes of a history of the Jewish hope".

and organized agreement between Pastor Boegner and Cardinal Gerlier in their interventions. Both practiced as much as possible a policy of presence, which their responsibility in their Church imposed on them. "The Council of the Protestant Federation", explained Boegner,[24]

> had directed me to remain in contact with the public powers. Whatever might be the authorities exercising—or believing to exercise—power in unoccupied France and maintaining diplomatic relations with most of the nations in the world, I thus had the duty to go to Vichy in order to make present and alive to everyone the French Protestant reality, to demand for our churches the freedoms recognized by law, to make their protest heard each time it was necessary and above all to bring their witness into circles where the tendency was only too strong to ignore them.[25]

The two consulted each other; both were concerned to act not precisely together but simultaneously and in the same sense. The presence of the Church of Jesus Christ, Boegner would further say, is made manifest at certain times "with a more persuasive force thanks to the communion of thought that we have put forward, the Archbishop of Lyons and I".[26] Both were for some time under an illusion about what they could expect from their action, but they did all that they could. Boegner has not been reproached for this, and with good

[24] M. Boegner, *L'Exigence oecuménique*, 136.

[25] France's Grand Rabbi Schwartz was to have a similar conception of his own responsibility. Boegner met him at Vichy (136–37). On the Protestants and their churches faced with the persecution of the Jews in France: Pierre Bolle, in *F.Q.J.*, 171–96. Cf. Marc Boegner, "Les Eglises protestantes pendant la guerre et l'Occupation", *Actes de l'Assemblée générale du protestantisme français*, October 22–26, 1945 (Paris, 1946).

[26] Cf. 275: "I recall the close relations that developed between the Cardinal and me during the years of the Occupation." When Boegner returned to Paris in 1943, "all the questions I had discussed with Cardinal Gerlier were examined in a similar climate of Christian community" with Cardinal Suhard (163).

reason: Why be so dead set against Gerlier on this subject, with a bitterness that more than once misses the truth?

On December 7, 1941, the Archbishop seized the occasion of a traditional pilgrimage of men to Fourvière to fight publicly against the ravages that a growing anti-Semitism, stirred up by propaganda in a thousand different forms, was making in some Catholic consciences. In his speech, he rose up against a blasphemous article by Montherlant, "Solstice de juin", which had recently appeared in the *Nouvelle Revue française*, which had fallen into the hands of the nazi occupying forces. Montherlant was giving notice to Jesus Christ, whom he meant to insult by calling him "the celebrated Jew". "Should there not be", retorted the Pastor of the diocese, "enough respect due to what is most sacred in the depths of our souls and to what can safeguard the brotherhood of hearts in our sorrowful France to preserve us from such remarks? Let us take care: such an aberration could well become more serious than defeat, for defeat is a catastrophe from which one can get back up again every day, while this anti-Christian work would become a poison from which one can die." An oratorical remark, undoubtedly, in Gerlier's own style, but it is indicative of one of his constant preoccupations. Approached through the device of literary criticism, and this time without any direct allusion to the government, the lesson was nevertheless clear and well adapted to "Catholic means". Yet we must remember that *La Semaine religieuse* of December 12, censored, was not able to record it in its entirety.

A few days later, on January 1, 1942, the Archbishop again alerted his diocese "against the present deviations from charity". Which was to say, essentially against anti-Semitic feelings, against "remarks and actions that stir up hatred, vengeance". This text, which appeared in *La Semaine religieuse* of January 5, has been quoted along with the following remark: "But the Cardinal said nothing of the basic problem." [27] It seems to

[27] Cf. *Colloque de Grenoble*, 161–62.

me that the essential reminder a pastor had the responsibility of giving to his people on that occasion was indeed given. And as we have seen above (Chapter 11), when new facts were revealed during that year of 1942, what is called here "the basic problem" was nonetheless vigorously treated, either by official addresses to the authorities, by personal support of those devoted to snatching away the victims of the agents of nazism or by a solemn pastoral letter. Nor do I see the pertinence of the following remark: "In fact, at the beginning of 1942, the Cardinal hesitated once again. The decisive outburst came, moreover, from a few priests and militants." Without denying, certainly, these influences, it must be noted well that the "decisive outburst" was provoked by a new, enormous, unexpected event, which could thus not have been the object beforehand of long "hesitations". The Cardinal, on the contrary, committed himself very promptly and deeply.

His attitude had already earned him more than once recognition by the Jews as well as violent abuse from the "collaborators". On May 13, 1942, in his speech to the assembly of the rabbinate, the President of the central consistory declared, in a rather solemn way but without giving any reason to suspect his sincerity: "Judaism could never be sufficiently grateful for what prelates, priests, pastors and faithful, both Catholic and Protestants, have done for us without any ulterior motive. And my gratitude is addressed particularly to the Prince of the Church, who is compassionate and charitable to all the unfortunate, who exercises with so much magnanimity today his title of Primate of the Gauls, both in name and in deed." [28] When, shortly afterward, the new efforts made by the Cardinal were known, this gratitude only grew, and it was again expressed in Lyons through new public testimony by Sylvain Goldschmidt. This was on September 4, two days

[28] Gerlier's cordial though powerless dedication consoled this old man for the attitude of Pétain, who had otherwise been his friend (cf. Marrus and Paxton, 87). Helbronner died after having been deported with his wife.

before the pastoral letter that was to be read in all the churches in the diocese.

On orders from the occupying forces, the press was unleashed in revenge. In *Au Pilori*, for example, one could read on October 8: "On account of his priestly authority, which he prostitutes, this man is a public danger, and he is one of those who deserves to be executed immediately. In the name of France, in the name of my beloved country, of all Christianity, I demand the head of Gerlier, Cardinal, delirious Talmudist, traitor to his Faith, to his country, to his race, Gerlier, I hate you!"[29] *L'Oeuvre*, during the same period, denounced with respect to him "the alliance of great, ambitious climbers in the Church with the Jewish community", a "total, absolute" alliance. But whatever the poor Cardinal said or did during those four terrible years, it seems that, even among those who really want to recognize his merit, some believe themselves nevertheless to be formally obliged to add a severe restriction, a reproving "but" to it, which, we must repeat, implies a lack of retrospective imagination, an astonishing ignorance of the circumstances and real possibilities.

Even as early as 1940, the censor was demanding omissions in text. Since the voids were too obvious, the censor demanded that the manuscripts be touched up, or the censor himself did some cutting. For example, Gerlier's speech of December 12, 1941, could not be reproduced as a whole either in *La Semaine religieuse* or in the journal of *La Chronique sociale*. On March 4, 1942, the editorial committee of *La Chronique* complained to the Cardinal that they could quote from him only the words chosen by the censor. When, gathered under the presidency

[29] Cf. P. Pierrard, 292, who also quotes Brasillach accusing Saliège in *Je suis partout*, August 21, 1942, of "a rather open revolt against the new order". Neither was Boegner spared: "Champion of Jewry", etc. (cf. 153). G. Wellers, 267, also quotes *Au Pilori* against Gerlier: "This infamous priest, in virtue of a pact concluded with the international Jewry, directs his clergy along the criminal path he has chosen."

of the Archbishop of Lyons, the Assembly of bishops denounced the massive shipments into Germany as "an attack on natural family rights", its text was mutilated. The German censor suppressed long passages of the official declaration of the A.C.A. of February 1944, which distorted its meaning.[30] It is well known that *La Semaine religieuse* of Bayonne was banned for having inserted without review the protest of its bishop in September 1942, and that Archbishop Petit de Julleville of Rouen "put an end to the existence of his *Semaine religieuse* on October 2, 1942, when the German authorities imposed the publication of an article on the measures of Paul IV against the Jews".[31] Another example: a book by the Grand Rabbi Kaplan, *Témoignages sur Israël*, was seized at the publisher's, and as the author had then tried to reduce it to a pamphlet containing only a few texts chosen from the most peaceable and signed by the most illustrious French authors, he received this simple notice: "French state. Refused, Central Censorship Service."[32] Conscientious studies have been made on "the reactions of Christians according to the *Semaines religieuses* of the five dioceses of the free zone", and this was with good reason, although the term *free zone* was hardly adequate; they are not without interest, and nothing should be overlooked. But, as Bishop Maisonobe of Belley, disciple and friend of Saliège, has recalled: "Of course, it was not in the official text of *La Semaine religieuse* of that time that one will find many traces . . ."[33]

All that is of the past. But why, when it is a question of Cardinal Gerlier, must we be obliged, in reading the historians of those terrible years, to beware so frequently of tendentious

[30] Paul Droulers, "Catholiques sociaux et révolution nationale", in *Colloque de Lyon*, 222. Guerry, 68. R. Bédarida, 121, etc.

[31] J. M. Mayeur, in *F.Q.J.*, 164.

[32] Kaplan, *Justice pour la foi juive*, 102–3.

[33] *Colloque de Grenoble*. The remark was made at the symposium (p. 59) by Msgr. Michel Mondésert, auxiliary bishop of Grenoble.

accounts and little evasions? "The underground press", we are told, for example, "published the letter addressed to the Marshal on August 20, 1942, by Pastor Boegner", but Gerlier's letter of the same date, also reproduced, is forgotten. It is pointed out that the B.B.C. quoted, in September 1942, the letters of Saliège and Théas as well as the address of the prelates of the occupied zone to Pétain; Gerlier's letters, the second of which at least was also quoted in London, are not mentioned. Moreover, they tell us that "the celebrated letter of Msgr. Saliége" was reproduced, but they do not say that that of Msgr. Gerlier was also—nor, of course, that "Cardinal Gerlier, in public opinion, incarnated the protest against the persecution", as has nevertheless been observed by a serious as well as equitable historian who is in no way given to excessive praise.[34] Further, we are told that "the Resistance had united in order not to hand over the [Jewish] children demanded of the O.S.E. (Union Mondiale pour la Protection de la Sante des Populations Juives et Oeuvres de Secours aux Enfants) and Cardinal Gerlier by the regional authorities", which is correct but incomplete, and which insinuates that Gerlier had nothing to do with it. Or, if one reproduces fairly the letter

---

[34] J. M. Mayeur, in *F.Q.J.*, 164, does not for all that forget that "a certain prudence and a deep personal affection for the Marshal, however, removed from his protest the prophetic style present in the protest of someone like Saliège". He likewise notes, with neither hostility nor scorn, "certain illusions of Pastor Boegner" (165). See also A. Latreille and R. Rémond, *Histoire du catholicisme en France*, 2d ed., 3 (Spes, 1962): 618: "Read from the pulpit, disseminated by the underground press, carried to the ends of the country by an extraordinarily prompt and effective oral transmission, the declarations of Cardinal Gerlier, Archbishop Saliège and Bishop Théas had a tremendous effect, and the protest of the pastors found an echo in the dedication of the priests and the faithful" (cf. Robert Aron, *Histoire de Vichy*, 506). In the *Revue d'histoire de l'Eglise de France*, 59 (1973), 1:244, "Specific aspects and problems in the history of the Jews in France", L. Landeau quotes for the summer of 1942 the letters of Saliège, Théas and Delay, but there is no question of Gerlier; a little before, he quotes a protest by Boegner but omits the parallel protest by Gerlier.

read in the parishes of the Lyons diocese on September 6, 1942, how could one immediately regret that it "rather gives the impression of condemning more the measures of execution of the deportation than the deportation itself"? Much subtlety is needed to arrive at such a judgment, which seems to us not only excessive but erroneous; which presupposes first of all a curious inversion in a text that is nevertheless correctly quoted: "The execution of measures" does not have the same meaning as "the measures of execution". Besides, these "measures of execution", in their immediate brutality, had been the first thing known, the only thing directly perceived by the population: first (as far as Lyons is concerned), on August 11, in the Perrache station, where the train coming from Rivesaltes had stopped, transporting around five hundred men and women in cattle cars, then from August 20 to 22, the nightly roundup in the Jewish quarters of the city. This is what had caused the emotional impact in the region. It is normal that the Archbishop had alluded to it—but he did not linger there. Pastor Boegner's letter to Pétain stresses these "measures of execution" even more, and no one dreamed or would dream, certainly, of reproaching him for it. Why, then, note with the severity of an inquisitor that Gerlier, in his letter to Pétain of August 1942, had spoken too timidly on the subject of the Jews, whose defense he was undertaking, about "anticipated treatment", instead of shouting plainly the truth that had just been revealed to him—although it is apparently found to be quite natural that, a few days later, with even more reserve, Saliège described these same Jews rounded up into camps as "embarked for an unknown destination"?[35]

Despite the esteem and even admiration one feels for men who sacrificed themselves in tragic times with great courage and who had to participate, under trying circumstances, in overheated discussions, one cannot help but find somewhat incoherent the remarks made in a quite recent symposium

---

[35] See above, Chap. 11.

by Eugène Claudius-Petit, with respect to the rescue of the Jewish children in Lyons in August 1942: "We went to see the prefect, . . . we went to see Cardinal Gerlier, both . . . to express our surprise about certain phrases and about a certain leniency, but at the same time to ask them to do the rest, that is, the impossible. The impossible, that was to do all that could be done for the Jewish children. True, we would perhaps have preferred a martyr, but he was what he was, and he did all that he could. Ah! If it were necessary to reject all who came to the Resistance only after the fact!" How are we to understand this? The Archbishop and the Prefect presented like associates against whom it was necessary to fight, and who are soon merged into one—who made the mistake of not dying as a martyr, but who was nevertheless recognized as holding his own against the Prefect and as having helped greatly in the rescue!

The author of these reflections, who belonged to the underground network of "Franc-Tireur" (increasingly dominated by anticlerical influences),[36] was not close to Cardinal Gerlier and he might, in good faith, not have understood him. Jean-Marie Soutou, who because of his work with l'Amitié chrétienne had more occasion to see Gerlier at close range, recalled in his account of a similar scene the disagreement he had one day had with him, a disagreement that in the end amounted to very little. It occurred at just about the same time, at the end of August 1942:

> Fr. Braun . . . was with me by one of the Archbishop's windows when Fr. Chaillet and Abbé Glasberg took the decisive step in relation to the children snatched from deportation by l'Amitié chrétienne. I remember that the Cardinal, trying to convince the Prefect of Lyons on the telephone, left the realm of morality where he probably should have stayed and had recourse to some juridical arguments. He said: "You have studied law. So have I.

[36] In F.Q.J., 372. On "Franc-Tireur et les Juifs": Dominique Veillon, 315–29.

I am a lawyer, and I can tell you that your thesis does not seem sound to me." Now, it is true: there was a juridical problem, since l'Amitié chrétienne had obtained the transfer of parental rights for each child in circumstances that were not in conformity with the law. But this problem was absurd, and it would have been better had he refused to speak of it.

One is free to think either that the Cardinal was in fact imprudent to appeal to a juridical argument for help or that Soutou perhaps gave proof of excessive purism in this instance. Was that truly a sacrilegious argument, unworthy of a noble cause? I will not attempt—it would be ridiculous—to serve as a referee in retrospect of a debate long since posthumous. Besides, as we can see, it was only a matter of one of those usual little clashes between companions in work and war. And Soutou himself continues: "I have been made to say in certain published texts that I had refused to give the Cardinal the addresses of refuges where we had hidden the children because 'I did not trust him'." He explains the difficulties in which each struggled, and he concludes, with a loyal and generous heart: "I do not believe I experienced any feeling of distrust at that time with respect to the Cardinal. I firmly believe that his action in this matter was very positive and that, without him, we would not have been able to do what was done."[37]

---

[37] In *F.Q.J.*, 252 (Symposium of March 10–12, 1979), J. M. Soutou returned to the question shortly afterward, on June 25, at the annual conference of the *Alliance israélite universelle*: "Without him [Cardinal Gerlier], what was done could not have been done. . . . There is one point I must clear up, for some things have been said about it with which I cannot agree. I never thought that Cardinal Gerlier would hand over the children entrusted to l'Amitié chrétienne. . . . But I was afraid that his inexperience with underground methods might make him unknowingly the victim of Vichy's machinations. We did not give the addresses [of the hidden children] even to ourselves, as it were. We had to be as little informed about them as possible, for obvious reasons" (typed text, July 9, 1979).

Those historians who have a tendency to set themselves up as examining judges without managing to reconstruct the atmosphere of the period would therefore be wrong in drawing arguments for their indictments from these memories filled with emotion or from other similar ones. They would also do well not to forget that in those tragic days, the Archbishop increased the steps, recommendations, indeed, the orders in order to assure a refuge for the Jewish children in the convents of his diocese, "while ensuring that they would be returned to their parents or to Jewish organizations" and making all necessary arrangements in union with André Weil and Chaillet. They should also remember that the following year, with respect to the S.T.O., on May 18, he went further than the declaration made jointly with the other two cardinals, in language at once more clear and more energetic: "Force can bend wills, but it cannot wipe away injustice or absolve the refusal to consider what is right."

Cardinal Gerlier intervened as much as he could with Pétain, in the stubborn hope of obtaining some effective gesture and of rallying around his name some large resistance to the "collaboration" party. Disappointed, he would no longer even mention his name. But for some historians, this fact immediately became another reproach: Gerlier went over to some less than honorable form of waiting game, condemning acts of violence. We think, rather, that there is to be seen here a gesture worthy of a true pastor. The warning was not only opportune but urgent. Like Gerlier, Saliège had made it understood, and likewise in February 1944 the Assembly of cardinals and archbishops: "We condemn these appeals to violence and these acts of terrorism that are tearing our country to pieces, provoking the assassination of people and the plundering of homes."[38] This was also the position of one of the last *Cahiers du T.C.*, *Exigences de la Libération*, which condemned terrorism and drew the line at "resistance", passive or active.

[38] In Guerry, 36. J. Guitton, *Le Cardinal Saliège*, 172–73.

Still another complaint had been put forward, one which we have already encountered from the pen of Rabi.[39] Although I could not begin to explain such an aberration, it had just been taken up again, three years later. When the Archbishop of Lyons, in July and August 1942, intervened as we have seen in order to defend the persecuted Jews with such persistence, he supposedly quite simply *"ran to the help of victory"*![40] Gifted with a political intuition that was keener than Laval's, he thus supposedly anticipated one year ahead of time the about-face of the French government, which in 1943 would endlessly delay and finally never publish the law that it had prepared under pressure from Darquier de Pellepoix. According to the terms of this law, French Jews naturalized after August 10, 1927, having become foreigners, would be immediately arrested and deported. "It was only too evident", states J. Delarue, "that Laval", in this retreat, which made the nazis furious, "had not been persuaded by a sudden awakening of conscience. . . . After Stalingrad in February, the retreat from Tunisia at the end of March, the Allied landing in Sicily at the beginning of July. . . ",[41] the moment was well chosen for this "abrupt reversal". Gerlier, more cunning, had thus foreseen all this one year earlier, at the height of nazi power. Why not say as much for Saliège, or for the whole French episcopate (with the exception of a few backward members)?

Cardinal Gerlier was not acting out of "very reckless courage"—about which André Latreille has insisted on reminding us—when, in June–July 1944, he stood up to the Germans and

---

[39] Cf. above, Chap. 5, p. 64.

[40] In *F.Q.J.*, 258. All rests on a remark supposedly made by Fr. Chaillet to the author in 1941, according to which Gerlier would not have supported him had he known of his contact with such friends in the Resistance as the author. Cf. the wise reflections by A. Latreille, *Colloque de Lyon* (1978), 246.

[41] J. Delarue, in *F.Q.J.*, 70–72; similarly, 140. Cf. the report by Roethke of August 15, 1943, Pétain's irritation, the discussions at Vichy itself of R. and Geissler with Laval and Bousquet: text and account in L. Poliakov, *Bréviaire de la haine*, 201–6.

the chief of the Gestapo,[42] only later becoming more circumspect and reserved since he was unable to protest: this was an
uncontrolled movement of the heart, which this time got the
better of his mind.[43] What does this mean if not that, according
to his basic thinking, he was for the established order, even
if nazi, against all resistance, even the purest, and incurably
anti-Semitic? There we are, in another form, brought back
to that "Maurras trend", from which he undoubtedly made
efforts to "dissociate himself" but with which his mind, one
supposes, despite the experience of those four atrocious years,
still remained impregnated. Pure invention, an absurd fable.[44]

---

[42] *Documentation catholique*, September 24, 1944, 14. This was following
the massacre of 110 prisoners from Fort Montluc, at Saint-Genis-Laval. Roger
Radisson was one of the victims. On R. Radisson and the weekly *Position*
1942–1944: Renée Bédarida in *Colloque de Lyon* (1978), 421–33.

[43] Although not going as far as the odious suggestion that appears here,
it seems to me that more than once there has been an abuse of such expressions
as "in general hearts reacted better than minds", or "hearts that were more
Christian than minds". Applied with arbitrariness, they would allow a kind
of recognition in passing, as if between parentheses, of the "courage" or the
"charity" of Gerlier and other pastors who in fact were very active in their
work to save the Jews and hostages and to protect members of their dioceses
or parishes. These formulas might be applied with great appropriateness, and
without any depreciating ulterior motives, to many of the French, Christian
or not, who, without having had the means or the occasion to form any idea
whatever of Israel, simply turned one day to the persecuted beings whom it
was necessary to assist in their misfortune.

[44] Letter from Cardinal Gerlier, which he personally carried and read to
Commander Knap, on August 22, 1944, on his return from Saint-Genis-Laval:
    "I have the painful duty of bringing you, along with the expression of the
indignation I experienced in the face of a spectacle that words cannot portray,
a solemn protest against the abominable cruelty of the execution carried out
there on August 20 and that continues, alas, to be carried out against many
others.
    " . . . I have seen in the course of my life many horrible spectacles. I have
never seen any that revolted me as much as that which I viewed there a
moment ago. . . .
    "I am convinced that you yourself are not aware of the refinement of
savagery that marked that atrocious execution, but I do not hesitate to declare

As if this had been the occasion for coolly spouting forth some dissertation refuting erroneous doctrines![45]

Soon after the death of the Cardinal, the Grand Rabbi Kaplan, in a broadcast of *Ecoute Israël* (January 28, 1965), gave a talk, "Homage to Cardinal Gerlier", in which, after having recalled a certain number of facts, he concluded:

> Justice, according to our Sacred Book, is more than justice. The Just One, for us, is as much a man of goodness as one of equity, a man of piety as one of charity. In the same spirit, Judaism, in numerous texts, mentions the "just from among the nations". Cardinal Gerlier was one of those. He occupied a place of honor among them. This is why his memory will always remain present in our community. As we read in the Talmud: "The just, after their death, continue to exist in thoughts and in hearts."[46]

that those who bear the responsibility for it are forever dishonored in the eyes of humanity.

"May God deign to pardon them!" [in summary].

[45] Scarcely several days after the beginning of the grave events that I have just set forth, the Grand Rabbi Kaplan was to be a victim of the Gestapo. His work *Justice pour la foi juive*, 106–123, gives the passionate account of that day, August 1, in Lyons, when he was tracked down, arrested, led to and detained at his office, searched and, after various incidents across the city, finally released. (At that time, there were in the city of Lyons alone four hundred collaborators of the Gestapo on the hunt, doriotists and others.)

[46] Recorded in *N'oublie pas*, 155–58.

Chapter 13

"Submission to the Established Authority"

What leads one not only to distinguish "churches" and "Christians" in their attitude and their action, when they find themselves in direct contact with situations created by events such as the territorial occupation by nazi Germany and the "national revolution" of the Vichy government—a distinction that is in itself perfectly legitimate and imposed by the merest glance at the facts—but in a way to set them in opposition and thereby to distort the lived reality, is a certain conception of the "official Church" (I am speaking here only of the Catholic Church) and of her doctrine on the authority of the state. It is set forth, for example, in a report presented by Jean-Paul Cointet at the Lyons symposium in 1978.[1] The author draws his statement from the encyclical of Leo XIII promulgated on November 1, 1895, "The Constitution of the States":

> Invoking the authority of St. Paul ("*Non est potestas nisi a Deo*"), Leo XIII was led to consider that the one who is invested with any legitimate power whatsoever is as if clothed with the very authority of God, who gives, so to speak, a sacred character to his own authority, whoever might be the one in whom this authority resides ("*quamvis eam potestatem in persona esse constiterit*"). Two consequences result from this axiom: wholehearted submission to superior authorities and the fact that he who refuses obedience to legitimate authority refuses to obey God himself and deserves punishment.

---

[1] "L'Eglise catholique et le Gouvernement de Vichy, Eglise et Légion", in *Colloque de Lyon*, 1978 (P.U.L., 1982), 435.

This doctrine, which is in fact from St. Paul, is far from expressing the whole doctrine of the Church, herself founded on Scripture, on this subject. Certainly, within the framework of such a report, we cannot demand a complete exposition. But the fact of retaining only one point, even if it be fundamental, inevitably falsifies the whole. It is very true that the Church teaches submission to legitimate authority—and even, in one sense, simply to the "established" authority, within the limits necessary to assure the minimum of social life, of authorities of foreign occupation. But the author has not pursued his reading of the Acts of Leo XIII very far; otherwise he would have read, among others, in the encyclical *Rerum novarum*, of May 15, 1891: "A law deserves obedience only insofar as it is conformed to right reason, and thus to the eternal law of God." Nor does he seem to be very well informed about Catholic Tradition in the matter.[2] That Tradition tells us everywhere that the power, regime or government is one thing and its various acts are something else. The Christian must never take as an absolute rule of conduct an *unconditional* submission accorded in advance to any of its acts. For "in the final analysis, it is neither to a government nor to a regime that one's obedience goes, but to the common good and finally to God in whom that common good is rooted."[3]

So the Christian can agree to submit to an unjust act in his regard or even in regard to a whole group, in order to avoid a greater evil; but he has the duty to refuse to give his assistance to any unjust act, whoever might be the authority that claims to impose it. It is not a question here of debating the legitimacy of the origin upon which one regime or another might pride itself: in most cases that is arguable, and it is less the origin

---

[2] It is to his credit that he was able to gather information from several scholars of the period, who were strangely forgetful, as we will later see.

[3] Roger Heckel, S.J., *Le Chrétien et le Pouvoir* (Le Centurion, 1962), 38; cf. 50.

of a power that renders it legitimate than its capacity to ensure the common good.[4] St. Augustine had no illusions about the origins of Rome: it was founded, he said, "like another Babylon", in crime; yet, after having "subjected the whole earth by force, it brought peace everywhere by uniting it in the society of one single republic ruled by the same laws", and its power assured "the tranquility of order"; it was in this measure that it was legitimate.[5] The question envisaged here is different. It was resolved clearly, in principle, by the authority of the Church. I will cite only two attestations of it.

The celebrated *Catechism of the Council of Trent* teaches, in the chapter on the Fourth Commandment of God: if, among those who have authority over us,

> one encounters some who are wicked, it is the divine authority that resides in them that . . . we revere, not their malice. . . . Consequently, the knowledge that they have an irreconcilable enmity against us is not sufficient reason to dispense us from rendering them . . . obedience. . . . Nevertheless, when they command us to do something bad or unjust, we must not obey them, because in that they are not acting through the legitimate authority entrusted to them by God but through the impulse of their own injustice and from their own malice.[6]

In a more sober style, and with extreme cases in mind, St. Thomas Aquinas taught no less clearly: "A tyrannical government is not just, since it is not ordained to the common good. . . . Thus the overthrow of this regime does not have

---

[4] "When a constitution, written or unwritten, goes back into the darkness of time, we easily forget the vices of its origins or we idealize them"; the same is true when it is a question of recent changes: thus the numerous regimes that succeeded each other in France during the nineteenth century have all been contested, "because practically all were established in a confused climate and because some original fault could be detected at the beginning of all of them": R. Heckel, 15–18, who quotes Leo XIII, *Notre consolation*, May 3, 1892.

[5] *City of God*, l. 9, c. 12; l. 18, c. 22.

[6] French trans. (Paris, 1686), 468–69. Cf. Marveau-Carpentier trans., 1905.

the character of sedition, except in the case where the overthrow is carried out in such disorder that it leads to greater damage for the people than the tyranny itself."[7]

We should also recall the conduct of the early Christian generations in the midst of an empire that often persecuted them. Recall the exposition and justification that St. Augustine gives of it, particularly with respect to an instance closer to his own time, that of the emperor Julian. Julian was an apostate, iniquitous, idolatrous; soldiers faithful to Christ nonetheless served this infidel emperor; they opposed him only when he wanted to make them apostatize.[8] We should also read that reply of a German bishop to his sovereign Frederick II: "My life belongs to my king, but not my conscience." (The Bishop of Münster, Msgr. von Gallen, quoted these words in his sermon of July 20, 1941, reproduced in its entirety in the second *Cahier du T.C.*, *Notre combat*.) If there is one case, in fact, where the duty to oppose injustice can obviously be applied, it is certainly that of the extreme anti-Semitic measures imposed by Hitlerism. Nevertheless, of course, such a duty was not imposed in the same way or with the same imperative force on everyone. That depended on the situation, the competence, responsibilities, vocations of each one. On the other hand, every time an action of resistance was necessary, it inevitably gave rise to a lack of understanding from various sides. The *Témoignage chrétien* was not always spared this. But there were also many fervent supporters among those who did not have the means for undertaking any action whatever.

The essential distinction we have just seen has always been maintained by the Church, both in theory and in practice—whatever the individual weaknesses or errors, of course, may have been. This was what inspired Cardinal Tisserant, in December 1940, to express the wish to see the appearance of an

---

[7] *Summa theologica, Secundo Secundae*, q. 42, art. 2, ad tertium.

[8] *In psalmum* 61, 8; cf. 51, 6. See H. L., *Théologies d'occasion*, 274–76.

encyclical setting forth "the individual duty to obey the dictates of conscience".[9] This was also what the Catholic Champetier de Ribes had in mind when he wrote on October 29, 1940, in his journal *Le Patriote des Pyrénées*: "A man born French and Christian owes loyalty to the government, whatever it might be, but he owes only a conditional loyalty. No government can demand more than it has a right to. As for the French, a man of this country must be loyal insofar as the government serves the profound interests of the country."[10] The same distinction dictated the formula adopted by the bishops of the occupied zone on July 24, 1941, in Paris, which was later ratified by the episcopate of the entire country on September 5, but with a significant reversal in the construction of the sentence: "It is our wish that, without servility, a sincere and complete loyalty be practiced toward the established authority."[11] It is the same doctrine, but with a different emphasis—all the more so as the bishops then immediately said: "We venerate the chief of state." Their formula assuredly remains susceptible of more or less elastic applications, and its application could more or less tilt in one sense or another. The lesson learned from events that were at that time unforeseeable by most made it lean more and more to the side that human and Catholic fidelity demanded. For in reality, despite a first interpretation that gave too much credit to either the curiously charismatic personality of the head of state or the real feelings of his whole government and to its relative independence, the "without servility" had not been a mere stylistic clause for the episcopate. Increasingly, through the

[9] Cf. Charles Klein in *Colloque de Lyon*, 584.

[10] Quoted by J. Duquesne, 147.

[11] The A.C.A. of Paris, followed by that of Lyons, had already made known to the Pope, on January 15 and February 6, 1941, their loyalty toward the new regime. But several historians seriously distorted the meaning of the texts when they wrote (such as J. Duquesne, 277): "The recognition by the episcopate of the legitimacy of the authority of Vichy, which implied the obligation to obey its laws . . ."

evolution of circumstances, it proved to be urgent. From the beginning, it barred the way to any form of "collaboration". One day when a lawyer had thoughtlessly asserted that "collaboration", seeing that it had been advocated by Marshal Pétain himself, might be recommended by the "two cardinals of Paris" (he was thinking of the aging Baudrillart, who had no pastoral authority),[12] Cardinal Suhard, recounts Fr. Riquet, "asked me to say and to have repeated: 'There is only one Cardinal of Paris, and he is not a collaborator.'" Fr. Riquet goes on to say that Cardinal Suhard never in the days that followed "reproached me for taking a position in favor of the Resistance, nor did he ever give in to the pressure from the German authorities, who many times asked him to have me silenced".[13] It was again in virtue of the same principles that a vigorous letter was written by the Belgian episcopate, on March 15, 1943, against the imposition by the occupying authority of obligatory work service for the youth of the country, and that on May 9, despite the delicate situation that the intermediary existence of the Vichy government created for them, Cardinals Gerlier, Liénart and Suhard had read from the pulpit in the churches of France a text declaring that workers "are being subjected to force, a force that the French government is trying to render more human but that does not constitute for them an obligation of conscience". To the violent protests of the German minister Schleier against "this

[12] Only the enfeebled mind of the elderly Baudrillart can explain such a reversal. In "Les Racistes peints par eux-mêmes" (*Cahier* 4–5, February–March 1942), the *T.C.* reproduced (26) the forceful article that he had published on May 7, 1938, against the anti-Semitic Hitler; cf. Yves Marchasson, "Autour du cardinal Baudrillart", *Colloque de Lyon*, 227–35.

[13] *Chrétiens de France* . . . (S.O.S., 1972), 44–45 and 61. Well before this period, Fr. Michel Riquet had made his debut by leading, in *Etudes*, under the title "Sa Majesté la Loi", an inquiry about the right to oppose oppression. In it, he published the replies of lawyers Léon Duguit, Maurice Hauriou, François Geny and Henri Barthélémy and of theologians Vermeersch, Fallon and Garrigou-Lagrange as well as of Jacques Maritain.

new provocative declaration", which was one more thing, he went on, to be added "to the positions already taken by the Church up to this time in opposition to the Relief [levy of French workers sent to Germany]", Vichy apparently replied that the instigator had been Gerlier, supported by the nuncio.[14] Whatever the German minister may have said, the declaration of the three cardinals, although it stated what was essential, was not very vigorous; but in Lyons, Gerlier did not mince words; he spoke of an "attack made on natural family rights and on the prerogatives of the human person" and in particular proclaimed the term *deportation* prohibited.[15]

To avoid artificial oppositions and ill-considered judgments, moreover, we must never forget, as Fr. Heckel has recalled in the work I have already cited, "that the contribution of the Church", in her leaders and in the whole body of her pastors, takes, and must take above all in troubled times just as always, "the form of spiritual nourishment and the general formation of consciences. This is what many forget, failing to value this contribution until after a number of solemn declarations."[16]

In the same work, Fr. Heckel also stated: "To accept the present regime, loyally, does not constitute an unconditional recognition for the future", and he wondered: "With regard to a legally constituted authority that has become powerless,

[14] *Colloque de Lyon,* 389–90 and 585. Cf. Guerry, 68–73.

[15] The censor mutilated the text of the episcopal Assembly of Lyons, gathered on February 6, 1943, under the presidency of Gerlier.

[16] Op. cit. Cf. Bishop Jean Calvet, *Journal inédit 1939–1945* (Paris: Dessain and Tolra, 1970), 9: June 8, 1940: Rectorial advice: "In a few days . . . from the moment when you know that the Germans are the masters of Paris, tell yourself that I am a prisoner . . . , all that they tell you I have said no longer counts", p. 30, September 20, 1940. Visit to Cardinal Baudrillart, our old rector (82 years old) gives us the example of courage, p. 38, November 22, 1940: "I have seen the cardinal. Between the man whom I saw in September and the man of today, there is an abyss. He is crushed. He sees the Catholic Institute closed forever. . . . He suffers from an obsession; he is dying of it."

incapable of being exercised on a long-term basis, at what moment can one say that it loses its legitimacy?"[17]

Throughout the Occupation, the question naturally had to be asked, but in paradoxical forms. "Vichy" was a mixture of multiple and rival tendencies that sometimes coexisted and sometimes succeeded each other: "National revolution", "realism" of the admirals, the indecisive ambitions of the "synarchy", old-style politics, grandiose plans for European integration; there were also the fanatics of nazism, those of anti-Bolshevism, and even traitors.[18] "Vichy" was a government that was less and less free, or rather more and more enslaved. The French who were clear-sighted could thus see "the needle that marked its legitimacy progressively decline on the scale of justice".[19] During the first two years, discussions and criticisms were certainly not lacking; the most severe were those of the summer of 1942. But beginning with November 1942, when the "southern zone" was invaded, the "prince" appeared to all eyes to be a "slave". Then, without public manifestation, the episcopate allowed itself to express its thought to the old Marshal. It was too late to speak of sailing to Africa, and besides, such advice would have been improper interference. But Bishop Chappoulie, delegated by the Assembly of cardinals and archbishops, came twice to express privately to Pétain and to his entourage "the feeling experienced by a very large number of Frenchmen: that the head of state, in a territory occupied almost entirely by the enemy, had to renounce the exercise of his functions and to consider himself a prisoner".[20]

[17] Ibid., 17 and 40.

[18] See J. B. Duroselle, "Réflexions sur la France face à la 'guerre totale' d'Adolf Hitler", in *Mélanges offerts à André Latreille*, 355.

[19] G. Fessard, "Journal de la conscience française", *Etudes*, January 1945, 87. Cf. J. M. Mayeur, in *F.Q.J.*, 166, on the "necessity of studying the chronology closely, particularly essential in a time of crisis".

[20] Cf. Guerry, 275, n., and 360.

But beginning with this period, a new, more serious problem was posed to the conscience of the bishops, one that directly concerned their pastoral responsibility and became more acute every day. A good idea of this can be grasped by rereading the orders, which some must have at first thought surprising, given by Cardinal Suhard to the principal representatives of the Catholic movements, called together in his archdiocese on December 11, 1942:

> Nothing [he tells them in substance] of what we declared in July 1940 has been modified. The Church carries on her activity on the spiritual level without servile submission and in complete loyalty to the civil authority. She has the impression, in fact, that it is the only way for her to maintain, as far as possible, the indispensable, fundamental stability for her own mission and, at the same time, to help the civil authority itself in the very precarious position in which it is placed.

"The Cardinal", comments Fr. Michel Riquet, who related these remarks to us,[21] "frankly recognized that the authority of the Vichy government was, even before the last events, 'a diminished authority', and that this was more and more the case. In answer to the question posed by more than one, about the loyalty due to an authority thus diminished", the Cardinal and his colleagues replied that to refuse one's support, given the fact of our internal divisions, would be to expose the country to anarchy. He admitted that each one, in the face of his particular situation, must make the decision dictated by his conscience, but he "did not want to compromise the Church in the intrigue of an insurrection that would breed anarchy, which the occupying power could drown in blood", "nor did he want to involve her in the equivocal ways of a collaboration with national socialism".[22]

That was wisdom. (This, as we will see later on, was the great concern of Fr. de Montcheuil.) But at the same time—

---

[21] *Chrétiens de France dans l'Europe enchaînée* (S.O.S., 1972), 126–27.
[22] Ibid., 128.

and not at all through some base opportunism, which was very unjustly attributed to them—that the bishops were insisting on avoiding "servility", Catholics who were "resisting" the occupying forces felt more encouraged, and three days after the promulgation of the so-called law of the S.T.O., the episcopate itself was to become, as Archbishop Guerry wrote, if not entirely a "conscientious objector", at least a liberator of consciences: "In the two declarations of the A.C.A., April 1943 and February 1944, the only two official documents destined for the faithful during this period, there was no longer even a single reminder of the duty to submit to the established authorities. This silence . . . was intentional. Even more, it was in 1943 that the A.C.A. opposed a law of the French state"; above the positive law, the Church recalled "the sovereignty of moral law".[23]

On February 19, 1943, thanks to a thousand dangerous precautionary measures, these words launched by Vatican Radio could be picked up here and there: "The Church does not accept regimes built on forced labor, nor on the uprooting of populations, nor on collective or individual deportations, on the exploitation of peoples, on the dispersion of families." *Cahier* 17 of the *Témoignage chrétien*, which was distributed in June, quotes this text and takes its inspiration from it. It also quotes the Declarations of Cardinal Liénart (March 21), the three cardinals of France (April 7 and 8), of Cardinal Saliège (April 18), of Archbishop Dubourg of Besançon and of the four bishops of his province. Of course sometimes a complaint could be heard from the young Resistance workers about what

[23] Op. cit., 360; cf. 362. From the end of 1942, says M. Ruby, 392, "there would no longer be any collective declaration of allegiance to the regime". The word *allegiance* is not very fortunate, for it suggests more than simple loyalty. The old Bishop Chollet, who was undoubtedly a completely exceptional case, declared on September 1, 1941: "We do not have the right to discuss the person of the leader or his commandments; the subordinate obeys without seeking or asking the reason."

they called, in their lack of experience, "the ecclesiastical circumspection of the episcopal body": that in no way detracted from the profound understanding between this "episcopal body" and *Témoignage chrétien*, each freely playing its own role.

In August 1943, Bishop Chappoulie was again delegated to go to Vichy to protest against the law already signed by Laval (but which would never be promulgated), which would remove en bloc French citizenship from Jews naturalized after 1927. "The Church", he explained, "considers herself as it were committed to taking up the defense of the weak and oppressed; she also considers herself the guardian of the natural law, and to dislocate families is to attack this law."[24] On November 16, in his address at the beginning of the school year for the Catholic Institute of Toulouse, Bishop Bruno de Solages, rector, treating principles of "moral theology", demonstrated once more, according to the traditional Catholic teaching, that the basis for the legitimacy of a regime or legislation is not the "established authority" but the "common good" (he would soon be deported).[25] In his pastoral letter

[24] Quoted in Deroo, 90.

[25] See his text in the small volume published in 1946: *Discours interdits* (Ed. Spes). This little volume contains speeches given by Bishop de Solages that had been censored during the time of the Occupation. "From the time of our first conflict [with the censor] with respect to the publication of the speech at the beginning of the school year [of the Catholic Institute of Toulouse in 1942] on truth, I had written to the censor that I was protesting against the very principle of a censorship that was both dishonest—because it did not allow any indication that a passage had been removed—and abusive—because while pretending to be military censorship, it was in fact a political censorship that went to the point of preventing the spiritual authorities from making the Gospel truth heard. It even attacked, constantly, the declarations of bishops and cardinals, indeed, even pontifical texts." He refused every time to publish a text that had been censored in this way, thereby making it a "forgery". A few titles: "La Vérité" [The truth], "La Théologie moral" [Moral theology], "Bergson, témoin spirituel" [Bergson, spiritual witness], "Le Pape" [The Pope], etc. In conclusion: "La Liberté des âmes" [The freedom

for Lent of 1944, Bishop Blanchet of Saint-Dié, is also prudent with respect to a government that lost what legitimacy it might have had when it fell completely into the hands of the occupying power, but the preservation of which despite its faults might still spare the country, to a certain point, a civil war and anarchy followed by definitive domination by one of the two totalitarianisms: the red or the brown. On the other hand, he insists with vigor, quoting Leo XIII, on the essential difference between the regime and its legislation.[26] The exemplary value of this pastoral letter derives from the fact that its author renews the same teaching that had already been given to the members of his diocese in September 1941.[27]

On September 17, 1944, in the form of a reply to one of the members of his diocese, Archbishop Roques of Rennes would publish a letter in which the principles of Catholic doctrine in this matter are set forth once more with great clarity. It is a long catechism lesson, whose interest this time stems from the application made to the new situation created on the day General de Gaulle entered Paris. Its author recalls there in particular, in the "application of principles", in reply to an objection that had been made to him, that "the presence of a diplomatic representative at Vichy was only the de facto

---

of souls], given at the Easter Mass, on April 1, 1945, in the concentration camp at Neuengamme: "We are celebrating this Easter morning our interior freedom, that freedom which, as prisoners, we have been able to maintain, with regard to everything and despite great odds, that freedom which no external power, not even the firing squad or the gas chamber, can take away from a human creature without his own consent, that freedom of souls . . . which we owe to Christ." An explanation of the Paschal mystery followed. On Bishop de Solages, 1895–1984, Catholic Institute of Toulouse, Supplement to the *Bulletin de littérature ecclésiastique*, Chronicle no. 9 (1985), 72 pages.

[26] Cf. Leo XIII, "Lettre au clergé de France" [Letter to the Clergy of France], *Au milieu des sollicitudes*, February 16, 1892. Texts in *La Documentation catholique*, October 1, 1944, 3–8.

[27] Reproduced in *La Vie catholique, documents et actes de la Hiérarchie 1940–1941*, 96–97.

recognition of Marshal Pétain's government. For if the Church preaches subordination to established authorities, if she deals with them, . . . she does not for all that interpret this as investing them with a title of legitimacy that they might lack";[28] she accepts without any ulterior motive the civil authority in the form in which it exists, for "the supreme criterion of the common good and public tranquility imposes the acceptance of new established governments, in fact, in place of former governments that, in fact, no longer exist".[29]

For almost twenty centuries, the relations between the Church and what I would in brief call the state have always been turbulent.[30] But never, without doubt, has the antagonism been so absolute in our country as in these years when the Third Reich occupied our land. Two concepts were at war with each other and both were intransigent: that of the Church, defending man and his conscience; that of modern totalitarianism, reviving for a more inhuman undertaking, with incomparably stronger means, the claims of the old pagan authoritarianism. One maintained, in fidelity to the Gospel, that the authority of the state comes from God; the other supported the unappealable authority of the deified state. The heralds of the second were often fanatics: one of their compatriots could say of them that they were "master executioners, possessing a kind of clairvoyance based on demonic instincts".[31] They were served by misguided minds, committed to the principle of the unconditional oath, or intoxicated by

---

[28] The author quotes the Apostolic Letter of Gregory XVI, *Sollicitudo*, of August 7, 1831, recalling that "through the official recognition of those who preside in any way whatever over public matters, no rights have been attributed to them, established or approved".

[29] The last text is borrowed from the Letter of Leo XIII, *Aux cardinaux français*, of May 3, 1892.

[30] I have treated this problem briefly in *Méditation sur l'Eglise*, chap. 5, "L'Eglise au milieu du monde", 2d ed., Théologie, 27 (Aubier, 1952), 139–73.

[31] Ernst Jünger, *Journal de guerre et d'Occupation, 1939–1948*, Henri Plard trans. (Julliard, 1965), 222; cf. 280, on "the nihilism in Chief Heydrich".

202 CHRISTIAN RESISTANCE TO ANTI-SEMITISM

propaganda, or simply motivated by self-interest. For others, their sight was obscured by the screen of the Vichy "authority" (about which one could always debate the measure in which it might be a "lesser evil"). Some seem to have seen the reality only in memory or in their dreams (whence journals such as *Voix françaises* and *Soutanes de France*). A certain number of bishops gave an example of a "personal loyalty that was very little restrained" (Latreille) toward "the Marshal", in whom they placed too much hope; both were the victims of aberrations and at times inconsistent besides,[32] but should this be too surprising? Many of them were ill prepared by even the most elementary teaching to face complicated and completely novel situations. These cases were, moreover, much more rare than we would be led to believe by a legend, based on excessive complaints about which André Latreille has said, with full knowledge of the situation, that they give "an idea of the climate of confusion that could reign at the time of the Liberation in the midst of Catholic Resistance workers who thought themselves to be well informed".[33] It is possible, if one wishes, to pick up some relative weaknesses in tone, stemming from the fear of a greater evil, in one declaration or another, judged to be too soft, like that which provoked, on February 26, 1944, the (private) thundering letter from Cardinal Saliège to Cardinal Liénart.[34] We can still be surprised

[32] One of them, soon after Montoire, naïvely preached "collaboration", in terms that signified quite the contrary of the real meaning covered by that word. Cardinal Suhard, more of a realist, expressed the morally unanimous opinion of the episcopate in a note of April 1941: "Collaboration is not at all possible today, since to submit cannot be to collaborate. Now we are submitting" (quoted by J. Duquesne, 174). Cf. A. Latreille, in *Colloque de Lyon*, 592–93.

[33] Ibid., 65. Latreille also says: "At the time of the Liberation, some Resistance workers held complaints against the bishops based on very inaccurate, very partial and fragmentary memories: people were far from having known everything about their behavior; they knew one striking or excessive word better than hidden acts of courage and dedication."

[34] Saliège's letter and Liénart's reply are quoted by F. Delpech, *Colloque de Lyon*, "Les Chrétiens et le S.T.O.", with a brief remark about "collegiality"

that anyone thought the presence of a nuncio at Vichy meant an absolute guarantee of the legitimacy of the regime, indeed of all its legislation, involving, under pain of sin, without distinction, the duty to support it: besides the absurdity of the doctrine, how could they ignore the fact that there was a nuncio at Berlin? What is most important not to forget, in an overall judgment, is that we were all in a situation that was without precedence, full of ambiguities, in which each one had to untangle in his own way, and often in the dark, what share of responsibility the government had and what share the occupying forces had; in a situation that furthermore never ceased to evolve, with jolts, from the meeting at Montoire to the formation of the "militia". Some were more quickly perceptive about the development of events and their consequences; others were slower to understand, from which arose many differences in appraisal and behavior. But the Catholic fidelity of the "spiritual resistance", like that of the episcopate, to the traditional doctrine of the Church did not, as a whole, substantially change.

I would like to recall, in concluding this section, the case of two priests, Jesuits, who were among the most perceptive observers of events and the most penetrating judges of their deepest meaning.

One, Fr. Fessard, who had opened, as we saw above, the series of the *Cahiers du T.C.*, wrote some notes in 1942–1943 that were to appear in part after the Liberation in *Etudes*, under the title "Journal de la conscience française" [Journal of the French conscience], as well as a voluminous confidential memoir "La conscience catholique devant la défaite et la révolution" [The Catholic conscience in the face of defeat and revolution], the title of which ended up being "Du Prince-Esclave" [Of the slave-prince]; various extracts, in summary or adaptations, were circulated clandestinely. (At the beginning

---

that gives witness to the eccentric interpretations spread in France on the subject of episcopal collegiality, which was called to mind by Vatican II.

of 1943, a condensation of six typed pages was studied by different groups, notably by the Federal Committee of the J.O.C.) [35] It had its origin in a long conversation between Fr. Fessard and Cardinal Suhard in September 1942, on the occasion of a pamphlet by Maurice Lesaunier, director of the university seminary at the Catholic Institute of Paris. The latter, in the simplism of the submission that he taught "without any hesitation" to the government of Marshal Pétain and "without recrimination" toward the occupying authorities, seemed close to the positions of his rector. Now he said his attitude was "commanded by the purest Catholic doctrine", and he had received the Imprimatur of the archdiocese, which impressed even some of the bishops. [36] At the end of their conversation, Cardinal Suhard, very impressed, had asked Fr. Fessard, for whom he had great esteem, to set forth his thinking in writing, so that he could examine it at leisure. One of the priests of the archdiocese would later say to the author of the memoir that his reading of it had troubled the sleep of the archbishop for several nights. In his prudence, the latter did not send any acknowledgment in reply, but neither did he send any sign of reproval or even disagreement. It is besides quite normal, as I have stated above, that in his difficult position the Cardinal would feel obliged to adopt a more circumspect attitude than that of a mere theologian who was committing no one but himself. In any case, the texts that he signed, even if they appeared inadequate to some, obviously prove that he had in no way adopted the theses advanced by Abbé Lesaunier. (The latter, moreover, gave evidence of naïveté rather than a "collaborative mentality", for the pamphlet in question had been drafted around September 1941, a time when many illusions could still haunt a timid soul.) Through

---

[35] Cf. Pierre Bolle, "Les Chrétiens et la Résistance", in *Colloque de Grenoble*, 228.

[36] Cf. Archbishop Marmottin of Reims, in *Notre Journal* (reproduced in *La Vie catholique, documents et actes de la Hiérarchie*, 97–98).

his silence, the good Cardinal discreetly safeguarded Fr. Fessard,[37] just as he had already shielded Fr. Riquet—and undoubtedly, too, he himself was encouraged, through the reading of this memorandum, to resist contrary influences.

Neither the two Fessard articles that *Etudes* made public in January and February 1945 nor the memorandum about the "Slave-Prince" were improvisations. They applied "to the concrete situation of that time and to its slow evolution the general principles" concerning the leader and authority that Fr. Fessard had been studying in depth since the years before the war. After having participated in 1939 in the philosophical group of the journal *Esprit*, he had set forth these principles on May 24, 1941, in a communication to the Lyons Philosophical Society. In February 1942, he had finished a more developed draft of his work, the first part of which, treating authority and the common good in general and avoiding any too explicit allusion to fascism and to national socialism, was able to appear in the volume *Science religieuse, travaux et recherches* (the substitute, during the time of the Occupation, for *Recherches de science religieuse*). In 1945, Aubier would publish, in the new series launched by the scholasticate of Fourvière under the title "Theology" (no. 5), the volume *Autorité et Bien commun* [Authority and the

---

[37] "I had the sad surprise", Fr. Fessard was to write in 1968, "of noting that my work had served no purpose." His disappointment is understandable, but this report of failure is too pessimistic. His work surely made others reflect. It helped to change what had still been only tolerance or fearful interest in more than one instance into approval and tacit support for activities such as the *T.C.* But it was necessary, for the safety of all concerned, that no visible link be suspected. Cardinal Suhard was surely encouraged himself by this reading in his almost daily resistance to solicitations, traps, threats and blackmail attempts of the occupying forces and their "collaborators". We know, for example, the blame he incurred by his presence at Henriot's funeral; the historian must not forget that, despite great pressure, he refused to speak there.

common good], whose value, which was immediately recognized, gave rise very quickly to a second, enlarged edition.[38]

Fr. Jules Lebreton belonged to this same *Etudes* community, living at 15, rue Monsieur, then directed by Fr. René d'Ouince, in whom he as well as Fr. Fessard and Fr. de Montcheuil confided. He was certainly no longer a young fanatic! Professor of fundamental theology for more than thirty years, at the Catholic theology faculty in Paris, he had become its dean. He had published at the beginning of the century a series of important articles directed against modernism, which had earned him some strong enmity but also the warm gratitude of Pius X. In 1910, with Fr. de Grandmaison,[39] he had founded the *Recherches de science religieuse*, the importance of which immediately compelled recognition. His works, in particular his *Histoire du dogme de la Trinité* [History of the dogma of the Trinity], in two large volumes, were authoritative. Deeply spiritual, he enjoyed a kind of veneration in his order and among the clergy.[40] From 1939 on, in *Etudes*, he had warned the Christian conscience against the nazi perversion that was threatening it. In 1940, he published there on March 5, during the "drôle de guerre", an article on "national socialism in conquest of the world"; another, on May 5, on "the swastika against the Cross of Christ"; still another, at the most critical time, on June 5, on "the German Occupation in Poland; the fight against the people and their Faith". Then, in two *Cahiers* of *Construire* (the successor of *Etudes* in Paris), 4 and 8, he published, as a historian, "Jesus and his people under the Roman domination" and "Saint Augustine and an invaded

---

[38] Which appeared, again through Aubier, in the series "R.E.S." ("Recherches économiques et sociales") in 1969, thus long afterward and in a different context.

[39] In his *Mémoires* (Stock, 1974), 83, Cardinal Jean Daniélou recalled that General de Gaulle "had loved Fr. de Grandmaison very much".

[40] On Lebreton: Joseph Lecler, in the encyclopedia *Catholicisme*, vol. 7, col. 140.

Africa", two articles that, at least in their substance, would escape the censor. For Christmas of 1942, he had just put the finishing touches on a long "consultation about several cases of conscience posed to the Catholics of France by the German Occupation".

Like Fessard's "Slave-Prince", obviously, it was a clandestine writing. But it was no more clandestine in relation to the episcopate than the "Slave-Prince" had been. It was not even "unsolicited". It was in fact a reply to a request—it would be still more accurate to say to a "command"—received from Msgr. Courbe, auxiliary bishop of Paris and secretary of the Assembly of cardinals and archbishops, after the invasion of the southern zone in November and the new demands of the occupying authority. I will not reproduce here the text of this consultation because it will soon be published, I am told, in the acts of the symposium held at Biviers (near Grenoble) in September 1984. It is of exemplary vigor and clarity from beginning to end. Its author quotes several lines in it written in 1908 by the future Cardinal Baudrillart: "There is no greater evil for a people than to be conquered on the battlefield, at least when the defeat is as disastrous as that of 1870 was for us, because in this collapse the conquered lose confidence not only in their power but in their national spirit, and they aspire to take on even the same spirit as the conqueror, along with his methods." He shows how much more serious still was the disaster of 1940 and how much more perilous its consequences for the Christian faith. He recalls the recent persecution against the Jews and "the immense danger" of a "spiritual vassalage" that "enlists all the French under the swastika". He ends with the recently proclaimed prayer of Pius XII: "Stop the invading deluge of neopaganism!"

When the A.C.A. gathered for the first time as a whole, in Paris, the consultation of Fr. Lebreton was available to it. It attached a certain importance to it, particularly with respect to the S.T.O., but timidly, too timidly in the eyes of many.[41] (The agreement of the whole Assembly had to be obtained.) It was then that Robert d'Harcourt, a regular visitor at "rue Monsieur", having noted that the exact arguments enunciated by Fr. Lebreton had not been retained by the A.C.A. declaration, which weakened it, persuaded Fr. Lebreton to summarize his text in more succinct terms that would be more accessible to the public at large, and he had this new version printed. "Thirty thousand (?) copies were stored on the *Etudes* premises when the police appeared for a search. A lay collaborator of the journal, the journalist Joseph Brandicourt, carried all those papers away on his bicycle before the Germans had time to inquire about them. The text then began to circulate all over France."[42] It was the object not of critical discussions but of insults among the collaborationists and of hesitations among the more restrained. It reinforced the declaration of the episcopate by founding it on the most explicit reasons, drawn from the nature of nazism, which it had been difficult for the episcopate to set forth in all their harshness.[43]

---

[41] It was in this regard that there was a series of letters between Saliège and Liénart (see above, n. 34). At Fribourg, Abbé Journet, having first of all declared himself disappointed, nevertheless admitted that "a father who senses that he has many fainthearted ones among his children does not speak as if he knew he could count on their clear-sightedness and steadfastness". Cf. *Exigences chrétiennes en politique* (L.U.F., 1945).

[42] According to J. Duquesne, 294, who must have been informed by a good source.

[43] To recall the seriousness of the cases of conscience that were posed to many from June 1940 on, and particularly to the bishops, concerning the questions of legitimacy discussed in this section—questions too often treated lightly and in too emotional a way—one can call General de Gaulle himself as witness. "De Gaulle's action on June 18, 1940, was not only the rebellion *of an officer* against those in power but also the will to substitute a new legitimacy for the old. 'What wrench of conscience did he experience when he decided to disobey? The call of June 18, which stirred all of us, produced in him a horrible drama, he told me' (Joxe)." J. B. Duroselle, *L'Abîme* (1982), 518.

Roger Heckel, S.J., *Le Chrétien et le Pouvoir*
(Ed. du Centurion, 1962), 128–31

France from 1940 to 1944

June 1940: Military collapse, general confusion, breakdown
of the institutions of the Third Republic, in fact as well as in
spirit, all made worse by the occupation of a tyrannical power:
one can indeed speak of a vacuum.

Two Analyses of the Situation in 1940

1. In the beginning, for the majority of the French people,
the vacuum that had suddenly appeared seemed partially filled
by the establishment of new institutions, according to a pro-
cedure that seemed to them to offer all the guarantees of
legality: Chamber and Senate joined in congress and restoring
full powers to Marshal Pétain by a more than comfortable
constitutional majority. For this majority of the French, there
was no doubt that the presumption of legitimacy was in Marshal Pétain's favor, and they had to draw the consequences
of this: obedience to those in power—not idolatry or unconditional obedience, of course—and concern to favor the
national renewal under the management of the power so constituted.

2. From the beginning, a minority of men assessed things

210 CHRISTIAN RESISTANCE TO ANTI-SEMITISM

differently: for them, *France was and would remain in a state of institutional vacuum*, a vacuum simply *veiled* by the new organisms established at Vichy. Whether or not the transfer of authority had been truly constitutional—there were some who doubted it—was of relatively little importance in such an event. If, on the basis of serious information, the French arrived at the reasoned conviction that what *truly* characterized the situation was a *radical impotence* of the new authority to administer the national good, they could legitimately draw the conclusion: insubordination to that apparent authority, to the "Slave-Prince"; they themselves did not claim, however, for the moment, to constitute a government. Simply, in view of the existing vacuum, they *took* the responsibilities for public order that seemed to them the most urgent—they were of the military order—to prepare a situation in which the country could freely produce new institutions.

In accordance with the analysis of the situation that he judges to be good, the Christian should orient himself in one of these two ways, taking full responsibility. The religious authority has neither the office nor the particular light to make *the analysis of the situation* in his place. *That authority, for its part, should enlighten consciences in the various situations.* If the great majority of citizens were convinced in 1940 that the good of the nation was bound up with the Vichy government, the bishops cannot be blamed for enlightening them on their duties in this perspective; that does not mean that the bishops gave them this perspective and, even if they did, they did not invest it with their full authority. Those who have serious reasons for analyzing the situation differently will draw different consequences from it, without for all that being in a true state of insubordination with respect to the religious authority.

Evolution of the Situation

1. Those who rallied to the Vichy government and who gave it obedience progressively noted that the vacuum glimpsed

in 1940 had not been truly filled by the existing legal structure, or at least that the vacuum quickly deepened once again, that larger and larger zones were developing in which the government itself judged that it could no longer exercise authority or in which they could no longer obey in conscience.

The head of state made it explicitly known that he did not always have all the freedom he desired, which was a formal invitation not to apply without caution the principle of presumption in his favor: citizens were invited to make a supplementary effort of discernment and, correlatively, of personal responsibility in arriving at the conviction that an order given was not enacted for the national good.

Effectively, some clearly unjust laws and orders appeared, which the citizen had the right, and at times the urgent duty, to disobey—everything that concerned the pursuit and denunciation of the Jews, to cite but one incontestable example.

Now, under the conditions of the Hitlerian Occupation, limited disobedience could oblige one very quickly to a more general insubordination. More and more numerous men, in a larger and larger part of their life, were cast outside of what was legal. Visible and invisible zones of insubordination developed. The twofold duty to defend oneself against the occupying power and to organize oneself to avoid anarchy and what was arbitrary imposed serious initiatives. The men who took responsibility for it had to exercise it with respect for the moral laws: all means were not legitimate, and there remained the usual duty not to make the general life of the country needlessly difficult.

2. Parallel to this erosion of the situation, the responsibilities of men from London and Algiers increased. They became, in fact, and increasingly, the focus for national reintegration. They had the possibility—and therefore the duty—of helping to organize visible or invisible zones of insubordination over the national territory, of introducing a first cohesion there. This duty without question included the indispensable right to implement it effectively. (This is not a question of justifying

the abuses that, during the Occupation or at the time of the Liberation, were grafted onto initiatives that were legitimate in principle.)

All this brings out the personal responsibility of men. According to the elements of assessment at their disposal, according to the evolution of the situation, they were led to make extremely different choices, to review them periodically, to change them when necessary, as painful as that might have been. Insofar as there was no treason, their eventual opposition to each other must not keep them from respecting each other.

The religious authority cannot be a substitute for the laity: it has neither that office nor that competence. Christians are responsible for the concrete analysis that they make of the changing situation in which they are implicated, each in a different way. Moreover, their personal decision is *never a simple application* of abstract moral principles but *a truly personal way of living these principles*. Animated by the doctrine and the life that they draw from the Church, it is up to them, in their responsibility before God and men, to make the decisions that seem best to them for serving the good of the nation.

When, through these various studies and these confrontations, a power in fact emerges and is constituted, it is henceforth to this power that the obedience of all must be directed. The common good is linked to it, and, the exceptional situation being overcome, political activity will henceforth be situated within the new institutions.

Fr. Roger Heckel
Future bishop coadjutor of Strasbourg

When he wrote these pages, Cardinal de Lubac did not have at his disposal a number of elements contained in the archives of his friend Fr. G. Fessard. A note by the latter, undoubtedly written in 1952 or a little later, furnishes us with the following information. Besides the printed texts brought together in his bibliography, G. Fessard wrote, between 1940 and 1944, the following works, all typed by him, some of which must have been circulated in this form and recopied in whole or in part:

1. October 1940: "Deux compagnies de pionniers dans la bagarre" (Two pioneer companies in the fight); May 10–June 25, 1940: "Souvenirs" (Memories), 214 typed pages in four or five copies.

2. 1941–1942: "Réponse à l'abbé Lesaunier; la conscience catholique en face du devoir civique actuel" (Reply to Abbé Lesaunier; the Catholic conscience faced with the civic duty of today), second revision; forty-seven typed pages.

3. August–October 1942: "La conscience catholique devant la défaite et la révolution" (The Catholic conscience faced with defeat and revolution), 105 typed pages in twelve copies.

4. "Argument [from the preceding text], tract sur Prince-Esclave" (Argument . . . treatise on the Slave-Prince), six typed pages, reproduced.

5. 1942: "Force et justice. Comment un pouvoir de fait devient-il autorité de droit?" (Force and justice. How does a power by fact become an authority by right?), 142 pages.

6. "Appendice [to the preceding text]: Qu'est-ce qu'un pouvoir légitime?" (Appendix . . . : What is a legitimate authority?), thirty-three typed pages.

7. March 1943: "Participation à la guerre totale? ou bien.

213

. . ." (Participation in the total war? or else . . .), clandestine treatise; thirty-nine typed pages.

8. Same year: "Croisade pour la civilisation chrétienne?" (Crusade for Christian civilization?), clandestine tract; forty-three typed pages.

9. May–July 1944: "Paternité et fraternité" (Fatherhood and brotherhood), about a hundred typed pages.

10. 1944–1945: "Avant-propos pour *Au temps du Prince-Esclave*" (Foreword for *In the time of the Slave-Prince*), book before reuniting the preceding treatises, which were to be published by Maryse Choisy in *Cahiers de la IVe République*; twenty-four typed pages.

11. 1945: "Journal de la conscience française (1940–1944)" (Journal of the French conscience [1940–1944]), 125 typed pages, excerpts from which appeared in *Etudes*.

12. "Conclusion" to the *Journal de la conscience française (1940–1944)*, 229 typed pages, numbered 126–354, excerpts from which were published in *Cahiers du Monde nouveau*.

13. May–July 1945: "Libéralisme, nazisme et communisme" (Liberalism, nazism and communism), three articles intended for *Etudes*, but not published; ninety-six typed pages.

Additional information on Fr. Fessard's activity during the Second World War will be found in Gabriel Marcel and Gaston Fessard's work, *Correspondence annotated by Henri de Lubac, Marie Rougier and Michel Sales*. Introduction by Xavier Tilliette (Paris: Beauchesne, 1985). Cf. also Gaston Fessard, *Eglise de France, prends garde de perdre la foi!* (Paris: Julliard, 1979), 292–94. For G. Fessard's bibliography during this period: ibid., 301–2 and 310–11. The text entitled "Collaboration et Fidélité", which appeared in the clandestine *Cahiers* of the *Témoignage chrétien*, October–November 1942, reproduces in substance the text of the first clandestine *Cahier* (*France, prends garde de perdre ton âme!*), very slightly revised by Fr. Chaillet to take the date of publication into consideration.

Note by Fr. Michel Sales

Chapter 14

Yves de Montcheuil

While Fr. Fessard was writing his first *France, prends garde . . .* in Lyons, on rue Sainte-Hélène, and Fr. Chaillet, from the hill of Fourvière, was continuing the clandestine preparations that were to end in the launching of his *Cahiers*, Fr. Yves de Montcheuil, their confrere and friend, could not participate in the enterprise, for the demobilization had led him directly to Paris, to the *Etudes* house directed by Fr. d'Ouince, from which he wrote me on July 3, 1940: "So here I am, safe and sound, but, as you can imagine, very sad"; with no illusions about the "honorable façade of an aged and circumvented Pétain", he further told me: "Perhaps we will have occasion to know what it means to take a risk in order to assure the freedom of the word of God; this will be the moment for proving that all we said before the war was more than the sterile chatter of people living in security." Soon his initiative was going to outstrip that of his Lyons friends, for at least by November 1940 he was composing and having distributed a treatise against the mortal danger of Hitlerian racism and anti-Semitism.[1] But the "demarcation line" kept us from knowing about it, just as it kept him for some time from knowing about the first numbers of the *Cahiers du Témoignage*

---

[1] "Reflections on several themes in order to orient ourselves in a Christian direction in the problems raised by the outbreak of anti-Semitism in the contemporary world." These pages would be published in 1945 in *l'Eglise et le Monde actuel* (Ed. of the T.C.), 2d ed., 106–23. (In the table of contents this text is entitled "Le chrétien en face de l'antisémitisme".)

chrétien; later, he was to be one of the principal organizers of their distribution in the occupied zone. Around the end of 1941 or the beginning of 1942, he had duplicated in order to circulate a conference that he must have given in various youth groups. It is a very carefully written, very tight text, from which I will quote here only a few lines:

> In its overall tonality, German racism . . . is profoundly foreign to us. This pantheism of race, this rooting of man in nature, this importance given to "blood" and "soil", . . . are difficult for us to absorb. Yet it would be wrong to believe that it is going to remain without any influence on us. . . . Racism is built on the admitted rejection of Christian values . . . and it has, on the level of force, managed to succeed. . . . Now success is always a temptation [examples . . .]. The whole Christian spirit is being attacked by this en bloc. It is not only religious practice or belonging to the Church that is disappearing, but people are seeking a scale of opposite values. . . . [Now] what is essentially necessary is to reject the criterion adopted for judging Christianity. The primary goal of Christianity is not temporal success but the spiritual transformation of man. . . . When we see again the circumstances of the Cross, Christ surrounded by a small group of faithful alone in the midst of a hostile crowd, that should not shake our faith. . . . Nazism has obtained its success only by ruining man. . . . There is no time for flirting with it or being hesitant about it. It must be clearly shown that the grandeur it gives is not pure, and the moral monstrosities that it not only tolerates but provokes must be emphasized.

Then follow a warning against all anti-Semitic propaganda and a critical analysis of the measures taken by the occupying power against the Jews; then against "the total separation of morality and politics", with supporting examples. Another danger was that of the "divinization" of the state and its leader, leading to a "resignation of personal conscience"—a danger particularly for the young, whom they wanted to recruit into a "unique movement" to make them "accept in full knowledge of the case the necessity to submit to the dominant conscience of the collectivity" (quotation from Pélerson, delegate to the propaganda office of the Ministry of Youth).[2] "The modern totalitarian dictator wants not only to obtain external obedience but to bend souls in interior allegiance; one must have captives who think they are free"; this was the reason for that "incessant, brutal hammering", aimed less "at convincing than at suggesting", using "lies in all forms". If some still resisted, "nazism resorted to systematic, recorded, glorified informing, to the multiplication of police forces", and the like.

> All this threatens to break out and develop in us under the influence of nazism, in those who believe themselves at times shielded from its influence or who think they have made a distinction between what should be rejected in it and what can be accepted: Let the Catholics fight its symptoms.

In the typed copy I have before me, this duplicated text is untitled; but the title given by Pierre Bolle to a typed text to which he refers and which would date from the end of 1941: "Ce qui risque de passer du nazisme chez nous" [What threatens to pass from nazism to us], corresponds so perfectly that I believe we can say that the two writings are identical, or at least we can attribute them both to the same author.[3] In fact, in both pieces the criticism is based on the anti-Jewish measures of the occupied zone, quotations are borrowed from Paris publications and one can recognize Fr. de Montcheuil's

[2] This long paragraph on youth justifies the firm insistence of the episcopate and particularly of Cardinal Gerlier with respect to the public powers against the "uniform regimen for youth" projects—especially in connection with the A.C.J.F.

[3] I have no memory of this typed text and do not go along with M. Bolle in attributing it to me. One slight difficulty might make one hesitate about the identity of the two texts: M. Bolle speaks of fifteen pages; my copy comprises only six, but they are so compressed, without any space between the lines, almost without margins, that a copy less tightly spaced might well comprise about fourteen or fifteen pages.

style of language as well as one of his usual themes: the relationship of politics and morality.

With respect to the Jews, François Delpech also pointed out a "note on anti-Semitism", "without an author's name", found by him in "the Guerry files"—undoubtedly a working document for the use of the A.C.A., like the "Doctrinal Note" by Fr. Joseph Bonsirven that is attached to it. He "believed he could recognize the style and the ideas of Fr. de Montcheuil". In this he is quite right, but according to the lines that he quotes from it, this would seem to be simply one part of those "Reflections on . . . the outbreak of anti-Semitism . . ." that I pointed out earlier, concerning the existence, the nature and the Christian conditions for an examination of the "Jewish problem". We should note the brief commentary that Delpech adds to his quotation: "This poses the true question very well, at least for what concerned the French Jews, for this author, too, left aside the case of foreigners, which clearly shows the damaging effects of xenophobia, even in the most lucid of minds."[4] This is a fine example of the kind of quirk often noted already in our author. Three things at least have escaped him: Montcheuil was in Paris, cut off from the southern zone; and the problem of foreign Jews—who were nearly all packed into the camps in the South of France, a problem that was undoubtedly urgent but local and temporary—was to elude him. The note in question was a *doctrinal note*, as must have been requested of him, or as some reader must have taken the initiative to make known to the secretariate of the A.C.A.; it was not a call for help: no one can do or say everything at the same time. Finally, in these Guerry files, Delpech also found and pointed out immediately after the Montcheuil note, "the integral text of the famous declaration" of the Lyons theologians, which seems certainly to indicate that a file had been put together to help the Assembly reach a judgment on

[4] Compare F. Delpech, *Sur les Juifs*, 289–90, and Yves de Montcheuil, in *l'Eglise et le Monde actuel*, 108–12.

the recent law of October 1941 concerning the statute of the French Jews, as we saw in sections 4 and 5.[5] In any case, in the long "Reflections" of Fr. de Montcheuil, from which the note that reached the A.C.A. was extracted (more or less literally), it is indeed any kind of anti-Semitism, and not only that which attacked the French Jews, that is radically criticized. To evoke, in this respect, "the damaging effects of xenophobia" is absurd.[6] Let us rather conclude from the preceding remarks that, in order to enlighten the members of the Paris Assembly that Cardinal Gerlier had joined, the contribution of two Parisians at least, Riquet and Montcheuil, had been added to that of the Lyons theologians.

When war broke out, Fr. de Montcheuil had been since 1936 a professor of dogma at the Catholic theology faculty of Paris, where he regularly carried out his work until the summer of 1944. He had first been assigned to teach in our theology scholasticate in Fourvière, but a ridiculous incident, which took place while he was preparing himself at Rome, had made him change his destination. Maurice Blondel had charged his former student and faithful friend Fr. Auguste Valensin with preparing a little volume of pages of moral doctrine extracted from L'Action for the series "Christian Moralists" edited by Abbé Baudin. With the agreement of his mentor and Superiors, Fr. Valensin had had Fr. de Montcheuil help him, and the book, as edifying as it was innocent, appeared at the beginning of 1935, achieving a rather quiet success: "Beautiful and stimulating reading", Fr. Joseph Maréchal, S.J., of Louvain, had written. But a year later, in a solemn session of the Pontifical Academy of St. Thomas in

---

[5] Which is confirmed by the "last document" of the same dossier, "a brief anonymous note of a slightly later date, entitled 'The French legislation on the Jews [to December 15, 1941]', which also dates prior to the meeting of the A.C.A."

[6] The same reproach against the Lyons theologians: "But once again, it was a question of the French Jews." The law they were criticizing did in fact concern the French Jews.

Rome, Fr. Garrigou-Lagrange, O.P., inaugurated with a roar a new campaign against the whole of Blondel's work: "The new *Action* by the philosopher", he declared, "confirmed everything he thought of him: Kantian, immanentist."[7] It was the sign foretelling that Blondel would be placed on the Index. In the audience was Bishop Mulla, a Turk and former Moslem who had become a Catholic and priest during his studies of philosophy at Aix under Blondel's influence. According to what was made known to me later by a reliable witness, Fr. René Arnou, a professor at the Gregorian, Mulla (himself a professor at the Oriental Institute) was able to intervene with Pius XI, who was opposed to this maneuver. Some in the Society of Jesus, however, were fearful. Father General Ledochowski, alerted, had a new assessment made of the little work, already published, which, while recognizing that every detail could be defended, concluded that it was a "danger". The result was that Fr. de Montcheuil, turned down by Fourvière, was assigned to the Catholic Institute of Paris, where Cardinal Baudrillart, rector, who had already asked for him, was all too happy to receive him.[8]

---

[7] Cf. Blondel to Valensin, April 9, 1936: "Several witnesses have been dumbfounded by the misinterpretations, isolated or abbreviated texts, fictitious anecdotes and invented words that have been attributed to me. . . . Knowing the strong irascibility of Fr. Garrigou, I wonder if the best thing would not be for me to recite once more the psalm: Qui habitat in adjutorio Altissimi . . . "

[8] In 1942, he would publish through Aubier, Fr. Valensin having entrusted the complete project to him with the agreement of Blondel, *Maurice Blondel, Pages religieuses, extraits reliés par un commentaire et précédés d'une introduction.* Some sought to quibble with him about this and even disturbed Blondel himself, who was already blind; but when the latter subsequently got hold of the book itself, he proved to be very satisfied with it (and wrote that to me). On December 19, 1946: "I am infinitely grateful for the perception and precision with which the dear Father discerned, specified and clarified the effort I had made to establish the human part in grace." And to Fr. Valensin, on November 3, 1948: "I did not remember that the Introduction [by Fr. de M.] was so penetrating."

Fr. de Montcheuil had a mind and spirit that were anything but excitable or rash. In everything, he applied himself to what was essential, and, to the degree that he had not completed the twofold effort of study and in-depth reflection necessary to form a judgment on any given subject, he could appear rather taciturn. After his death, his courses in dogma were for a long time used by others, so that in the papers I received I still found only one "thesis", written with care, from his course on the Eucharist ("*Christus fit praesens per transsubstantiationem*"), which could be called a model of its kind. On the characteristics of his teaching, his thought, his relations with his students, see the testimony of one of them, Fernand Guimet, in Appendix 1 following. With a few colleagues, he also organized, in his last years, a series of lectures for the students of the Sorbonne. This was the C.U.C. (Catholic University Center), the first seed at the origin of the C.C.I.F. (Catholic Center of French Intellectuals). These lectures were true theological teaching, placed within reach of the young student but always substantial. He discussed there, in succession, the Trinity, Christ (the Incarnation and redemption), the Church and the sacraments.[9] His apostolic activity was very quickly practiced with greater scope. He was the chaplain of the "J.E.C. [Jeunesse Etudiante Catholique] literature group": this is what was to lead him, during the years of the Occupation, to reflect more deeply not only on the doctrinal and spiritual problems that followed but also specifically on the varied cases of conscience that confronted the young, as well as to warn them even more against nazi infiltrations, under what were at times ambiguous forms, into thought, morals and French institutions than against nazism itself in all its horror. But above all, it was the foundation of

[9] The *Leçons sur le Christ* and those on the Church (*Aspects de l'Eglise*) were published after his death. The manuscript on the sacraments was still too rough to be published without reworking. I have not been able to locate the part concerning the Trinity.

faith, the meaning of Catholic fidelity, the concrete demands
of the Christian life that he sought to implant in these young
people who had such trust in him.[10] Those were the fine years
of Catholic Action.[11] Under the influence of the J.E.C., there
were conversions. Here, for example, is what he replied to a
young girl, a recent convert, who wrote to him from a vacation camp to ask his advice:

> The manual of Christian initiation by Canon Masure will give
> you an overall view of Christian doctrine. . . . If something
> still seems particularly obscure to you, note it, and I will try
> to explain it to you in September. The other books will be
> valuable for your spiritual formation. . . . Also read the Gospels
> and the Acts of the Apostles with great care. You will not
> understand everything the first time through, and you will have
> to come back to it. . . . It is indispensable reading for a Christian
> at the beginning of his Christian life and something to which
> he later returns without ever tiring of it. . . . With what you
> have at hand, you have something to prepare you for the great
> joy and the great grace of your first Communion. Pray to our
> Lord, who has himself placed in you this desire to receive him,
> to know him and to love him more, that he might help you
> accomplish that. Recommend yourself to our Lady, who will
> prepare you to receive her Son. Apply yourself with all your
> heart to your task every day; this is the best way to use the
> time that separates you from the fulfillment of your desires. I
> am praying to our Lord for you: I thank him for having drawn
> you to himself, and I ask you to complete the work that he has
> begun. —July 31, 1943

The inner principle of his apostolate with the young was
none other than that of his own interior life: total love,

[10] Several testimonies about the students' chaplain have been collected in
the foreword of his posthumous *Mélanges théologiques* (Aubier, 1946; 2d ed.,
1951) and of his *Problèmes de vie spirituelle* (Paris: J.E.C.F., 1945; several
reprintings, Ed. de l'Epi, 1967).
[11] On the J.E.C. during that period, see Yves-Marie Hilaire, paper for the
Biviers Symposium, September 1984.

unconditional gift, an attachment of his whole being to God, revealed in Jesus Christ our Lord. In this, of course, he was indebted to the entire Christian Tradition stemming from the first apostles, but more particularly to that of the Society of Jesus and governed by the Spiritual Exercises of St. Ignatius of Loyola. Very early on, he was surprised to see it somewhat softened in the practice of preaching. A letter that he addressed to me from Jersey on November 24, 1923, seems very significant to me in this regard. It is a letter from his youth, his expressions are a bit awkward, it was written as his spirit moved him and besides, Fr. de Montcheuil was never a stylist. But the passage I will quote helps to give a better understanding of his actions in later life. In his letter, he had just told me about what had happened to him during the exercise, to which each of the young philosophy students was in turn subjected: a sermon in the refectory:

> I had practiced it rather well. I will admit to you that I have something against that kind of preaching where they find a way of commenting on the Gospel without saying a word or nearly any word about our Lord, without considering that it was from him that it comes. The sermons I heard in Paris during my military service left me with the impression that not enough is said to the faithful about our Lord and about the place that a personal love for him must hold in their religious life. I could say the same of those I heard in college. Yet I believe it is especially when you are addressing the young that you can make people understand easily what a personal attachment to our Lord is, and by doing so you would make their Christian life deeper and stronger. Perhaps there is an effort to be made in that respect. All that is perhaps a bit fanciful, but anyone who has not even had a few dreams in his head when he is young will do nothing very new or original. —When I was in recollection[12] I reread Fr. Lebreton's *Dogme de la Trinité*: there is nothing to be said, it is superb; with Fr. de Grandmaison's

[12] This was the name then given, in the scholasticate, to the time set aside on certain days for silent and meditative reading outside of the hour of prayer.

Jésus-Christ and Fr. Rousselot's *Christus*, one has something with which to begin to understand one's religion without waiting for one's theology, where perhaps we will learn heaps of things that will make us go much less deeply into it.[13] So when they say to me about these books: "It is very beautiful, but wait for theology to read them; you will not profit from them", I want quite simply to shrug my shoulders.

A little further on, he said to me: "If it is not a matter of becoming intellectuals in our spiritual life and in our manner of praying, which would please me less than anyone else, neither is it necessary that the ideas that nourish our spiritual life and, so to speak, make up its framework lag behind while all the rest of our intelligence develops."

Personal attachment to Christ proceeding not from some sentimental blaze in danger of being extinguished but from reflection ripened by intellectual effort, suitable for preparing a firm Christian commitment, that in my opinion was the fundamental trait, and one that could be detected very early on, of Fr. de Montcheuil's personal spirituality; it was also the characteristic underlying the formation that he endeavored to place at the base of his apostolate. One mimeographed page, dated March 1944, which was a part of a "Bulletin of Team Leaders" from which only this one trace remains, will give us some idea of this. Written with some haste, its title is "Les Bases spirituelles de notre engagement" (The spiritual bases of our commitment). It dates from five months before his death. I reproduce it in its entirety:

It is not to a human cause that we are making the gift of our person, to which we are consecrating ourselves without reserve,

[13] Jules Lebreton, *Histoire du dogme de la Trinité*, 2 vols. (Beauchesne, 1910 and 1928). Léonce de Grandmaison, "Jésus-Christ", in *Dict. apologétique de la foi chrétienne*, edited by A. d'Alès (Beauchesne, 1911). *Christus*, a handbook of the history of religions, edited by Joseph Huby; all of the last part was edited by Fr. Pierre Rousselot, with the assistance of one of his confreres for each chapter.

but to the Kingdom of God, to the continuation, consequently, of the work of Christ. This spiritual enterprise must, then, have spiritual, not human, bases. One must take care, for the call to work for the Kingdom of God can arouse one who sees only the exterior of the work to follow a human enthusiasm. Examples are not lacking. Recently, a young man who, before the war, held an important role in the Belgian Catholic Action, Raymond de Becker, wrote a kind of autobiography, *Le Livre des Vivants et des Morts* [The book of the living and the dead], in which he recounts how he passed from Catholic Action to nazism. Reading it, one can see at what point it was the relish and the need to act that had drawn him to Catholic Action and how he progressively turned away from Catholicism because he found in nazism something more exhilarating, because it flattered the tendencies of his nature more than had Catholicism. Without doubt, all those who put something too human into their commitment will not end in such catastrophes, and that human part can be very variable besides. But in the very measure in which the motives of our commitment are not supernatural, it will be ineffective. This is one of the fundamental lessons of the Gospel: the Kingdom of God is found only by those who live by the spirit of the Kingdom of God, who seek it for itself.

How will we remain in this spiritual atmosphere? By recalling the fundamental truths that must enlighten *this commitment*. We must first of all not forget that *it is only a response to a call*. It was not we who thought of it first; it was our Lord who called us to it. He can say to us as he did to his disciples on the evening of the Last Supper: "It was not you who chose me; it is I who chose you." Left to ourselves, we would never have turned this way. We would have taken different routes according to our character, our inclinations, circumstances; we would never have taken that one, we would never have loved the Kingdom of God for itself. And much more: *we are only following an inclination, an impulse given to us by grace*. Our Lord not only shows us the road; he gets us to walk it. Our progress is always only an acceptance and, as it were, an abandonment to the impulse that he communicates to us. All that we give to him comes in reality from him.

If our Lord asks our help, it is not that he needs us. He could do the work by himself and for himself. He can overcome all external obstacles and change hearts without any assistance. *If, then, he calls us, it is through love for us; he wants to give us this grandeur and this dignity of being his assistants.* His demands sometimes seem hard to us, and sometimes we come to regret that he did not leave us in our ignorance and inertia. Yet it is we who gain something, not he. We must thank him for having wanted us, for not having grown tired of our delays, of our negligences, of our laziness, for having wanted even so to make useful instruments of us and for having insisted until we decided to respond. We must never forget those words of our Lord in the Gospel: "When you have done all that has been asked of you, say: we are useless servants." We are not to say to ourselves: "We are useless servants", and then, "Let's do nothing", but on the contrary, after having worked with all our strength, to say to ourselves that we are useless servants. In that way we will remain in humility.

If we walk with generosity, our Lord will ask much of us. He will ask more and more of us, we can be certain of that, because he will want us always to grow more. *But we must not be afraid of that.* Let us not say only that our Lord knows us and that he will not impose too heavy a burden on us. Let us think that in asking something, our Lord gives the grace to do it. In that, we see one of the ways in which Christ is incomparably superior to all human leaders. The latter can ask heavy things, but they have only a weak and at times very limited part in making others capable of doing these things. Our Lord is for us he who asks and he who gives the strength to accomplish. So we can be assured that there will never be a conflict between the two, if we pray as we should. We can live, then, in serenity. Let us repeat with St. Augustine: "Lord, give what you command, and command what you wish." We do not have to commit ourselves with respect to Christ in proportion to our strength, since we expect from him the strength to serve him. Our commitment can and must be without reserve, so long as it is humble and trusting. If we never forget what our real situation is in relation to Christ, we will purify our commitment each day of what might have been too human in it at the beginning, but we will protect ourselves from any danger of taking anything back, and we will give more to the Lord every day.

On the last page of his *Leçons sur le Christ* [Lessons on Christ], in expressing the substance of his faith, he literally anticipates, with marvelous precision, what would be set forth twenty years later at the Second Vatican Council, in the first chapter of the constitution *Dei Verbum* on divine revelation:

> The revelation of Christ is definitive; it contains the ultimate truth, because it is the revelation of charity. There we find the rule of all our Christian thought and all our Christian action, that is, of all our thought and all our action as disciples of Christ. But we must still add one essential thing: Jesus Christ is not only he who announces and preaches charity, he who reveals it by his words, as if it were a message different from himself. He is, in Himself, in his Person as God-man, the revelation of charity. He is, through his life and through his death, the charity of God become visible in the action it takes to uproot sinful man from his misery. We can know this charity of God only through him. And we can receive him and possess him effectively only by associating ourselves in his action, only by imitating him as much as we can, or better, by letting ourselves be led by him. This is why the Christian religion is the religion of Christ, in the two inseparable meanings of that expression: not only in the sense that Christ is its initiator but also in the sense that he is its object. It is impossible to separate the Person of him who reveals from the revelation he brings. It is impossible to claim to guard the ideal of charity by rejecting as a provisional envelope or as an unseemly addition the worship, adoration, the absolute love of Christ. Let us repeat the words of St. Irenaeus with which we began: *Omnem novitatem attulit, Semetipsum afferens* [he brought all that is new, bringing himself]. That is what we must never forget.[14]

---

[14] *Leçons sur le Christ*, 184–85. Vatican II, Dogmatic Constitution *Dei Verbum*, chap. 1, no. 2: "*Intima autem . . . tam de Deo quam de hominis salute veritas nobis in Christo elucescit, who mediator simul et plenitudo totius revelationis existit*" [The most intimate truth this revelation gives us about God and the salvation

From this it follows that one can never pass beyond the Christian faith, confided since the beginning to the living Tradition of the Church. It is an inexhaustible spring that, as it flows forth, to use the words of St. Irenaeus again, never ceases to bring fresh life to the vase that receives it: Fr. de Montcheuil loved that comparison, following Fr. Lebreton, who had given much emphasis to it. He often used it to express himself. Faced with the problems of all kinds that always recur, true fidelity can only be creative, "like a constant docility, under the direction of 'the holy hierarchical Church', to the guidance of the Holy Spirit".[15] Each of us, under this guidance, is called to transcend himself.[16] For those who placed themselves in his hands, the very example of their chaplain was the echo of this call, when they heard him say to them: "Great causes are strong in the sacrifices they demand and not in the concessions they make for the mediocre in order to hold them."

In so brief a summary, I am forced to mix many things together that a more complete study would distinguish: the question of the homogeneous development of dogma, which is not to be confused with some foreign addition, change or continued revelation; the question of the relation between initiative and obedience; that of the respective role of the laity and the hierarchy; the human problems on every level that arise in the course of one's life, whose solutions the Christian can find, according to the situation, from more or less

---

of man shines forth in Christ, who is himself both the mediator and the sum total of revelation]. (Cf. H. L., *La Révélation divine* [Cerf, 1983], 16 and 43–48. Pius XI had said in 1936 in a similar expression: "In Jesus Christ, the Son of God made man, has appeared the fullness of divine revelation" [*Mit brennender Sorge*].)

[15] Cf. René d'Ouince, Introduction to the *Problèmes de vie spirituelle* (Ed. de l'Epi, 1963), 14.

[16] This call *to transcend ourselves* in order to remain faithful to the growing demands of Christ should not be confused with the call "to transcend" in any way the Gospel of Christ and his Church.

direct inspiration in the Church's doctrine; the evangelical call
to the Christian soul, a call that, to the degree in which it is
perceived, enables it to transcend itself in peace by giving it
its strength. But in their extreme diversity, these problems
all rest, within the Church, on the foundation of the unsurpass-
able revelation of Christ, and it is that which Fr. de Montcheuil
set forth, according to the occasion, with respect to each of
them, with equal strength and balance. He was a marvelous
educator.[17]

In the course of these years 1940 to 1944, he would continue
to carry out in a normal way his theological teaching,[18] at the
same time as his work as a writer and his ministry to the
young.[19] From the time that the *Cahiers du Témoignage chrétien*
were able to reach (and then also begin to be printed in) the
region of Paris, he became one of their principal distributors,
along with Frs. Gonzague Pierre and Jean Daniélou.[20] He was
naturally in close contact with Fessard and with Chaillet, when
the latter came secretly to Paris. But events rushed forward.
With the direct seizure by the German army and the Gestapo

[17] Bishop Bussini, who did not know Fr. de Montcheuil personally, nevertheless gives us a very accurate idea of him, thanks to a long consideration
of his writings: "I have always been struck by the tone of his works. Vocabulary is used with a rare sense of the particular appropriateness of terms. The
syntax is fluent. Yet nothing flashy. . . . In familiarizing oneself with Fr. de
Montcheuil's style, one learns to understand and to appreciate without mis-
interpreting a deeply evangelical virtue: humanity." Biviers Symposium,
September 1984.

[18] On this teaching, see in Appendix I following the authoritative testimony
of Bishop Fernand Guimet. It was reproduced in part at the beginning of the
Mélanges théologiques, 13–15. See also that of Suzanne Duchemin, at the beginning of the *Problèmes de vie spirituelle*.

[19] Let us point out the little trilogy issuing from this ministry, part of the
Editions de l'Orante, the first two pamphlets of his life: *Pour un apostolat
spirituel* (cot. 42), *Vie chrétienne et Action temporelle* (2d trim. 44), *Le Rôle du
chrétien dans l'Eglise* (1945).

[20] The first of these two was appointed to help Fr. Riquet with the "Con-
férence Laënnec", whose premises served as a storehouse for the *Cahiers*. Cf.
M. Riquet, 142 and 178. R. Bédarida, 192–95.

of the territory as a whole and the more and more demanding requisitions of "relief" troops and the S.T.O., a new problem arose for young people. For many, this was at first a serious problem of conscience. By declaring itself to be against the legitimacy of the requisitions, which Cardinal Gerlier and others with him described as "deportations", the episcopate was thereby authorizing young Catholics to evade them.[21] Most of the draft-dodging "conscripts" scattered as they could and went into hiding, but at the same time they intensified their efforts toward an effective Resistance. In the wooded or mountain regions that lent themselves to it, various "maquis" (the generic term that quickly came to be used) were formed. "While the Resistance was being organized," Archbishop Guerry writes, "there was not one word in an official document from the episcopate against its leaders or any prohibition made to Catholics about entering into it."[22]

But there were maquis and maquis (not to mention certain groups who became gangs of looters). Not only was the relationship between them and the outside very difficult, but the Resistance itself was deeply divided. To simplify, let us distinguish between the two extremes: the maquis under communist obedience and the maquis more or less trained by the secret army. The former advocated immediate action, organized assassination attempts that provoked reprisals; they constituted a force within the hands of the party, and one could wonder whether their principal objective was not to prepare in that way for a national insurrection within the climate of

---

[21] Appeals that were perhaps at times indiscreet or presumed too much on their moral strength were however now and then addressed to Catholic Action groups to ask them to go, in the name of the apostolate or of solidarity. See on the other hand the wisdom (and at the same time the supernatural heroism) that someone like Fr. Dillard showed (above, Chap. 8, n. 4).

[22] Op. cit., 361. Perhaps Archbishop Guerry was exaggerating, as some have complained, when he said that in its declaration on the S.T.O., the episcopate itself had practiced conscientious objection. At the very least, it not only tolerated but positively authorized it.

civil war that would facilitate their taking power.[23] The latter, from the end of 1943, sometimes took on military objectives, but above all they were preparing for D-Day, in view of cooperating with the Allied forces,[24] early enough to take an effective part in the liberation of their country.[25] The propaganda from Vichy mixed all the groups together under the label of "terrorists" and thereby justified the necessity of the "Militia" and its excesses. This reinforced the confusion that

[23] Cf. M. Riquet, 179. H. Amouroux, *La Vie des Français sous l'Occupation*, 319–20; *L'Impitoyable Guerre civile* (Laffont, 1983), 153–90 and 237–40. Charles de Gaulle, letter to General de Bénouville, May 14, 1948 (in *Lettres, notes et carnets* [Plon, 1985], 269–70).

Various clandestine groups of young communists had been organized as early as June 1941, and after the requests of the S.T.O., their number had considerably increased.

[24] M. Riquet, loc. cit. On the maquis: H. Noguères and J. L. Vigier, *Histoire de la Résistance en France* (Laffont, 1969), vol. 2. In the *Revue du Nord*, no. 238 (July–September 1978) (*Colloque de Lille*, 2:540–41), Robert Vandenbussche, used to classifying men, their feelings and their actions according to sociological criteria, wrote: "The Catholic militants seem to have preferred forms of personal engagement or 'peace' movements more than violent actions, at least up until 1943, and perhaps even until the time of the Liberation approached. These middle-class youth were probably not ready for sabotage actions nor undoubtedly for daring strokes. Their Christian formation prompted them to choose violence as a last resort." (These last words are the most accurate. Cf. the following note.)

[25] See the wise advice that Fr. de Montcheuil gave, on the other hand, to French youth in the *Cahier du T.C.* of May 1944, *Exigences de la Libération*, 168–70 in the facsimile edition, vol. 2: "Vers le soulèvement de la nation." "A country like France does not let itself be liberated passively when it can aid in its liberation. . . . There is no shame in accepting the help of allies. But it is a dishonor to allow others to fight in one's place. That would be to accept the position of a country under a protectorate." "Justice is indivisible. . . . Duty is imposed on every man, but it would be still more inexcusable for a Christian to evade it." Then he warned against any spirit of hatred or vengeance: "We can give witness that there is no need to light the fire of hatred in man in order to obtain total sacrifice from him."

from the beginning the nazi power had worked to maintain between communism and Catholicism.[26]

The maquis of Vercors (in Dauphiné) was among the latter group. It was a "military maquis". General Delestraint, leader of the secret army in contact with London, had come to inspect it in April 1943. The following year, the number of people involved rapidly swelled, going in the first six months from about four hundred to more than four thousand. Its history was unfortunate and was terminated by a catastrophe.[27]

The leaders of the A.C.J.F. had opted for the Resistance. A number of students known by Fr. de Montcheuil had joined the maquis. An appeal had come to him from Vercors.[28] He took advantage of a vacation period, in 1943 and 1944, to answer it. Some have spoken in this respect of a "theologian in the maquis": the expression can be defended, but three

[26] See, for example, Alfred Rosenberg, Nuremberg address, September 6, 1938: "Catholic authorities are allied with Marxism, which they pretend to fight mercilessly but whose universalist attitude they in fact share. . . . A senile doctrine does not want to yield to the vision of a new horizon. At present, it is under the sign of the racist ideal that the great process of the purification of the European awakening is unfolding." (Quoted by H. L., *Le Fondement théologique des missions* [Seuil, 1946], 80.) "Nazi Germany and its French collaborators tried to lead Christians into an anti-Bolshevik crusade in the name of the values of Christian civilization in contradiction with Marxism. The faithful, priests, let themselves be taken in. Young Christians became involved in the *Waffen SS*, others in the 'Militia' " (M. Riquet, 179).

[27] H. Amouroux, *L'Impitoyable Guerre civile*, 243–60. *La Vie des Français sous l'Occupation*, 320. Fr. Fraisse, who was an officer at Vercors, gave more information: "This 'maquis' in the end was comprised of two distinct groups: one on the plateau itself, comprising about twenty-five hundred men; the other, for the rest of the Drôme, with about five thousand. There was a twofold military command. The parachutists were inadequate and, the last ones, too late."

[28] Following the text quoted above (n. 22), Archbishop Guerry adds: "It was in this period that chaplains were given to the 'maquis'." (At the same time he was assisting his bishop, Msgr. Lebrun, as vicar general of Autun, Fernand Guimet was "chaplain" of the maquis of Saône and Loire.) There were other similar, though rare, cases.

points should be added. First of all, Fr. de Montcheuil did
not stay for long periods of time in the maquis; he was not
strictly speaking the chaplain there; he did not come there
in the first place as a theologian. It was as a priest, to bring
his spiritual assistance to young Catholics and to administer
to them the sacraments of the Church, that he went twice,
or even three times, if I am not mistaken, to Vercors. The
first time, in the summer of 1943, I saw him for rather a long
time when he passed through Lyons. He had stopped there
to go to the chancery office to obtain the necessary faculties
for his ministry. He had contacted, through secret channels,
a certain number of young people scattered about the Lyons
region, who came to meet him in our house at Fourvière.
There, in a secluded corner, he had several conversations
with them to place them on guard against the communist
danger,[29] which worried him greatly, just as it also worried
his friends Fessard and Chaillet.[30] (The question was taken
up at that time, in May 1943, in the first *Courrier du T.C.*)
This was a danger that was all the more formidable for
young minds, as anticommunism was the standard that had
been raised everywhere in order to make them submit to
the nazi yoke, against which they had rightly taken a stand.

The following year, around Easter, Fr. de Montcheuil had
come back to the Southeast for a few days. I was at that time
absent from Lyons, and I was not to see him again. On July
15, having ended his school year in Paris, he left again for
Lyons and for the Vercors plateau. He was to make, in the
exercise of his ministry, a brief tour of inspection there in
order to report some accurate information to the ecclesiastical

[29] I have a precise memory of this because I was, at least for a moment,
present at one of these conversations, and Fr. de Montcheuil confided his
concern to me.

[30] It is known that, on December 15, 1940, in Vichy, Fr. Fessard condemned
both nazism and communism.

authorities.[31] I have in hand a typed "note on the clandestine ministry", whose author (surely a priest) is unknown to me, addressed undoubtedly to some bishop. (It is impossible for me to remember how it happened to reach me.) It is a very intelligent report, rather pessimistic as to the "spiritual decline" of the young people in the maquis and as to the almost complete "temporalization" of their idea of the Kingdom of God. This second observation coincides so well with one of the major concerns of Fr. de Montcheuil, as attested by the recollection day he had just given to one group of students preparing for their teaching examinations in mid-Lent of 1944,[32] that I would be tempted to attribute this brief note to him if he were not mentioned at the end of it. The author, whoever he was, concludes that the presence of a few chaplains in the maquis would be very desirable—but, for various reasons of a practical order, he judges that the organization of such a chaplaincy was scarcely possible. What is of interest to us in this report is the advice he gives in conclusion: that the leaders of the group and the priests they are able to meet should "address to Fr. de Montcheuil" all questions about morality, the spiritual life and contact of the young with the priest. This bears witness to the reputation for priestly wisdom that Fr. de Montcheuil had. With him, no mistake about the Kingdom of God was possible.[33]

I will not go back over his tragic end, in that July of 1944, since I have already recounted it on the basis of the testimony

[31] In its first form, this was in October 1943, the preaching of a camp retreat of Sévriennes at Solesmes: *Le Royaume et ses exigences* (Ed. de l'Epi, 1957).

[32] "It was in order to inform the ecclesiastical authorities and to have chaplains sent to the maquis that, solicited by the young people engaged in the Resistance, Fr. de M. had undertaken that trip to Vercors" (Fr. Lucien Fraisse, *Colloque de Biviers*, 1984).

[33] There is nothing in him, or in those like Fessard or Chaillet, that proclaims what one author calls "a new type of Christian" or any variety whatever of "Christians of movement". Bishop Bussini wrote: "He teaches the way of the most rigorous theocentrism."

I was able to gather for my preface to his *Mélanges théologiques* (2d ed., 1951), and then in 1980 in the second part of a little book entitled *Trois jésuites nous parlent* (*Three Jesuits speak*).[34] Perhaps the symposium that will be held in September 1984 at Biviers, close to Grenoble, and that will commemorate the fortieth anniversary of his death, will contribute either corrections to the little we believe we know or a few new significant details. In closing, I will simply recall his concern for the Church and for her unity during the whole horrible drama brought about by nazism. In a conversation about "collaboration", he once said: "There is not a German Church and a French Church: there is the Catholic Church, which is one, because she is the Body of Christ in the world. To touch the Catholic Church in any one particular place is to touch her everywhere."[35] Or again, in opposition to the frequent claims regarding our religious individualism: "We are able to return to God only because he came to seek us: the inevitable result of this is that we can join him only by the ways he has set for us." To those who always find reasons to complain of the Church, he asked: "What is the proportion between what the Christian has to suffer from the Church and what the Church gives him?" To the various "progressives" who want to impose their plans for her reform: "It is from the Church herself that the great reformers of the Church have made flames burst forth to renew her. It is only in the holiness she possesses that there lies a remedy for the sin that afflicts her."

In thinking over his life and death, we recall this thought of his: "The Passion of Jesus was not only the consequence of his testimony; it was also its culminating point."

Finally, these last words in concluding our remarks about him: "The knowledge of God sets everything on fire."

[34] Henri de Lubac, *Trois Jésuites nous parlent* (Lethielleux, 1980), 57–96: "Yves de Montcheuil, 1900–1944" (with a series of excerpts from his thoughts); English trans.: *Three Jesuits Speak* (Ignatius Press, 1987), 15–60.

[35] Reproduced in *L'Eglise et le Monde actuel*, 2d ed. (Ed. du T.C. and l'Epi), 102.

Varennes-Saint-Sauveur (S. and Loire)
April 6, 1945

My Reverend Father,

It is with gratitude and emotion that I take the occasion you have offered me to confide a few memories of Fr. de Montcheuil to you.

All his students, when they learned of his death, had the sense of an irreparable loss—for them, toward whom he was the kindest, most authoritative guide—for the Church of France as a whole, of which he proved to be one of the most remarkable theologians.

The only thought that can console our grief is that this heroic death was the only one worthy of him. It will remain as an infinitely precious witness—that of a priest who did not betray. Fr. de Montcheuil's nobility of soul, of which his teaching bore the mark, is wholly revealed in the sacrifice of his life.

What was perhaps the most striking in Fr. de Montcheuil's teaching was surely its simplicity and its soundness. Without any artifice, whether literary or dialectical. But the simple, strong presentation of truth. Without any attempt, skillful or not, to mask the difficulties inherent in the exposition of a thesis. But an admirable intellectual loyalty, an integrity that brought peace and that had its source in an unshakable confidence in truth. Newman said something like a thousand difficulties do not make a doubt. Fr. de Montcheuil's assent to revealed truth was of such an impressive firmness that he could then, with a singularly penetrating lucidity, enter into the exposition of the historical or conceptual difficulties raised by the problems studied. The certitudes of faith, which he placed with luminous precision at the sources of theological knowledge, appeared to us to be of an entirely different order than the dust that, here and there over the course of the centuries, had come to conceal them.

Nor did Fr. de Montcheuil give in to the easy temptation to make concessions to current events and more or less suspect agreements. He had a magnificent sense of Tradition.

That is perhaps one of the aspects of his thought that strikes me the most, in a mind as well informed as his was about the tendencies and trends of contemporary thought.

It often happened that, after a course, his students would come with trust and freedom to discuss with him the problems that concerned them. Beneath his rather cold exterior—one which never sought to capture sympathy by artifice—they had very quickly understood that such an open soul was hidden that they did not hesitate, sometimes with a kind of youthful naïveté, to tell him of their aspirations, their difficulties, their plans. And Father, with a kindness that never tired, assumed that role of intellectual director—a role that is more delicate at times than that of spiritual direction itself. What was surprising, often, was to see how such and such a daring, even revolutionary proposition—or at least we thought it to be so—when we had submitted it to him, found itself, as if on its own accord, taking its place in the whole of revealed truth, set forth in its most traditional sense. With one word, one phrase, Father had gone over it, corrected it, situated it. And our intellectual audacities, without ever being disappointed or having to "plead at the bar" with humiliation, found themselves "converted", invited to seek in a deepened knowledge of God and ourselves the extension they hoped for.

Understood in this way, the teaching of theology was truly an apostolate. It is not surprising that Fr. de Montcheuil knew better than anyone how to define, in an invaluable little pamphlet, the demands of a spiritual apostolate.

If I wanted to capture in one word the memory Fr. de

Montcheuil's teaching left in his students, I would freely say that he incarnated for us the very rare ideal of the theologian-philosopher.

As a theologian, he had the very sure sense of Tradition, the filial submission to the authority of the Church, which became for him, in the distinctive domain in which he exercised his thought, the first rule of method—the still more rare, properly theological, spiritual as much as intellectual, habit of envisaging from the very point of view of God himself the fundamentals of the science he taught. Fr. de Montcheuil's spiritual personality, about which he kept an extreme reserve and modesty, was revealed in this characteristic: the teaching of theology was never for him separate from the exercise of the virtue of faith, which in a certain way places our spirit in continuity with the divine truth such as it is known by God himself. In a book review in, I believe, *Cité nouvelle* of the *Post-scriptum* by Kierkegaard, Father, with respect to this work, distinguishes between a book on religion and a religious book. Supernaturalized in this way by the faith that made him see in their very source the truths that he taught, the teaching that Father gave was truly religious teaching.

And it was not only the general atmosphere of his courses that was transformed in this way—but, quietly, here and there, the very choice of the personal positions of Father, who showed himself to be influenced by this basic theological orientation of his thought. One sensed that his preferences were drawn to that which, respecting the mystery more integrally, preserved the itinerant character of developments in theological knowledge, poised between the faith that prepares for them and the vision that completes them. This was undoubtedly the reason why, with a marked predilection, he returned, in his essays of systematic speculation, to the expositions by the great Franciscans, in particular by St. Bonaventure.

When the life of faith reaches such a depth, to the point of determining a new mental regime and a new vision of the world, it no longer presents any obstacles to rational speculation. It too has its place in the itinerary of the soul toward God. Spontaneously a philosopher—and a philosopher who could have been formidably armed for criticism—Fr. de Montcheuil left us a fine example of that vital coexistence in a soul of the most solid faith and the most open, the most honest investigation.

As a philosopher, he had the essential gifts: a horror of mere wordplay; a sense of the whole, of the connection between problems; the ability to discern beyond formulas and congealed systems the spiritual attitudes that inspired and, at times even without their authors knowing it, controlled them; a sense too of the complexity of doctrines and of the levels of different depths that can be recognized in them. His lucid criticism was exercised with skill: his insights into the thought of Malebranche, which we can hope to see once again in the book he prepared about that philosopher and which friendly hands have undertaken to put into a posthumous edition, give the measure of his gifts as a historian of doctrines.

The general direction of his thought seems to have been oriented toward a vigorous personalism, in which the influence of Maurice Blondel can be easily recognized. But if Fr. de Montcheuil made no secret of the debt of gratitude he owed to Blondel, his fidelity was creative: it did not at all stop with an elaboration of the work of some scholastic, even Blondel; it entered with a free assurance into open paths through the philosophy of Action. When necessary, it made a choice among them. Never, even with respect to his most beloved masters, did Fr. de Montcheuil consent to give up his freedom as a philosopher.

This man who was so sensitive to greatness of mind, was—and this was undoubtedly the secret of his life and of his death—even more open to the greatness of charity. This passionate search for truth which his courses and his personal work put into action before us, like a witness and a very high example, was for him a form of attachment to this God who is love, and no one understood better than he, along with Pascal, that truth without charity is only an idol.

Executed for having given his care to the wounded of the maquis, Fr. de Montcheuil gave the measure of his charity.

Fernand Guimet
Superior of the Ozanam School, Mâcon

Bishop Guimet was vicar general of Autun, chaplain of the university parish for higher learning, ecclesiastical adviser to the French ambassador to the Holy See. His last publication, *Existence et Eternité*, appeared through Aubier in 1973.

APPENDIX 2

Fr. de Montcheuil gave in Paris, at the "St. Michael Conference", in January 1938, a talk on the Immaculate Conception. He explained there the meaning and doctrinal importance of this dogma of the Catholic Faith, retraced in broad outline the history of its maturation in the course of Tradition, and he made use of it as an example to show his audience "the true place that the faithful can and must occupy in the life of the Church, and even in the life of her doctrine". As this text is not well known, even though it was printed, and has not been included, as far as I know, in any of Fr. de Montcheuil's posthumous works, I reproduce it here as the concluding page. It seems to me to be useful in throwing light on one aspect of his thought and in making better known the Catholic sense with which he was penetrated.

The movement that ended in the definition of the Immaculate Conception came neither from theologians nor from the center of the Church but from the mass of the faithful. Certainly the decision of the Magisterium was needed in order to be sure that the path entered was a good one . . . ; certainly theologians had their role in the study of the dogma defined in order to clarify the Faith . . . , but the faithful are far from being a passive mass in the Church. . . . Many of the devotions universally accepted and recommended today by the Church or even included in her official liturgy came from the initiative of private persons. . . . They were born in ardent hearts where the Church recognized a true inspiration of the Spirit. . . . Because what is human can so easily be mixed with the best desires, deviations can creep in, and the Church must pass judgment and proscribe. . . . Truly faithful souls submit themselves, then, knowing that

241

they are weak and that the Church is there precisely to effect the necessary discernments and to keep them from losing their way. The example of the Immaculate Conception shows that this role of the faithful in the Church extends to the doctrinal and dogmatic sphere: it would be folly to want to give an absolute value to all that nourishes our piety, to everything that seems worthy of God; but the Holy Spirit, the soul of the Church, present in every faithful soul and not only in that of the leaders of the hierarchy, can use all faithful souls to initiate a new step forward in the penetration or deepening of the revelation received, which the Church will one day, in one form or another and not necessarily in that of dogmatic definition, sanction and propose to all as a necessary food for their spiritual life. This grandeur of the faithful soul, like all Christian grandeur, has a corresponding obligation: that of making itself an instrument that is docile to the Spirit by purifying itself, by detaching itself from all egoism, all pride, by removing all obstacles to its action.

The history of the dogma of the Immaculate Conception is one of the most striking illustrations of the eminent place of the faithful in the Church, a place that they occupy worthily only if they make themselves worthy by making themselves docile to the Spirit and docile to the Church, which must in the end discern between the divine gold and the impure dross that our still unhealed nature mixes so easily with it.[36]

[36] The same theme, in more elaborated form, will be found in the writings of the following years. See, for example, *Aspects de l'Eglise*, eighth lesson, "La situation du chrétien dans l'Eglise", January 15, 1943, Unam Sanctam, 18 (Ed. du Cerf, 1951), 96–108.

Epilogue

In the anguish of the 1930s, then under nazi domination, we had felt at the same time uplifted by the great breath of catholicity. This was true of Chaillet, Fessard, de Montcheuil, each according to his temperament. . . . I mentioned above our common admiration for Pius XI. By encouraging the churches of different rites within the one Church of Christ (which was sometimes later confused with petty, so-called unionist politics), he made us grasp with renewed intensity both her catholicity and the healthy pluralism of her earthly rootedness. By his great missionary encyclical, completing that of Benedict XV and immediately applied in Rome on the very day when he consecrated the first Chinese bishops, he confirmed and deepened this same teaching, at once so simple and so essential. He had thus shown the Church, in the rapid evolution of the world, to be well ahead of the nations, always exercising her salutary action over those who really wanted to hear, always "*Mater et Magistra*". Then had come the stunning condemnation of the twofold totalitarianism that already held part of the earth beneath its yoke. He had reminded all Christians of their spiritual origins, which they could not deny without denying themselves.

Now, using all possible means remaining, tortured by the insoluble cases of conscience confronting him, having to face the most varied and unforeseen situations, Pius XII continued where Pius XI left off. We could not know all that he did or even all that he said, but from the time just after the French disaster we knew enough about it not to risk letting ourselves be caught up in blind recriminations—or, later, in the reprobations and tumultuous turbulence that succeeded in creating for a time a new "Dreyfus affair". In our unusual action, we felt ourselves to be, more than ever, sons of the Church; some happened to be satisfied with, better disposed to understand, at times to excuse, the apparently excessive prudence of our bishops, their concern not to provoke a state of anarchy from which a worse evil would result. Among the better informed and more reflective of us, even the pontifical documents that seemed foreign to the burning problems of the hour, such as the two encyclicals *Mystici Corporis* and *Divino afflante Spiritu*, were of great importance for maintaining the supranationality of the Church, based on her origins and her Faith of all times: every soul could thus breathe, even under the worst restrictions, and on the other hand find preserved intact the Judeo-Christian patrimony without which there would no longer be a Church or security or dignity recognized for every man.

The very tragedy of the situation made us feel all that intensely. At times our strength seemed to be increased tenfold. An immense pity overcame us for so many misfortunes, but at the same time, in fear and despair, it became possible for us to act with a kind of peaceful exhilaration.

Fessard, de Montcheuil and Chaillet were not dreamers or visionaries; they were profoundly religious men who breathed the great air of catholicity, and their doctrinal work already invited those whose path they were striving to enlighten to a better-informed, more profound fidelity. This was one of the lasting fruits of their joint action. In this sense, one could say that they had contributed less than anyone to forming some "new type of Christian" who would be "Christians of movement", who "would no longer take traditional ecclesiastical structures into account" in order to clear a way for themselves and "to seek in the world of men the true questions asked of the Church of today". That would be a total misinterpretation, spread by those who had not known them. Those who understood their effort and who were associated with it in the same spirit understood at the same time that the true questions that governed everything—without dispensing from more immediate questions and from the particular tasks required of each one—are the fundamental questions that the Church, by her very being, never ceases to recall to us, and that political men, anxious to dismiss the Church—as experience shows—no longer even know how to ask themselves.

When the Liberation came, darkened by so much hatred, so many crimes, and thick with other threats, Yves de Montcheuil had consummated his sacrifice. Three or four years later, in the course of an unbelievable theological quarrel, the real history of which is not yet publicly known, impassioned men crushed his memory, accusing him of heresy and hypocrisy.

Pierre Chaillet left to its fate a weekly of which he was not the master, and fading little by little in the face of various teams of young laymen who took over the future of the journal,[1] he founded the independent *Editions du Témoignage chrétien* in order to publish (in spite of lively opposition) the new work of his friend Fessard, with whom he remained in full communion of thought: *France, prends garde de perdre ta liberté!*

---

[1] One author has spoken of "the Society of Jesus' seizure of the *T.C.*" after the war, a seizure accompanied by the "normalization, within the Jesuits, against the Jesuit participants in the Resistance". He seems to want to explain in that way its participation, "at the beginning of 1947, in the creation of the Union of Progressive Christians"—whose premises date from before the war and whose spirit was completely opposed to that of the *T.C.* It would not be worth the trouble to revive this subject if a general spokesman at the symposium at Lyons in 1978 had not allowed himself to be misled by this. (*Colloque de Lyon* [P.U.L., 1982], 469. Cf. 505 and 550.) Fr. Michel Sales, better informed, recalled that, after the Liberation, under other influences, "the weekly *T.C.* would take a direction that, without public stir, would repudiate its principal founders". (In a postscript to the edition of G. Fessard, *Eglise de France, prends garde . . .* [Julliard, 1979], 293, n. 14.) In his reserve and goodness, Fr. Chaillet suffered certain degradations, which made him lose nothing of his optimism, which was founded in God. "Tenacity, realism, courage, thoughtfulness as a friend; the sharp sense of the responsibility implicit in the name Christian, an ardent love for Catholic unity, ingeniousness in easing all misery, such are some of the characteristic traits of his moral physiognomy" (*Compagnie*, n. 59, June 1972).

[France, take care not to lose your liberty!][2] (then, in order to associate me with them, he published two opuscules by me). He also founded the monthly *Cahiers du Monde nouveau*, which proposed to give a Christian impetus to the examination of the great social problems that arose after the war. Gaston Fessard, Gabriel Marcel, Fr. Teilhard de Chardin, Alexandre Marc and others wrote for it. After years of residence in the kindred house of *Etudes*, he was superior at Grenoble and at Dijon. But from the first day of the Liberation of Paris until his fatal illness, he was to bury himself completely in the hard labor of the social works of the Resistance,[3] which absorbed him to the extreme limits of his strength; he thus renounced any return to his theological research in order to respond to "the love of Christ which surpasses all knowledge".[4]

As for Gaston Fessard, who had narrowly escaped the police, at the beginning of 1944, over the roof of the *Etudes* house (thanks to the dedication of Fr. d'Ouince who was arrested in his place): he went on, with a courage that was as calm as it was fearless, to pursue, without any seeking after personal success, his fight for truth, begun at the beginning of the 1930s, against the lie of totalitarian ideologies. In the foreword of his *Libre Méditation sur un message de Pie XII* (Christmas 1956), published in 1957, he would recall "the

---

[2] *France, prends garde de perdre ta liberté!* by G. Fessard, author of *France, prends garde de perdre ton âme!* first clandestine *Cahier* of the *Témoignage chrétien*, 1st and 2d greatly augmented edition (Paris: Ed. du Témoignage chrétien, 1946).

[3] The "C.O.S.O.R.", founded secretly during the Occupation, in union with Jewish associations, and which he managed to protect against political exploitation. His most serious duty was to assure the education of children whose family had perished. At the end of some number of years, the establishments created for this purpose were transformed into schools for children who were poor, emotionally disturbed or from broken homes. When death neared, he had them ask me to come to the Lyons hospital where they were taking him, but by the time the ambulance arrived, he had died.

[4] Renée Bédarida is preparing a *Vie du P. Chaillet* [Life of Fr. Chaillet].

light and the hope that the word of the Vicar of Christ brought to us at the time; that same word", he would repeat, "brought us no less encouragement and comfort" than it had fifteen years earlier.

I do not want to place too much emphasis on what these three friends had to suffer from misunderstandings, indeed calumnious accusations, or on the injustices of which their memory is still the victim: that would be too contrary to their spirit. The disciple is not greater than the Master. For that, too, I give thanks to God.

Abbreviations

A.C.A.	Assemblée des cardinaux et archévêques (?) (Assembly of Cardinals and Archbishops)
A.C.J.F.	Action catholique de la Jeunesse française (Young French Catholic Action)
B.B.C.	British Broadcasting Corporation
C.C.I.F.	Centre catholique des intellectuels français (Catholic Center of French Intellectuals)
C.F.T.C.	Confédération française de Travailleurs chrétien (French Confederation of Christian Workers)
C.G.Q.J.	Commissariat général aux questions juives (General Commission for Jewish Questions)
C.U.C.	Centre universitaire catholique (Catholic University Center)
F.T.P.	Francs–Tireurs Partisans (Partisan French Marksmen)
J.E.C.	Jeunesse étudiante catholique (Students' Catholic Association)
J.E.C.F.	Jeunesse Etudiante catholique français (French Catholic Student Youth)
J.O.C.	Jeunesse ouvrière catholique (Young Worker's Catholic Association)

L.U.F.   Library of the University of
             Fribourg (Switzerland)

O.S.E.   Union Mondiale pour la Protection de la Sante
             des Populations Juives et Oeuvres de Secours
             aux Enfants
                 (World Union for the Protection of the Health
                 of Jewish People and Children's Aid)

P.P.F.   Parti Populaire Française
                 (French Popular Party)

S.T.O.   Service du Travail obligatoire
                 (Obligatory Work Service)

Index

Mayeur, Jean-Marie (*cont.*):
on *Israël et la Foi Chrétienne*,
108; on Jewish immigration,
175*n*; on Pétain, 74; resistance
efforts, 127–28; on Saliège,
149*n*, 166*n*; on Vichy regime,
196*n*
Ménétrel, Bernard, 20
Merklen, Father, 160
Michel, A., 22*n*, 115*n*
Michelet, Edmond, 117, 135
Michelin, Alfred, 24*n*, 160
Miguet brothers, 142
Millard, A., 110
Minéry, Jean, 142
Mirabeau, Honoré de, 101*n*
Mistiaen, Father, 118–19,
120
Moch, M., 156*n*
Moehler, Jean-Adam, 37, 42*n*,
48
Molette, Charles, 29*n*, 62*n*,
66*n*, 80*n*, 96*n*, 107*n*
Monchanin, Jules, 16–17*n*, 23,
24, 58, 174*n*
Mondésert, Michel, 180*n*
Montclos, Xavier de, 64, 122*n*,
130*n*, 154*n*
Montherlant, Henry de, 177
Montini, Giovanni, 95–96
Moré, Marcel, 46*n*
Mounier, Emmanuel, 43
Moussaron, Bishop, 159
Mulla, Bishop, 220
Mussolini, Benito, 121

National Council of the Re-
formed Church, 159, 175
Naudet, Abbé, 59
Nemoz, Adrien, 142, 145*n*
Neumann, Theresa, 117
Newman, John Henry,
236
Neyra, Jean, 44
Nietzsche, Friedrich, 100

Nobécourt, Jacques: on Bérard
report, 84*n*, 86, 91*n*, 93; on
Chaine declaration, 63*n*; on
French episcopate, 129; on
Lyons faculty, 63*n*; on
roundup protests, 162*n*; on
Vallat, 89, 100*n*; Vatican
broadcasts and, 119
Noël, Léon, 153*n*
Noguères, H., 231*n*

Ory, Pascal, 19*n*
O.S.E., 181
Ottaviani, Cardinal, 28*n*
Otto list, 38, 39

Pacaut, Marcel, 112*n*–13*n*
Pacelli, Cardinal, *see* Pius XII,
Pope
Paillot, Claude, 99*n*
Pallière, Aimé, 58*n*, 174*n*
Parti Populaire Française, 17
Pascal, Blaise, 240
Paul, Saint, 189, 190
Paul IV, Pope, 89, 180
Paxton, 164*n*, 170*n*, 178*n*
Pedroncini, Guy, 50*n*, 74, 85
Péguy, Charles, 49, 111, 113,
114, 115, 117, 120
Pélerson, 217
Pellepoix, Darquier de, 55,
158*n*, 186
Perrin, Jules-Xavier, 118
Pétain, Phillippe: anti-Semitism
and, 178*n*; Bérard report
and, 74–77, 80, 84, 94–97;
censorship complaints and,
24*n*; deportations by, 107*n*;
Gerlier and, 167–70; Jewish
statutes and, 19–20, 21,
186*n*; myth associated with,
73; political allegiance and,
194, 196, 202; protests to,
78, 79, 146, 150, 181, 182;
reinstatement of, 209;